SACRED STORIES OF ORDINARY FAMILIES

SACRED STORIES OF ORDINARY FAMILIES

Living the Faith in Daily Life

Diana R. Garland
Foreword by Dorothy C. Bass

JOSSEY-BASS
A Wiley Imprint
www.josseybass.com

Published by Jossey-Bass
A Wiley Imprint
989 Market Street, San Francisco, CA 94103-1741   www.josseybass.com

Jossey-Bass books and products are available through most bookstores. To contact
Jossey-Bass directly call our Customer Care Department within the U.S. at
800-956-7739, outside the U.S. at 317-572-3986 or fax 317-572-4002.

Jossey-Bass also publishes its books in a variety of electronic formats. Some content
that appears in print may not be available in electronic books.

Credits are on page 266.

Library of Congress Cataloging-in-Publication Data
Garland, Diana S. Richmond, date.
    Sacred stories of ordinary families: living the faith in daily life /
Diana R. Garland; foreword by Dorothy C. Bass.—1st ed.
        p. cm.—(Families and faith series)
Includes bibliographical references (p.) and index.
    ISBN 0-7879-6257-0
    1. Family—Religious life—United States—Case studies. I. Title. II. Series.
BV4526.3.G37 2003
261.8′3585′0973—dc21   2002155634

Printed in the United States of America
FIRST EDITION
HB Printing   10 9 8 7 6 5 4 3 2 1

THE FAMILIES AND FAITH SERIES

The Families and Faith Series is devoted to exploring the relationship between the spiritual life and our closest human relationships. From one generation to the next, faith and families are deeply intertwined in powerful ways. Faith puts all of life, including family life, in such a large perspective that it invites the gratitude, wonder, and hope so badly needed in the middle of the complexities and struggles of existence. On the other hand, faith becomes real only as it lives through concrete human relationships. Religion needs families and communities where the generations gather together and share and celebrate what it means to love God and to love others. At their best, faith and families are immersed in grace, and this series hopes to be a resource for those seeking to make love real in their families, congregations, and communities.

Diana R. Garland
> Director, Baylor Center for Family and Community Ministries
> Baylor University

J. Bradley Wigger
> Director, Center for Congregations and Family Ministries
> Louisville Presbyterian Theological Seminary

SERIES EDITORS

*To my family and to the 110 families
who opened their homes and lives to me,
giving me the privilege of telling their stories
and hearing the melodies of their faith*

CONTENTS

FOREWORD

In a time when the difficulties families face are so frequently in the headlines, I am grateful for this book full of the sacred stories that ordinary families tell about their lives of faith.

I say this not because the families to whom Diana Garland introduces us have faced few difficulties or have overcome them so serenely. In fact, among the 110 families she interviewed, we find a full complement of human hardship and a fair amount of questioning and continued need, besides.

Why, then, be grateful? First, I am grateful that Garland invited these families to tell their stories of faith and then listened to them with such generosity. Readers will learn from these tales about small acts of care that in fact were huge in their significance, about the lingering hold of loss and threat, about the changes within families that can come over time. And many will also learn about listening itself. I will treasure Garland's realization that in listening to a story of how a divorcing family showed care for one another she had allowed this family to tell the church about its faithfulness, though the church defined it only as "broken."

I am also grateful for the way in which Garland discerns the presence of God in these stories. Sometimes the theology comes in testimonies from the family members themselves, of course—and when this happens, we glimpse a form of "lived theology" to which theologians should attend. Beyond this, however, Garland weaves the stories she hears in these families' homes into the story of God as Christians know it in scripture. A frantic parent searches for a lost child as the shepherd searches for a lost sheep. Two "unrelated" people become a family, as Mary and John did when Jesus, as he died, instructed them to henceforth be mother and son to one another.

Faith, as Garland understands it, is *active,* a matter of doing as well as believing. And this book about faith is active as well. Garland wants to get readers talking—within families and among families—and also to get them *doing.* In the end, this generous and appreciative account also delivers a challenge to families, urging them to disciplined engagement in the practices of faith. Garland also challenges congregations to embrace all the families they encompass—not just the "of course" families—and to resist the age-group separation that so often cuts into the time family members spend together beyond the church.

Valparaiso, Indiana   Dorothy C. Bass
February 2003

PREFACE

The work that led to this book actually began in the early 1990s. Churches were asking for guidance in developing family ministries that would strengthen the families in their faith communities and reach out with support to families in their larger communities. I was teaching social work and family ministry in a Baptist seminary and directing a center of family ministry there. At that time, researchers were discovering that strength in families seemed to be related to having a faith they shared and to being involved in a community that supported that faith. When families were faced with crises and challenges such as unemployment, the loss of a family member in war, or natural disasters and chronic illness, those who seemed to weather the crisis best were those who had an active spiritual dimension to their life together and who belonged to faith communities.

All that research encouraged my efforts to help congregations develop family ministries. But the research did not go far enough. It didn't show *how* congregations and families could strengthen this dimension of families' lives. Is it simply a matter of encouraging families to be active in church activities? Or are there more specific ways we can help families connect with the sacred in their lives in such a way that we tap their reservoirs of strength, resilience, and joy? The question that I found myself coming back to over and over was: What characterizes faith and spirituality in family life? How could we build family ministries without answers to that question?

James Fowler, the most influential researcher and theorist in exploring faith, has a definition of faith that emphasizes cognitive processes, how persons understand and find meaning in their life experiences. Fowler has defined universal stages of faith development, even though the content of faith varies greatly across cultures and religions and individuals. In other words, Fowler has theorized that all people have faith, because all people develop and revise ways of understanding their world. Others have challenged and built on Fowler's theory of faith development. Christian educator and theologian Craig Dykstra has suggested that faith should be defined not just as how we understand our world but also as the way we choose to act on that understanding, lining ourselves up with what we believe is the activity of God in the world. So faith is not only what people put their faith in and the process through which they developed that faith. It also involves the ways people act based on what they believe.

Fowler, Dykstra, and others see families as one of the most significant contexts in which people develop and live their faith. In an article titled "Faith Development Through the Life Cycle," Fowler describes families as "ecologies of faith consciousness." Family is the environment, with both its nurture and its challenges, that shapes the individual's faith. Through the more or less consistent care of the primary adult figures in their lives, children learn to trust—first parents and then God; trust is a necessary foundation from which faith emerges. At the same time, children are highly influential participants in the faith of adults. Parents report that the birth and raising of children profoundly influences their sense of meaning and purpose. For many parents, children are the reason for returning to or seeking out for the first time participation in a faith community.

ABOUT THE RESEARCH STUDY

In 1996, the opportunity came for me to explore the question of what characterizes faith and spirituality in family life and to learn more about the lives of families in Christian congregations. Louisville Presbyterian Theological Seminary provided me with an opportunity to serve full-time as a research scholar there; with the support of a generous grant from Lilly Endowment, Inc., I was able to begin a research project, named Faith Development of Families in Congregations. The study included thirty-two congregations in four regions of the United States. In each region, I selected two congregations in each of four denominations: Southern Baptists (Southern Baptist Convention), National Baptists (National Baptist Convention), United Methodists, and Presbyterians (USA). I conducted whole-congregation surveys to learn about the demographic and interpersonal processes of families in congregations. In addition, however, I interviewed 110 families in these congregations about their life together and their experiences of faith. I talked with the families in their own homes, with as many family members participating as they could gather at one time. Each interview lasted an average of two hours.

Either the pastor or a congregational committee helped select families for the project. I asked them to help me locate some families who were very active in the congregation and others who were more on the fringes, even only occasional attendees. I also asked for families that represent the range of family types in their congregation: two parents with children, remarried families with children, single parents, single adults without children, childless couples, empty nesters, and senior adult singles and couples. In short, I tried to find as many different kinds of families as I could, both in their structure and the extent to which they were involved in congregational life.

All of the tapes of the interviews were transcribed, and I studied them, looking for ways to understand what families had told me about their life together as families and how faith was a part of that life. Long after the first interview with them, I continued to have conversations with several of the families and wrote letters to all of them about what I was learning from them, seeking their confirmation that I had understood what they had told me.

This book tells the stories of these 110 families. I have changed names and identifying information to protect their privacy. All of the stories told in this book are true, in the sense that they are stories that these families told me. Although I have edited their stories to turn them from the tumbling conversation of a family to a written narrative, the stories are their own words. In early drafts of the book, I wrote about each of the families individually, but I soon realized that, although I had clear pictures of all these families in my own mind from talking with them and then reading over and over the transcripts of our conversations, readers would be quickly overwhelmed by trying to keep the characters straight in over one hundred families, with more than 270 individuals taking part in the family storytelling. Reviewers also cautioned me to try to limit the number of families that readers would have to keep straight in their memories from story to story and chapter to chapter. Therefore, I have often combined stories from one family with those of one or more other families that share similar histories, structures, and experiences, trying to balance readability with honor for the uniqueness of each of these families. I have also taken the liberty of sharing some of the stories from the life of my own family. My family has given me permission to share these stories with you.

An Overview

In the first chapter, I will explore the significance of stories in the lives of families. Chapter Two tells stories about how these families identify themselves and some of the challenges even of defining who our families are. The third chapter explores stories of family strength and resilience, that which brought them together and keeps them together, even and especially when the going gets rough. The fourth chapter describes how these families experience faith in their daily life together. Ways they attempt to practice their faith, the disciplines to which they have committed themselves, are the substance of the fifth chapter. Chapter Six tells the stories of how they have felt God's presence both in the ordinary and critical times of family life. The final chapter of the book will explore how you can help your congregation become a community where people know one another not only by name and occupation but also by family and by story, where families are encouraged to practice their faith with one another.

I hope you will have opportunity to talk about this book with others. Ideally, your family will be able to talk about the families you will meet in these pages along with other families in your community of faith. Congregations need to be places where we share our family stories with one another, and I hope this book will be a resource for such storytelling in your congregation. You can begin by talking about the stories you will read here, and that will undoubtedly lead to thinking about and perhaps sharing family stories of your own. If you are reading this book on your own, I hope you will find ways to talk about what you read with your family, even if that is not possible in the context of your congregation. You will find guides for thinking about how each chapter applies to your own family and for conversation at the end of the book. One guide provides ideas for conversation with your family at home or in the car or wherever else you happen to be able to talk about what you read. The other guide helps groups use this book for conversation together in the community of faith.

WITH GRATITUDE

My profound appreciation goes to the many families who gave so freely of their time, a scarce commodity in family life today. I wish it were possible for me to identify them all by name; many are the unsung heroes that daily weave the fiber of church and community life. As is customary in research such as this, however, I agreed with them that they would remain anonymous so that they could speak unguardedly. Indeed, many allowed themselves a surprising level of candor with me, a gift not only to me but to you, the reader. They will of course recognize themselves in the stories they told me.

This project developed with the nurture and support of a host of colleagues and friends. Lilly Endowment, Inc., made this project possible with a generous grant that allowed me to devote a full year specifically to this project, with support for all the travel and resources I needed and ongoing support for two more years while I completed the initial research project. I am grateful to Craig Dykstra for his encouragement and invaluable guidance in shaping the project.

In 1997, I moved to Baylor University, in Waco, Texas, where I found continued support for this project with release time to finish the initial research and then for summer sabbaticals to complete this book. One of the wonderful outcomes of this project has been the partnership forged between Louisville Presbyterian Theological Seminary and Baylor University. That partnership can be seen most clearly in the joint projects of Louisville Seminary's Center for Congregations and Family Ministries and Baylor University's Center for Family and Community Ministries. Lilly Endowment, Inc., was generous in providing funding for the development of both of these centers and now in funding the Congregational Resources Project, which has included the resources for developing the Families and Faith Series being published by Jossey-Bass, to which this book belongs. My dear friend and colleague J. Bradley Wigger, director of Louisville Seminary's Center for Congregations and Family Ministries, has been a steady source of encouragement, vision, humor, and balance for the past five years of work together.

In the beginning stages of this project, a group of colleagues gathered with me to refine and strengthen it. They included Dan Aleshire, Nancy Ammerman, Don Browning, Bob Dempsey, Andrew Edwards, Ian Evison, Delia Halverson, Joe Leonard, Jim Lewis, Jack Marcum, Penny Marler, Bonnie Glass McDonald, John Roberto, Eugene Roehlkepartain, and Merton Strommen. Carol Lytch and Pamela Yankeelov served as wonderful research partners, full of encouragement and helpful insight, in the Faith Development of Families in Congregations Project, of which this report of interviews of families is only one part. Amy Lerner and Jeff McFarlane, both graduate students at the time at Seattle Pacific University, assisted me in making connections for the project in the Pacific Northwest.

April Armour, Peggy Foskett, and Sue Fridenstine provided capable office support and meticulous transcription of hundreds of hours of family interviews. They were wonderful partners in the work. After the initial phase of interviewing and transcription, Jeanie Fitzpatrick became the project manager for this and other projects of the Baylor Center for Family and Community Ministries. She has been a constant source of capable and reliable partnership, a gifted editor, and a tremendous friend who makes me laugh often and deeply. I am grateful.

Sarah Polster of Jossey-Bass encouraged me to consider turning this research project into a book for congregational leaders and families. This book, and indeed, the whole Families and Faith Series, began because of her belief that family ministry was of critical importance. Her untimely death was a terrible loss.

Julianna Gustafson of Jossey-Bass has provided invaluable assistance in shaping this book and has given generously of her professional talents in steering me through the editing process. She never let me become discouraged. Through it all, she has become a trusted friend, and I am grateful.

I subjected students in my social work classes at Baylor University to reading early drafts of the manuscript, and they generously gave me their feedback. I received many wonderful suggestions from them that guided the further development of the book. Six reviewers gave me invaluable constructive critique; the suggestions of Ray Anderson, Bill Doherty, Brian Grant, Don Hebbard, David Thomas, and J. Bradley Wigger provided ideas that strengthened and refined my work in the critical last stages of turning a research project into a book.

Ten of the families whose stories are told most prominently in this book read the entire manuscript, both editing the manuscript and confirming that I had understood them. The couple I identify as Bill and Peggy in the stories in the following chapters wrote me a letter saying, "We think you have 'hit the nail on the head' with your examples and experiences related to living the faith as it applies to average people doing this; we thank Almighty God for the small part we had in relating our part to you." I add my own gratitude to God for their story; it is powerful and has shaped my own life as I have sought to tell it well. Tess wrote, "Yes, you did understand the meaning of faith in our family life; this was shown not only in our story, but in others that I felt could have been ours." The blessing of these and other families in the project has been the most significant encouragement of all that this work could be of use to families and congregations.

I am also grateful to my colleagues at The Southern Baptist Theological Seminary, where I taught for the seventeen years prior to 1996. Most have scattered to other places now, but they are still beloved members of my larger community of faith, contributing significantly to my understanding of the importance of communities for families and their faith.

Above all, I thank my husband, David Garland, my biblical scholar in residence. David is professor of Christian scriptures and associate dean at George W. Truett Theological Seminary. We have been ministry partners and family for one another for thirty-two years, embracing one another's parents and my sister as family in the beginning and joined along the way by our children and friends, who greatly enriched our lives by becoming faith family for us. What I learned about biblical interpretation I learned from David. Our past writing together and our editing of one another's individual writings have refined my thinking. It is sometimes difficult for me to remember which thoughts first came from whom. On the other hand, he should not be held responsible for my biblical interpretations and theological musings. I am a social scientist by profession, not a theologian. My discussion of biblical content and theology in this book are my reflections as a believing Christian, shaped in a community of faith where I have lived and worked out my own understandings of how to put my social scientific self with my faithing self and my own family experiences.

Finally, I thank Sarah and John, my children; and my mother, Dorsie Richmond. They are incredible encouragers, reading and critiquing what I write, and, with David, allowing me to share the stories that carry the melodies of our life together. They have taught me more about joy and the nature of God's love through the love I have received and given to them than any one story can hold.

This host of people whose names I have written in gratitude is testimony to God's wisdom that goodness comes in not being alone in any task. Although the book cover carries my name as author, I am only a representative of this host of families and communities who are living sacred stories, the melodies that carry us through ordinary days and ordinary lives, connecting us to God. Certainly, this book is flawed; it is only a beginning attempt to understand faith as a dimension of family life. I hope others can build on it. I offer it, claiming the promise that God can work toward perfect ends even through "weak" efforts (2 Corinthians 12:9), as Marianne taught me so well. You will read her family's story in Chapter Four. Above all, it is my prayer that this book will help families to sing more boldly of the faith that carries them day by day.

SACRED STORIES OF ORDINARY FAMILIES

Chapter 1

MELODIES FOR DAILY LIFE

On the Sunday before I began writing this book, I was away from home and visited a church for Sunday worship. My work takes me to different churches fairly often, but the feeling of self-consciousness, of being not at home, always hits me when I walk into a church building where I know no one and they do not know me. That feeling of strangeness is even stronger in a church of a denominational tradition other than my own. This was a Presbyterian church; I am a Baptist. I chose a section of pew next to an elderly gentleman sitting alone. I sat a distance I judged to be close enough to be friendly but not too close for one stranger sitting next to another. *The things I think about!* I chided myself, as I realized I was calculating in my head the appropriate church pew distance. He turned his head and smiled faintly at me. The organist had already begun the prelude, and everyone was quiet. When time for the first hymn came, however, he reached to share my hymnbook. In a loud whisper, he said, "I don't sing very well, but I'll try." I moved a little closer and replied, "Me too!" And try we did, now holding the hymnbook together. All of the hymns were unfamiliar to me. A couple of the songs had words I did not know, but they were set to hymn melodies that are old standards, and once I caught the familiar melody, it was easy enough to put new words to the familiar tune. There was one hymn, however, with a melody I had not heard before. I wavered around, trying to find the notes, becoming less sure with each measure but determined to try

1

because he was trying too. By the fourth stanza, however, I got it, and I became less concerned about figuring out the notes and much more focused on joining my voice with my singing partner and the rest of the congregation. When the service ended, he turned and grabbed my hand and said, "You sing beautifully!" I don't, but that was not the point. What was important was that we sang together, the same song, the same melody. And he blessed me.

If we know the melody of a song, we can almost always sing along if someone gives us the words. A new melody, however, is different. We have to hear it, learn it, make it a part of us to be able to give it back with our own voice. It is the melody that makes music. It is the melody that makes the words come alive and gives them power. "Christ arose! He arose! Hallelujah! Christ arose!" Reading that line and singing it are two different things. To sing it means to reach for those high notes on "arose" and hold them, giving them all the wind within us. When we sing together, the words become more than what they say. They have a resonance that echoes through all the empty places in our bodies and our souls and in the spaces between our singing partners and us. The melody literally fills and connects us. When others stand mute in a congregation, perhaps feeling awkward because they "can't sing," I feel somehow cheated that they did not join their voice with mine. We did not connect with one another, and they left me singing alone.

As a young girl, I memorized great long passages of scripture, enough to earn the rank of "Queen with a Scepter" in the Girls Auxiliary organization of my Southern Baptist church. It landed me the terrifying honor of standing in a white dress and golden paper crown, holding a so-called scepter in my hand and spouting off those memorized scriptures to the whole congregation. Those passages have long evaporated from my memory. The scripture passages set to music that we sang in youth choir forty years ago, however, I can still sing. Those words have become a part of me. Perhaps I can't recite them, but I can sing them. Many older adults, including me, can sing all the words to the popular music of our adolescence; they are a part of us. The words are not all that important. What does "doo wop doo wop" mean anyway? But that isn't the point. The songs give us a sense of identity; we belong to a particular generation that has shared certain experiences, and so we in some sense belong to one another. We know that persons suffering from dementia may not remember who their children are or even who they are themselves, but they can sometimes sing along with old hymns that have become more a part of their lives than their own names.

This book is not about music and hymns, however; it is about stories. But stories have melody, too. The melodic nature of stories is most evident in the stories we read to children. Often the earliest stories are singsong rhymes that are more song than narrative. The words are nonsensical, playful, and musical; and the tone, rhythm, and drama of the voice are all important. Margaret Wise Brown's *Goodnight Moon* and the books of Dr. Seuss were favorites in our house, both for parents and children. As children mature, words become more important, and the melody is carried not only by the drama and expression of the reader but also by the meaning of the stories that reader and listener share.

This book is about the stories families tell about themselves. Family stories are not usually sung, of course, but they do have a melody nevertheless. The melodies are the meaning and purpose of shared lives and the faith family members have—in one another, in what they value together, in God. Although families do not usually sing or even write out their stories, they tell these stories to one another and to others outside the family. Stories help families remember what they want to remember. They say to others and to the family itself, "This is who we are." Because of that underlying melody of meaning, stories give families a sense of identity and of belonging. Storytelling, like singing, means joining our voices, except we do so by interrupting, correcting, and building on one another's words, telling a story together that becomes, in the process, *our* story, *our* song.

Hymn writers putting scriptures to music sometimes move the words around or use synonyms or in other ways fit scripture to music so that it can be sung, sometimes adding a few *Hallelujah*s or *amen*s. The words of the song may not be quite the same as the biblical text, but the hymn writer preserves and emphasizes the meaning of the words and deepens that meaning by putting the words to music. The Psalms were originally songs. Working like hymn writers, families may emphasize certain parts of their experience in their stories and leave out others, based on what is meaningful in that experience for the family. Family storytellers digress to add drama or exaggerate to underline what is important. The story takes on a subtle rhythm that almost resembles music. Once told, the story becomes a part of the family repertoire, perhaps to be told again and again. Even more important, by giving the family experience this shape, the story becomes a shared source of identity that will be remembered long after other unstoried experiences are forgotten.

Sometimes one family member tells a family story while others listen. One family member may be telling the rest of the family, or perhaps a friend or stranger provides an audience for the family story. Some families consider it impolite and inappropriate to interrupt or correct when another is speaking, particularly if an elder is speaking or the person carries more authority. Nevertheless, it is *their* story, about their family, and family members are taking it in and turning it over in their minds—perhaps even mentally correcting—and making the story their own as well. Sometimes one person tells a story about the family to outsiders. It is a family story, however, if the family itself has shaped the telling. In fact, the family is actually present as the audience in the head of the storyteller, silently judging, correcting, and interrupting.

A Sick Dog and a Sad Boy

The best way to describe family stories is to tell one. This whole book came out of my curiosity about family stories and out of a research project that took me into the homes of families who are active church members. I asked them to share with me the stories of their lives together. I wanted to know how their faith as Christians was a part of those stories, if it was. Families did share their stories with me, some stories they had told many times before, others that had never been given words until I showed up and asked them to tell me about themselves.

Renee, an Anglo-American Southern Baptist and a hospital medical technician, had given me directions to her home by saying, "Look for the house with the front porch railing that is completely rusted." And indeed it was. The house testified to the hard winters and hot summers of the Midwest; the paint on the siding was peeling in places. But it looked like a happy house, with children's bikes and skates in the front yard and a screened-in front porch with a large swing made inviting with pillows. Tim, age eight, came bounding to the door when I rang the doorbell and let me in. Renee came from the kitchen and invited me to come and sit at the kitchen table. Children's belongings and school papers and projects were strewn about the house. A large and very energetic dog poked his nose in my lap. I put my microphone on the big oak table amidst the school papers. Both eleven-year-old Susan and her younger brother, Tim, joined us for the interview, interested in the conversation.

Renee told me about her work at the hospital. A teenager from the church comes in the evenings to stay with the kids and spend the night while she works the night shift. It was early June; she and her husband had been in the process of divorcing since she had asked him to move out the previous November.

We talked almost an hour. The children told me about the activities they enjoy: dance class for Susan, Cub Scouts for Tim, and all of the activities in which they were involved in their church. Renee had talked about her marriage and some of the fun trips they had taken and the moves they had made. She gently described some of the difficulties leading to the decision to separate and divorce, aware of the children's listening ears, lightly touching the fact that her husband had a girlfriend. She has struggled with the loss of her marriage. Being a single parent was a turn in her life that she had never imagined. She and her husband had planned to become missionaries. That dream was destroyed with the end of the marriage. She said, "I'm not sure what God has planned for us next," and I knew this had been a real crisis of faith for her, perhaps more than she wanted to say in front of Tim and Susan.

At that point, I asked, "When things get rough, what keeps you going as a family?" Renee talked about the affection the three of them share and their involvement in the church and encouraging friends there.

Tim said, "I know this kind of sounds funny, but it's the dog. I think the dog helps me keep on going, because usually when we are really tired or just lazy, slumping around, and we need to get something done, she barks and scratches, and I get busy and take care of her."

I responded, "So she won't let you quit; she keeps you going."

Renee said, "Right before Christmas last year, our other dog got very sick. I think both kids were worried and pretty closed off at that point; they didn't talk a whole lot about it. Their dad had just moved out several weeks before. We knew the dog had cancer, and we discussed putting her to sleep. But Tim would not accept it. He just couldn't. He kept saying, 'You're going to kill her.' We explained that she was very sick and she would get sicker and sicker and she wouldn't eat. That she was in a lot of pain now. But he wouldn't agree to it." As I glanced at Tim and Susan, I could see that both had tears in their eyes.

Renee continued. "So my husband and I said, 'Tim, we will keep taking care of her the best we can, until you feel differently.' Tim kept hugging her and taking care of her, and she got . . . Well, you know, I was forcing food down her throat, and she couldn't swallow. She was just drooling, and it was just disgusting. Finally, it came to the point that we had to carry her outside so she could even pee. When she just wouldn't eat anymore, Tim said, 'It's OK now. She needs to go to heaven.'" Renee paused, fighting back tears (and so was I).

Tim mumbled, "She was just so sick."

Renee went on, "So we called the vet and had her put to sleep. That was such a hard time. The three of us wanted to put her to sleep before she got too miserable, but Tim just had a hard time accepting that. Maybe that was because he still had hope that she was going to get better."

Tim added, "It was hard to say good-bye."

Renee went on:

> With the separation in November, these kids were
> already wiped out. And then here came Christmas, and
> now we had to put the dog to sleep. I couldn't get a
> babysitter to stay with a dog with cancer, but my hus-
> band, who had already moved out, was willing to stay
> over here at night with the kids and the dog while I
> went to work. He would sleep here and then leave
> when I came home. All my friends thought I was crazy

for doing that, but it was the best I could do at the time. These kids were going through so much. How could I take away his dog?

As I listened to Renee, I pondered what she was telling me. After telling me that the dog had been put down, she backed up and began talking again about how hard the weeks had been after the separation while the dog was so sick. What must this have been like for her? Her husband had just moved out; her children were upset; and then their beloved pet became seriously, terminally ill. She had to force-feed the dog, carry her out to relieve herself, and allow her estranged husband back in the house to help out until Tim could reach the point that he could let go of his dog. Clearly her concern for her children's well-being and her love for them were the deciding factors for her in all of this.

What Makes a Family Story?

Stories tell a sequence of events that are happening to people and how those people are trying to influence the course and consequences of those events. The storyteller may reorder events to show what they mean, how what caused what according to a plot that is moving toward an outcome. And stories always have an outcome, an ending. In this story, it is an ending filled with ambiguity, but an ending nonetheless; the story stops with Renee's question, "How could I take away his dog?" as a summary. It began with a husband moving out, a terminally ill dog, and a very sad son. As we try to understand her story, what are the events in the story that she and her husband were trying to influence? What outcome were they trying to change? They knew that whatever they did, the dog was not going to get better. She made it clear that her stopgap measure of having her husband spend the night with the children and the dog was not an attempt to reconcile their marriage. The way she tells the story, it was the only thing she knew to do to accomplish—what? Her concern was for her son, for

7

his grief over losing his father as a member of the household and now his dog. The outcome she is concerned about is helping Tim with his grief, to somehow guide him through the loss of his father's daily presence in the household and now the loss of his dog.

Renee told this story in response to a question, "When things get rough, what keeps you going as a family?" as a part of a conversation with a stranger about faith and family life. I have pondered how the meaning of this story was a response to that question and to the larger question about how her family experiences faith in their life together. It is especially significant because she had just told me that their plans of living their faith together, of becoming missionaries, had been dashed by divorce. What was the meaning, the melody, of this story?

At a time when others might look at this family and say they are an example of faithlessness, the breaking of a marriage covenant, the mother tells quite a different story that runs deeper. These unhappy parents going through a major life crisis sense their child's grief and find a powerful way to communicate faithfulness to their children and even to one another. If they are willing to work together to care for a sick dog, how much more will they be there for their son when he needs them? Their story echoes the faithfulness of God, whom we can count on to care even for the sparrows (Luke 12:6) and for dogs and for us, God's children. Renee and her husband were sending that message of faithfulness to their children. The ending of the story, therefore, came when the son said, "It's OK now."

As I have thought about this story, it seems to me that he experienced and knew *he* was OK, safe in the care of faithful parents, even though their marriage was ending. If his parents were there for his dog, they were certainly there for him. This experience seemed also to have helped him realize that surely an all-loving God more powerful even than his own parents had prepared a safe place for his dying dog. He followed "It's OK now" with the statement "She needs to go to heaven," assuming that heaven would be there for dogs too. Of course, much of this meaning had not actually been spoken directly. The meaning was the melody of the story, the thread of family faithfulness in spite of the parental divorce and a beloved pet's death threatening its very foundations. The story said so much more than the words describing events could say.

Only a very small portion of our daily experiences becomes stories, because for an experience to become a story, we have to step outside of experience and reflect on it. Often we reflect on experiences that seem important to us or experiences we have a need to explain to ourselves or to others. We use words to give structure to the experience and to explain it. What causes what happens to us? Why do we do what we do? How does our world work, and what is our place in it? We choose parts of the whole experience to put into the story because they help us say not just what happened but *why* it happened and what that says about who we are. This mother could have said to me, "We are trying to be good parents to our children and examples of God's faithfulness, even though we are divorced." However, her story *showed* me that was true in a way that making a statement could not. We do not communicate faithfulness just by saying, "We are faithful." We live it; it has to be shown. And stories are ways of showing, of giving words to the melodies of daily life. One cannot fully tell what this story means except by telling it. One cannot describe a melody except by singing it.

Sometimes families have interesting arguments when they tell stories. They disagree about what parts to select. They sometimes dispute what really happened. No story tells all of what really happened; that isn't the point. A story communicates something beyond the precision of facts, a meaning embedded but deeper than the actual events. In their stories, families understand and explain experience together, and that often takes some negotiating, and even a lively argument. For example, a mother may tell her daughter the story about her labor and delivery that exaggerates the length of the labor and the danger of the delivery, with the story climax being her joy at first seeing the new baby and how beautiful she was. The meaning of the story may be "I wanted you so much that I really suffered, and you were worth it." If Grandma corrects her, "Now, honey, you were in labor eight hours, not eighteen hours," the storyteller may be more angry or hurt because the meaning of the story has been discounted than because the fact has been corrected.

The facts of a family story are therefore not so important as the meaning they communicate. Sometimes over time, the "facts" change. Was it six weeks or four that the dog was sick? Did the dog have cancer or heart failure? Perhaps the facts will change because some-one forgets and then substitutes another plausible "fact." Sometimes the story becomes more dramatic with each telling: how deep the floodwaters were, how far Grandpa walked uphill in the snow to school. Obviously, the facts are only important because they point to some truth far more important than the facts themselves.

Stories are true even if (or perhaps because) they are not simply historical accounts of events. Families select particular experiences and shape them into a story because they relate to a particular concern or event. Renee selected a story about their old dog to tell me, not their new dog, because we were talking about dogs in the context of what keeps this family going through hard times. Clearly stories are very different ways to get truth than history and science are. Stories explain and guide human experience just as history and science do. Science and history, however, are often developed by those outside the experiences who want to establish laws or principles that hold across different places and people. Stories, on the other hand, are deeply personal. They belong uniquely to the people who create them. Science and history study life and how living things function; stories tell who we living beings are in relation to one another, what we value, and what gives meaning to our lives.

Social scientists have studied the impact of separation and divorce on the emotional well-being of children and how different experiences have different outcomes for children. What difference does it make, for example, for the noncustodial parent to continue in faithful, frequent contact with children versus walking out and never coming back? Studies in social science question what we know about those differences for children in general. Renee's story has a different purpose—not to understand what is generally true but what is true for *this specific family.* Her story tells how these parents who are separating struggled and worried over the well-being of their children and how they attempted to communicate faithfulness in the process. It tells how divorcing parents can work together, not just that they should for the sake of the children. But even more, it is a story of what they value and, indeed, who they are as a family. It is not a story about all divorcing families; it is a story about this family in all its unique-ness—and faithfulness. At the same time, there is a depth of meaning in this family's experience that can help other families, as they confront similar challenges to family faithfulness, to create their own ways of beating the generalities, of being unique. They can weave stories of faithfulness too. The melody of faithfulness can have different stories in different families.

What Do Family Stories Say About Who We Are?

Whatever else a story means, it is always a way for a family to say, "This is who we are." Renee's story says that they are a family that is faithful in their care of one another, a family that is sensitive to one another's concerns and needs. So not only do stories reflect what it means to be this family, but they help connect family members to one another, whether separated by time, space, death, or divorce.

Sometimes families are the audience for their own stories. Families often tell stories during those special times: family reunions, holidays, funerals, birthdays and adoption days, graduations, and anniversaries of weddings or deaths. We tell stories during long car trips together or during those perhaps rare times when we just sit to watch a sunset or fish in a lake, or perhaps when we linger over the supper table because no one wants to have to wash dishes. Family stories are accounts of shared history, those moments of joy and sorrow, defining moments that have changed the course of our lives together. Children need and want to be told the special stories that surround their birth or adoption. Spouses want to hear how they were chosen as "the one" from all the other potential partners in life. We want to hear how others perceived and felt about our presence in the family. These stories say, "Your coming into this family was very significant. You are a vital member."

My husband, David, is an only child, and both of his parents died more than a decade ago. I know some of the stories from his childhood because I heard them over the first twenty years of our marriage while his parents were alive. Since his parents' death, he has felt orphaned, not only alone without parents but alone without others—brothers and sisters—who know firsthand the family stories of his childhood. Not long ago, we made a business trip together and decided to visit an older cousin he had not seen since childhood and whom I had never met. All afternoon, I listened fascinated as she told stories of their childhood and memories she had of David as a little boy. Since then, they have carried on a very entertaining and lively e-mail correspondence, reconnected by old stories, reclaimed as family, and now connecting stories of childhood with stories of their adult families and grown children.

Sometimes at a family reunion or during a reminiscent moment with a relative, we hear a story about the family we have never heard before. We may feel like children opening a new storybook for the first time, hearing the spine softly cracking a bit as we bend the covers back, smelling the new paper and pages, feeling the excitement of first reading. Most stories are not new to us, however. Most of what David heard that afternoon was not completely new to him, although there were recollections of forgotten experiences, and his cousin had a different perspective that reshaped some of his own stories. For the most part, however, family stories are rarely completely new information for the family members hearing them. And that is just the point. The stories belong to the family. Telling them is like reading the same book to a small child for the zillionth time: "Goodnight moon. Goodnight room." She corrects you when you miss a word or an inflection. She wants you to read the story not so that she will learn something new but to be comforted and rocked by the familiar rhythm and words and voice of someone who loves her. When adults tell family stories out of love, it is the emotional equivalent of being rocked in one another's lap, hearing words that, underneath, say, "I love you; you belong to me."

Theologian Louis Smedes calls a family a "community of memory." A family is much more than a group of people; a family is the current incarnation of a story that extends into the past and will have more chapters to come. Telling family stories turns memories into present reality and holds that reality as foundation for the future.

We also tell family stories to others: to friends, to our Sunday school classes, sometimes to our work colleagues over lunch. Telling a family story to outsiders has a different emotional content, but the purpose is the same—to say who we are, to claim a certain identity for ourselves. I do not know if Renee's family had articulated the story of the sick dog to one another before my visit. If they had, it would have been, no doubt, also a way to say to one another, at least in part, "We will be faithful to one another." Telling the story to me had that same meaning, but I was a different audience, and so their purpose in telling it was different. Telling the story to me was a subtle defense, a way of claiming an identity for themselves that the world—and the church—might deny them: "We are a faithful family."

The context of storytelling, therefore, has much to do with why a story is told and perhaps even how it is told. In my hearing of Renee's family story, I was a researcher studying faith and family life, coming to visit them under the auspices of her church. She probably presupposed that I had our society's and the church's perspective on what makes for a strong family, a faithful family—and that perspective does not include divorce. So when she told me a story about faithfulness, she was challenging our society's definition of what constitutes a strong and faithful family.

If we tell stories about only a fraction of our experiences, then all our stories never really can tell the fullness of our life together; they are only windows into what is within. Nevertheless, they are windows. Some families live in the dark! What if we had not made that visit to David's cousin, and someone had not said, "Do your remember when . . . ?" What if I had not visited Renee's home? Would she ever have had an opportunity to tell a representative of the church a story that says, "We may look unfaithful to others, but we are committed to being faithful to each other as a family"? When stories go unshaped and untold, families may lose out on opportunities to rock one another with a melody that says, "This is who we are" or to tell others the defining experiences of their lives.

CHANGING FAMILIES, CHANGING STORIES

A story—especially a good one—can take on many layers of meaning. We can, for example, read Jesus' parable of the prodigal son and focus on our likeness to the son who takes his inheritance and squanders it, picturing our own waywardness and the grace of God that welcomes us home. Or we can focus on our likeness to the older brother in his judgment of his younger brother, begrudging God's grace in the lives of others who have not worked nearly so hard to be righteous as we have. Or we can focus on the love and forgiveness of the father, and the goodness of God and how we are called to be examples of that love to others, even our own wayward family members. Many times, our focus comes from our own needs and struggles and concerns of the moment, and when those change, so may our understanding of the story.

The same is true with family stories. Stories may be told differently at different times in a family's life. Certain parts of a story may be embellished and dramatized; others may be downplayed or omitted, depending on the audience and the needs and concerns of the family at the time. For example, my family has a story about what happened one night more than ten years ago when my husband was out of town.

THE NIGHT I LOST JOHN

One cool Monday evening in early November, David was out of town, and I was juggling the family schedule: John, age eleven, had soccer practice at a field a twenty-five-minute drive away. Sarah, age thirteen, had a violin lesson about twenty minutes from John's soccer field, and I needed to do a quick visit with a client family in their home not far from Sarah's music school. I quickly strategized with the children. I would drop John at soccer practice first. He would probably finish before I could get back, but I told him to walk to the nearby store, which had a snack bar, and get something to eat and wait for me there. I would drop Sarah at her lesson, visit the client family, come back to pick up Sarah, and then circle back for John. It should work.

We were running late, so I did not go by the store to show John the snack bar where I wanted him to meet me, but I pointed across the soccer field in the general direction of the store. He was anxious to get to his practice, which had already started. He jumped out of the car, and Sarah and I were off to the violin lesson. I touched all the bases—dropped off Sarah, visited the family, picked up Sarah—and returned to pick up John an hour later. When I walked into the grocery store snack bar, however, he was not there. Sarah and I walked up and down the store aisles and then drove the half block to the soccer field, watching along the way. He wasn't on the way or still on the soccer field. There was nobody; everyone had gone home. My throat tightened, and I could feel the panic rising, "Where is he?" I said out loud, trying to sound calm for Sarah's sake. I went back to the store and had him paged. I alerted the store clerks to watch out for him and left Sarah in the front of the store to wait, should he show up. I quickly checked a couple of other stores in the area—a Target nearby that had a snack bar, a McDonald's—but he was not there either. Then I drove four blocks to the home of one of John's friends, to see if he might have walked home with his friend. The friend's father immediately pulled his coat on and went to walk the streets around the soccer field. By now, John had been missing almost an hour; I hurried back to the store. Sarah was stoically standing there, worry and fatigue scrunched on her face. I went to the store manager and asked to use the phone to call the police, fighting back the tears. After I told the police my son was missing, they promised to come right away, and Sarah and I returned to the parking lot, standing with our arms around one another by the car, looking in all directions for John. A police car pulled up beside me less than ten minutes later. The officer invited me to sit in my car and said she would pull up beside me to take the report so that I wouldn't have to stand there in the cold night air. Her kindness was the last straw, and the tears began to roll down my face. Sobs made it hard to give her John's description: eleven years old, blonde hair and blue eyes, navy-blue soccer shorts, and a red and white T-shirt. I was imagining his face on a milk carton. I thought about him in those thin clothes lost—or worse—on a night becoming colder by the minute.

Sarah was sitting beside me in our car in the dark parking lot, and once the police officer was through with the description and pulled away, I began sobbing uncontrollably, frightened and overwhelmed with guilt for not planning more carefully, for not being more protective, for trying to do too much and risking this disaster. Sarah was trying to comfort me, patting my shoulder, sobbing herself, and saying, "It's not your fault, Mama; he's just stupid." They were the only words she could think of to comfort me.

The police quickly organized search teams and concentrated on the nearby railroad track. A police helicopter flew low and back and forth with strobe lights. Sarah and I got out of our car and watched the helicopter, searching for any sign that someone had found him.

A colleague from work, innocently thinking he was going to buy groceries, drove into the parking lot, saw me standing near the several police cars now on the scene, and hurried over. I wept on his shoulder, and he waited with me. He slipped away for a moment and made a phone call to his wife. I didn't know at the time that she in turn called my teaching colleagues and my church. Word then spread quickly. Within thirty minutes, several other friends had gathered to wait with me. A lot was going on I didn't know about. Prayer chains and groups gathered in homes. The police had contacted the soccer team coach to see if he had any information about John, and the coach called the team's parents. They gathered in the home of one family who had a citizen's band radio, where they listened to the police messages about the search and prayed.

A nearby storeowner brought Sarah and me a cup of hot cocoa. The neighbor who had been walking the streets volunteered to take Sarah home, to wait by the phone should John try to phone. No one said it, but we were all hoping he would escape from his abductors and call home. Somebody needed to be there if he did.

AJ, the local police bloodhound, arrived just after Sarah and the neighbor left. "Do you have any of John's clothing?" the police asked. I would have laughed if I hadn't been so desperate and frightened. As many families can testify, children often use the backseat as a clothes closet and changing room in the fast-paced running from school to sports and music lessons. There was an ample supply of John's dirty socks on the backseat floor. With the whiff of John's sock, AJ tracked John, zigzagging all over the soccer field where he had played for almost an hour. AJ then took off across the street, nose to the ground,

16

through two intersections, and straight in the front door of the Target store. There was John.

When I first began my search, I had gone to Target looking for him, but he had been in the rest room when I hurriedly walked through the store. And I hadn't thought of that. So there he sat, waiting for me now almost three hours, alone and terrified. Where was his mother? He had seen all the police cars go by and the search helicopter floodlights. At first, he tried to call home, but Sarah was not there yet. Now it was 10:00 P.M., and the store was closing. I learned later that when I'd said "snack bar," John's mind clicked to the only snack bar in that area he knew about, the one in Target. I had meant the grocery store snack bar. But he had never been in that store with me. *How could I be so stupid?* I thought. "Sarah, it's your mother that's stupid!"

The police put him in their cruiser and brought him the block and a half to me. After we hugged one another and thanked everyone, John said, "Please, Mom, don't tell anyone what happened."

"I'm sorry, sugar," I responded. "But I think lots of folks already know. So maybe we had just better work on a really good story for you to tell at school tomorrow."

We went home. There, sitting on my front steps in the dark and cold, was the minister from my church. Someone had called him too. He hadn't realized that Sarah was inside. So he just waited and watched from the porch steps. He came in with us and listened to my story—and I cried all over again—and he hugged John. "I love you, man. I'm glad you are OK."

That was more than ten years ago, and my throat still tightens as I write this story again for you. It has always been my worst nightmare—to be responsible for harming those I love the most. The meaning of this story has changed over the years, however. The first time I wrote this story, I focused on the theme of the chronic stress of time demands in families of school-age children today. Even before that, however, I told this story to colleagues at work, to friends, to my mother on the phone. And before anyone else, I told it to my husband, who arrived home weary from a business trip, in the wee hours of the morning only hours after this episode ended. So what did it mean when I first told it to him and to my own family and friends? I first told it as confession: "Look what I did to our child." And in response,

17

I received in the shocked looks a confirmation that this was really a terrible experience; I had failed as a mother. I also received support, consolation, and acceptance rather than rejection. A few well-meaning friends told me I needed to slow down and get a cell phone. There was even an edge of anger in the voice of one friend as she stood vigil with me that night, because she loves John too, and this event scared everyone. Very soon, the story evolved into a warning, "Life is precious. We are always just half a step from tragedy, from losing one another. Hold on to one another." I know that many children on John's soccer team received parental lectures that night about listening to their parents and what to do if they should be lost. Our story became a cautionary tale for others—and for ourselves.

Over time the story has taken on other meanings. Five years after that experience, our family moved from Kentucky to Texas. I realize as I look back now that I began to hear a different melody in this story, one not just of danger but also of sadness. It became for me a story about the wonderful Kentucky community that gave our family support and encouragement. The scene of this story—the soccer field and grocery store shopping center—was a mile from our neighborhood, which is itself five miles from our workplace and church. Even so, a community of neighbors quickly surrounded me. Work colleagues; friends; church members; the minister sitting on my front porch in the dark, cold night; parents of my son's teammates; the police; and the kind storeowner who brought me hot cocoa sprang into action, each doing what he or she could do. All of these people had busy evenings that they simply dropped to come to our aid. My daughter's patient standing in that store waiting for her brother to please show up, sitting in the dark car with me, crying with me is testament that we are a family that loves one another even when we do stupid things, a family that supports one another and cries with one another. This story of community became especially meaningful for us when, five years later, we found ourselves uprooted to a new place, and that community was lost, and our daughter left us to go more than a thousand miles away to college. So at the same time that it is a story of community, it became a story of a community lost and the inevitable scattering of families as children grow into adults. Perhaps it is still, then, a cautionary tale, but the meaning is different.

SACRED STORIES OF ORDINARY FAMILIES

Sometimes family stories need to change, but they are stuck. A story may scapegoat a family member, emphasize failure rather than survival, embarrass rather than encourage. Family members may communicate to each other that there can be only one version of a family story, and to tell it another away is to be disloyal. It is very hard for individual family members who are being scapegoated or stunted by a story to change it in any way. Sometimes others outside the family can listen to the story with fresh ears and ask questions that help an individual tell it differently. For some, family counseling is a way of giving a new audience and input to family stories, and therefore new possibilities for change. The outsider, whether a counselor or a friend, validates the new story by being a witness to its meaning. The faith community can be a powerful witness to the stories of its families. In fact, although that was not my original intention in listening to Renee's stories about her family, I became a representative of the church who witnessed her family's story of faithfulness.

DIFFERENT KINDS OF FAMILY STORIES

All family stories are at some level stories of family identity. They say something about who the family is, about its character, about its history, about its values and virtues, about the family's place in the world.

Stories of Beginnings, and New Beginnings

The "how we became a family" stories are perhaps the most common. Often young couples share these stories with one another: how they met, the funny things that happened at the wedding. These stories, which are particularly valued if they can be humorous as well as romantic, become part of the fabric of family identity, even for children born long after, who try to imagine parents as dating couple and bride and groom.

There are also stories for all the ways people come into a family. Birth stories and adoption stories—for both children and adults—

are particularly powerful, because they say, "You were a part of us before you can even remember, but we remember." There are hilarious stories of first meetings between future sons-in-law and fathers-in-law. There are stories of the advent of stepparents into family life, of when Grandpa came to live with us. Clearly these stories give a family a sense of history and identity.

There may also be stories of beginnings and new beginnings of a different kind. "Do you remember moving day?" may help a family recollect the terrors and excitement of moving to a new house or community. Because community and the physical place of home is so important to defining family, changes in home and community are also important in our saying, "This is who we are." No doubt, you can remember vividly the day you moved into a new home, perhaps sitting on the floor surrounded by boxes, eating take-out food, wondering what life would be like in this new place.

Stories of Loss and Endings

Just as there are stories of beginnings, there are stories of endings, of grief, of loss. In my interviews, I heard many stories from family members about the experiences surrounding the illness or accident and death of their beloveds. Clearly these moments critically redefine what it means to be family. There are other kinds of loss and endings that profoundly affect family identity: illness and disability, retirement, divorce, and family alienation.

Stories of Heroes and Ancestors

Families also have stories of courage, of adventure, of heroic members, and, by extension, of the family they represent. These stories tell the family that it is courageous, strong, compassionate, smart, or just special. Sometimes stories of family members now gone are ways of keeping them a part of the family in the present; the family member is still alive in the story, still present to the family. Stories can be ways of holding on to those otherwise lost to us, to keep them a part of our lives—to "re-member," reattach them to ourselves. Writer and theologian Frederick Buechner suggests that stories make the distinction between past, present, and future ultimately meaningless and allow us to taste the eternity that God inhabits.

For example, family researcher Elizabeth Stone recounts a powerful family story from the life of Paulette Berry. Paulette Berry was eight years old when she was among the first African American children to attend a formerly all-white elementary school in Topeka, Kansas, in the 1950s. In 1954 the Supreme Court had ruled that segregated schools are inherently unequal, the case of *Brown v. Board of Education of Topeka.* As her grandmother took Paulette and her brother to school that first day, she told them a story they had heard many times before.

"She would tell me and my brother about my great-great-grandfather Dodge, who was a slave in Tennessee. He was an organizer, and to make an example of him, they cut his stomach open, just cut it right open. The last they ever saw of him, he was running up the road holding his guts in. He still kept his dignity."

The word *guts* is the key to the story. It suggests courage and, in the story, the power to contain oneself with dignity even when mortally wounded. The story is not of physical survival but of spiritual power and victory that transcends life itself, of not being spiritually conquered, even in death. Paulette Berry's great-great-grandfather did not "spill" his guts; he turned his back on the enemy and held himself together. It was a powerful image, powerful enough to help an eight-year-old girl cope with mean-spirited racism directed at her from taunting children and hate-filled adults. Paulette said that "When something came up where they didn't want me and my brother to waver, or where they were afraid we would waver, they'd tell us that story."

Not all heroes are ancestors, however. Sometimes family members tell these stories about themselves, attempting (sometimes successfully) to serve as a model of the values or characteristics that they want to instill in other family members. Or they may simply give a sense of historical identity that other family members might otherwise not have. These are the "I had to walk five miles uphill in two feet of snow every day to go to school" stories. Older family members want the young to hear these stories so they know that families do not survive without hard work or courage or faith or commitment to one another. Sometimes these stories locate the family in historical events—surviving the Dust Bowl days in Oklahoma during the Depression, the Trail of Tears, the Holocaust, the U.S. detention camps for Japanese-American families during World War II, the Vietnam War. Sometimes the whole family is heroic. Refugee families have stories to tell of the choices they made to leave a place, their sacrifices and perilous journeys, perhaps if not physically perilous, then perilous in the loss of everything familiar. Families together facing the care of an injured or chronically ill member have stories of quiet courage to tell.

Stories of Survival

In her research on family stories, Elizabeth Stone found that family stories often illustrate and give meaning to the cardinal rule that when people are *really* suffering, they can count on the family. Every family has survived some crisis or traumatic event, and many have stories to tell about that survival—of a war, a depression, unemployment, a natural disaster, three preschoolers in diapers at the same time. These stories may not be fodder for a movie drama, and they may not be all that gripping even to kind friends outside the family. They are the story equivalent of vacation slides—wonderful memories for us and a boring evening for others. For the family, however, these stories are important because they have come through the experience—together. And telling the story of that coming through is an important part of the survival itself.

Families work through pain and trauma by telling stories about it. As they shape words into a story, the family has become active in shaping the experience, preserving it in a form they can manipulate through the telling. Although the experience has shaped them in some significant way, telling the story also begins to give them some sense of control over the story—and the experience it represents. They define themselves as survivors, with the closure that comes from telling a story that has an ending.

Cautionary Tales

Still other stories are cautionary tales, such as my story of losing John on that cold November night. Cautionary tales may be told of the cousin who was badly injured in a motorcycle accident ("and I'd better never catch you on one!") or the uncle who became an alcoholic. Cautionary tales come straight out of our deepest worries and sorrows and have the purpose of trying to keep loved ones safe. We warn our loved ones not to make the same mistakes.

Cautionary tales can be healing. They turn the sin or foolishness or bad fortune of a family experience into a gift to others in the family or community: "Here is our experience; learn from us." Telling the story of losing John has been one way of dealing with my own guilt and with the horrible specter of what could have happened. I no longer squeeze my eyes shut and try to block out the memory but have transformed it through a story into what I hope will be a gift to others. The sad and sinful things that happen remain a part of us, but they are no longer as much of a burden of guilt and regret but perhaps more a source of wisdom and strength for the future.

Not only do stories deepen experiences, they also let us hold them differently. Telling the story enables us to put boundaries around an experience by providing a beginning and an ending, so it doesn't overwhelm or control us so much. Have you ever had a memory of an embarrassing moment come crashing in on you? You find yourself muttering to yourself, even out loud, which only adds to the embarrassment: "I can't believe I did that." But if we tell the story to someone else, that person shares it with us. We laugh together over it or cry over it, and it is not so powerfully shaming or embarrassing. We are human, and the other still accepts us and shares in our humanness.

The Funny Family Tale

For many families, having fun together provides a powerful and valued sense of identity. Many of the families I interviewed described with considerable pride how much they enjoy being together, "just laughing together." Often the fuel for that laughter is a story about themselves. One genre of family stories is the vacation or holiday disaster. These stories are usually told and retold with more zeal than stories of disaster-free vacations. They include, for us, the vacation to Maine with friends when it was rainy and foggy every day, and we could see none of the scenery we had driven more than a thousand miles to see. With those same friends, we journeyed another time to the Florida Everglades in August, where the climax of the trip was being seasick together on a miserable boat trip. These stories are important because they say that not only can this family (and friendship) survive adversity but we can laugh at it and keep on loving each other.

Humor depends on perspective. At the time, there was nothing terribly funny about waking up to fog every morning or being seasick on that boat off the Florida Keys—until we began to joke about it. An experience can be embarrassing, sad, or perhaps even tragic, but by turning it a different way in the telling of it, it can be funny. The great philosopher Hawkeye on the old *M.A.S.H.* television show once said something like, "Laughter means looking at the world sideways." Stories can turn the world sideways for us.

In a group of caregivers of persons with Alzheimer's disease, one middle-aged daughter told about the challenges her mother presents. The mother was dressing for the day and pulled on one leg of her panty hose. She then looked in puzzlement at the other leg of the hosiery dangling there. She couldn't figure out what it was for and cut it off with some too-handy scissors before her daughter realized what she was doing. The group of women laughed together at this story, understanding that it is terribly sad but also quite funny. Of course, this older woman had come to the age of wearing stockings long before panty hose had been invented. During her early life, she had worn stockings that only came "one leg at a time," held up by garters. Early memories outlast the shorter-term memories, so the memory of stockings and garters had endured when panty hose had been forgotten. One can either laugh or cry—or both—at stories like this. These women chose to laugh together at this story not at all to discount the tragedy that is Alzheimer's or to diminish the grief of watching one's mother lose her capacities, but instead as a means of defying tragedy and grief. This too is a story about family identity. As this daughter shared this story, she told a story about the humor and tragedy of caregiving, of her patience and her impatience—of the long-suffering faithfulness of loving and caring in what has been called the living death of Alzheimer's disease.

Sacred Stories

For many families, some of their stories clearly and overtly involve the sacred dimension of their lives. They are stories of experiencing God's presence or movement in their life together. The same God who called Abraham and Sarah to leave the familiar and strike out in a new direction, who led Noah to build an ark for protecting his family and all of the animal creation, who called Mary and Joseph to parent the son of God, and who worked in the lives of all the other very human, imperfect families of the Bible works in the lives of families today. Hidden in both times of crisis as well as our ordinary daily living, God is at work, if we can but open our eyes and ears. Just as we read the Bible to learn about God, so we should read our own experiences to find our perhaps small but significant role in the vast purposes of God. To keep our stories in mind keeps us open to the story that God is creating with every family—the story of their lives together.

Sacred stories do not necessarily use religious language, nor do they necessarily speak overtly of God. Yet they connect us to a sense of meaning and purpose in our own lives, and to the great truths of our faith. For example, from this perspective, one of the earliest sacred stories families tell to one another is the game of peekaboo with a baby. We cover our faces and then reappear with feigned surprise and exaggerated expressions of delight, often greeted by laughter from the baby. The language is not at all religious—there is no "language" at all, in fact. But there is a plot. Even when you can't see me, I am still here for you. I'll always come back. Children learn to trust the faithfulness of parents, and parents learn in a new way the cost and joy of faithful parenting. This experience of child-parent faithfulness connects us to the sacred truth of God's faithfulness, of Jesus' promise, "And know that I am with you always; yes, to the end of time" (Matthew 28:20 NIV). Even peekaboo is a story of faith.

Sacred stories may connect to many themes of faith, themes of love, joy, creation, rebirth, repentance and forgiveness, friendship, covenant, faithfulness, being lost and found. Because these are universal themes, sacred stories tell not only about how we are somehow part of the great story God is telling but also how we connect with and are like other families. Because many stories have more than one purpose in the telling, many are sacred stories at the same time they may be cautionary tales, or stories of beginnings or loss, or stories of heroes, or stories of survival. Two stories we have explored in this chapter are at their deepest level sacred stories. The story of the sick dog and the sad boy is a story of faithfulness; this family's actions said to each family member, "We will be there for you, no matter what." They connect in their faithfulness even in the midst of human frailty to the unfathomable faithfulness of God. My story of losing my son, my worry for him, and my joy at his being found connect with the biblical narratives of being lost and then being found, of God's grief when we lose ourselves, of a whole community searching for the lost sheep, the "little one" lost (Matthew 18:14 NIV).

Just as Jesus is the Word made flesh, we use our physical bodies through voice and gesture to give flesh and blood to words of experience. If we tell the story well, it lives on in the listener. Our language is limited when it comes to describing our relationship with the Creator God, infinite and holy and beyond our understanding. We therefore use pictures and symbols to help us say more meaning than our words can hold. Stories picture our relationship with the Divine when language is inadequate. They are the melody that gives the words depth and power.

All families have stories. All families also have *potential* stories; they have experiences stored in their collective memories that have not yet been shaped into stories. Family storytelling requires time together for just talking—while eating together, while doing chores together, or while barreling down the road in the car on a trip or an errand. Most often families tell stories in the midst of mundane daily activities. Of course, not every meal we share or trip we take becomes an occasion for storytelling. Sometimes they are times for arguments and problem solving and all the other items on the agenda of family life. But if there is no time together, there can be no time for stories. I hope as you read the stories of families in the chapters to come, you will be prompted to remember your own stories. Perhaps there will be moments for sharing those stories with one another again or for the first time.

Family stories also take on power with an audience, with a listening community beyond the family itself. In the act of witnessing the telling of a story, the audience contributes to the discovery of new meanings. The audience's experience of the story affects the storyteller and the telling, so that the story is revised, re-visioned. That is, a new vision or perspective is given to the story, both for the audience and for the storyteller. For this reason, congregations need to be places where families can share their stories. The faith community provides a rich context for storytelling, helping families experience afresh and perhaps for the first time the sacred in their stories. Renee needed to tell her story of family faithfulness to her faith community, and they needed to hear it. I needed to tell my story of parental failure to my faith community, to have them hear me and love me even though I had managed to lose one of my children and it took the whole community to find him. One of the many ways a congregation can support and strengthen families is to be a place that encourages them to share their faith stories.

For congregations to become communities of faith that encourage families to tell their stories of faith means that family members must be together at least some of the time in the life of the congregation. Splitting in all directions to age-graded programs may provide a place for individuals to tell stories about their families' lives, but that is very different from providing opportunities for family members to share in talking about their family and their faith to one another and to other families. In addition, family storytelling goes against the grain of how our culture uses stories. In many respects, our culture has professionalized storytelling. We use stories in literature and in the media to educate, to illustrate life principles, and of course to entertain. Although professionally told stories in books and in media are valuable, we need to reclaim our own family stories as the rich resource for knowing one another and learning the things that matter from one another.

This book came out of my search for faith as a dimension of family life, and in my work, I found family faith embedded in family stories. When families describe the ways they seek to live their faith in everyday life, how they find meaning and purpose in their lives together, and how they have experienced God in the midst of ordinary life, they told me stories. This book focuses, then, on the sacred stories of family life. The stories I have selected from the families I interviewed are not more important than any others I might have gathered and shared. Their significance rests in the chance that if I tell the stories well, you will recognize that their stories are also, in many ways, your own family story waiting to be told.

Chapter 2

THE CHALLENGE OF BEING FAMILY

Peggy and Bill were high school sweethearts a half-century ago. They married when she was twenty and he was twenty-one; the year was 1952. Anglo-Americans, they have lived all but the first three years of their marriage in a rural southern town a half-hour drive from the nearby city where they lived as children and met in school. Their home reminded me of the homes of my great-aunts and grandparents when I was growing up. Set back from a two-lane rural road, with a long gravel driveway under tall shade trees, their white frame house is located on more than an acre of land, with a substantial vegetable garden in a sunny plot behind the backyard swing and garage. An ample front porch with a swing conjured childhood memories of parents carrying their iced-tea glasses out after dinner for just sitting a while to talk and catch the cooler breezes of evening. Inside, family pictures sat on the tops of tables, and comfortable furniture communicated welcome.

For thirty-three years, Peggy and Bill were partners in a real estate business with Bob and Mary, the couple who lived next door.

The two couples began their business together when their children were babies. The wives each worked half a day in the business and shared responsibility for mothering the seven children they had between them. In the years before retirement, however, the men had an argument over some business matters. Bill and Peggy sold their interests in the company to Bob and Mary and then opened a competing company. When I asked what that meant for their relationship with Bob and Mary, Bill said, "For two or three years, we didn't speak to one another. Feelings were strained. We were still going to the same church. We spoke, but there was ill will. And then over the years, we drifted back together. Bob lost his mother and daddy, and his own health was deteriorating, and I lost my daddy meanwhile. We began to get back to the things that were basic. We drew back to each other. And then Bob died three years ago."

"But before he died, we were close again," Peggy added. "And Mary. We love her."

And Bill continued, "Bob was my best friend. Because he was an outsider, I could go and talk to him about anything, and I think he could me."

I focused in on one of Bill's comments, "You saw him as an outsider."

"Well, he wasn't a member of the family, you know," Bill replied. "Now, I guess, through his losses and our losses we developed a family relationship. In fact, his wife mentioned the other day, 'You're not an outsider; you're family.' Well, you know, you don't live with people this long without becoming that. I'd never thought about that. I commented to my wife that night, I said, 'You know, she considers us family.'"

Mary's naming them as family gave him a new way of thinking about what a family is. Through the daily life they lived together in their work and in the raising of children, he ponders, maybe they had become family. They went through a terrible time after they parted ways. Their anger and not speaking to one another must have hung heavy in the air of their congregation and small community. But families can act that way too; we get angriest at those with whom we are the closest. Abraham and Lot, an uncle and nephew, called one another brothers. Abraham took his wife and Lot with him when he followed God's call to a new land, but after a business friction led to family quarrelling, they parted ways (Genesis 11). But in a time of difficulty, Abraham dropped the quarrel and came to Lot's rescue (Genesis 14). As with Abraham and Lot—and many families—life crises for Bob and Bill pulled them back together; their lives had been so interwoven that they felt the need for one another as they faced the

SACRED STORIES OF ORDINARY FAMILIES

deaths of parents, the death of Peggy and Bill's son, and their own mortality. Bill and Peggy have pondered this together; the day Mary called them family, Bill said that they had talked about it later that evening, in one of those conversations couples have woven into the fabric of daily life, perhaps clearing the table or sitting on the front porch. "She considers us family." A statement, it also presented a question to turn over in their minds together.

WHO GETS TO WEAR AN "INSIDER" BADGE?

As we saw in Chapter One, families use stories to define their identity, who they are. One of the most basic elements of a family's identity is its membership, who is family and who is not. In Peggy and Bill's story, we see how they have defined themselves and are now in a process of redefining themselves. In our culture, we define family as those to whom we are related by biological kinship, marriage, or legal adoption. Typically, we define the nuclear family, a married couple and their children, as the norm, the so-called traditional family. In Bill's mind, he and Peggy have been a traditional family, married all their adult lives and now with grown children and grandchildren. But Mary, his best friend's wife, called his definition of Bob as an outsider into question. Can lifelong friends qualify too as family? And anyway, what difference does it make whether they call her a close friend or family?

When I go to conferences that have preprinted name badges handed out at registration, sometimes I am lucky enough to have a ribbon attached that says that I am somebody special at the conference—a presenter or a committee member of one kind or another, or perhaps a board member. It is embarrassing to admit that I enjoy the feeling of being special that such a ribbon gives me. Others evidently do too, or conferences would not bother attaching them to name tags. Those ribbons mean I am on the inside of what is going on. I have a named role (presenter, board member) that says I am an insider. I am not just an attendee, just another name on a badge.

In much the same way in families, the difference between being close friend and a family member does matter; being a family member is like having a ribbon with a named role. With that role as a family member comes not only a special identity but also major responsibilities and entitlements. We get to give and have to take advice and meddling from family members that friends would see as inappropriate. We can expect to be cared for and to care for others in a family in ways beyond what friends are expected to do. Friends certainly do take care of one another in a pinch, and sometimes in major ways, but usually for relatively short periods of time. Families, however, are expected to be there for one another for a lifetime.

The ribbons that families use to identify themselves can come in many forms. For some, they are the names we get simply by being born or married into the family: brother, wife, father, daughter. For others, like Mary, insider ribbons represent how people have *become* family to one another over time. If Mary had really become family to Peggy and Bill, they might speak of her as being like a sister, and the grown children might call her Aunt Mary. Names are important; they affirm and strengthen the bond as family rather than just friends. Moreover, naming and living with one another as family also is an important way we live the teachings of Jesus.

Family in Jesus' Life and Teachings

Jesus' own lineage, family relationships, and teachings challenge the limiting of family relationships to marriage and blood kinship. In the family tree that opens the Gospel of Matthew, we read fifteen verses of *begat*s by one father after another. When it comes to Jesus, the pattern changes. Joseph is not named as Jesus' father, because "before they lived together, she was found to be with child from the Holy Spirit" (1:18 NRSV). Instead, the writer calls Joseph "the husband of Mary of whom Jesus was born" (1:16). Despite the fact that Joseph was not Jesus' biological father, Joseph accepted him as his son by naming him, adopting him as his own (1:25). This adoption builds from the very birth of Jesus on Old Testament prophecy and prefaces the good news that Jesus himself would proclaim: in God's kingdom, no one has to be without family: "God sets the lonely in families" (Psalm 68:5–6a NIV).

When we follow Jesus, he teaches us, God provides a new family among the faithful. Jesus used an incident in his own family to bring home this point. His mother and brothers, like good family caregivers, have heard that his teachings may lead to real trouble and so have come to persuade him to come home and perhaps lie low for a while. They evidently cannot get close enough to him to talk because of the crowd, however, so they send word through the crowd that they are outside and want to speak with him. In response, Jesus says, "'Who is my mother, and who are my brothers?' And pointing to his disciples, he said, 'Here are my mother and my brothers! For whoever does the will of my Father in heaven is my brother and sister and mother'" (Matthew 12:48–50 NRSV).

Family now means *choosing,* choosing to follow Jesus and choosing to be family for one another. Our shared faith binds us together. We are no longer limited to family relationships defined by biological kinship or marriage. In looking at events later in Jesus' life, we see that Jesus was not severing family ties with his mother and brothers with these words. His mother was with him to the very end of his life, standing at the foot of the cross. His brothers became disciples and leaders in the early church. They *were* family, but they also *became* family to Jesus and to one another—and others—in their choice to follow him.

The Gospel of John (19:26–30 NRSV) records the last teaching of Jesus about family before his death. Mary stood at the foot of the cross with the other women, watching her son suffer. The beloved disciple stood beside her. Jesus looked at her and said, "Woman, here is your son." And to the disciple, he said, "Here is your mother." The very next verse states that Jesus knew that "all was finished." Proclaiming this adoptive relationship finished his ministry. This was part of the plan. Would they have cared for one another if Jesus had not spoken them into existence as adoptive family? Perhaps, but clearly, naming the relationship had power. "*And from that hour* the disciple took her to his own home" (italics added). Perhaps Jesus could have spoken to the group in good southern idiom, "Y'all take care of one another." But he was not telling the church to be the community of faith in this place; he was turning two people within the community into an adoptive family. Naming the relationship as family strengthens and transforms the

33

tie. That is what Bill started to realize once Mary, the next-door neighbor and his best friend's widow, named them family. Ribbons on name tags are significant!

NAMING FAMILY

How can we apply Jesus' life example and teachings to our understanding of family today? Every family I talked with answered my question "Who is your family?" by beginning with various combinations of spouses, children, parents, and siblings. These relationships are what our culture means by the term *family*. For example, single adults, particularly those who had never married, often began their definition with, "Of course, there are my parents and my brother. . . ." People related by blood and marriage are what I call the of-course family.

Adults who have been divorced find the of-course nature of family ruptured. Karen, an Anglo-American woman in her forties, has struggled to make ends meet for herself and her five-year-old son since her husband left a year ago. She and her son, Paul, live in a rented house in an older inner-city southern neighborhood. A stray cat has taken up residence on the glassed-in front porch, and Karen does not have the heart to put it out. Three more cats live inside the house, and two dogs live in the backyard. Karen is clearly a welcoming person, not only to animals but to people too. Shortly after her husband left her, a friend whose job is placing high school foreign exchange students in homes was desperate to find a home for a South American student. Karen cleared a place for him. When I asked Karen, "Tell me who your family is," she replied, with tears rolling down her face, "Since my husband left us a year ago, I guess I'm really not sure. Oh, I know that Paul and I are family. I consider my family my mom and dad and my sisters and Paul and me, and Jorge is now a part of our family. He's my exchange student. I'm crying because I feel like I'm still struggling with making a family with just us. My husband deserted us."

As the only adult, Karen is struggling to "make a family." For a long time, she had hoped her husband would return. In fact, she and her ex-husband still have not told Paul that they have divorced, just that he is away working in another city. The two of them have stayed in almost daily contact, as Karen's ex-husband tries to continue to be active and present in Paul's life. As important as his involvement is for Paul, in some ways it has made it harder for Karen to accept the divorce. She wanted to believe that perhaps he would change his mind, and their frequent conversations about Paul fed that false hope. Now she is facing the reality that she and her ex-husband have to figure out how to be coparents without being spouses—and explain that to Paul. In the meantime she has filled the house with pets and an exchange student. She has, in essence, begun to create a revised family.

Many families remake themselves after a divorce through remarriage. In twenty of the 110 families I talked with, one or both spouses had been previously married. They used language such as "mixed," "blended," and "a yours-mine-and-ours family" if there were children involved in the household. They also included in their families children living elsewhere, whether grown or living with the other parent. Like first-marriage families, they named their own siblings and parents, all living elsewhere, as family members. But they also had to work at defining themselves much more than of-course families did.

Patrick and Tess live in a beautiful home they had custom built, nestled in a rural wooded area, a twenty-minute commute from the city where they both work. Patrick grew up Catholic and attended seminary before deciding that the life of a priest was not his calling and became an architect. Tess grew up Baptist and is a teacher. They are Anglo-American and each have two children from their first marriages, ranging in ages now from seventeen to twenty-one. They have been married to each other for twelve years, so their marriage began with all four children in the preschool and school-age years. Tess's children have lived with them, and although Patrick's children have lived with their mother, they frequently visit. Patrick and Tess talked about all the difficulties of forming their family, the conflicts among the children, and a couple of rounds of counseling for their marriage.

In blending families with children from two previous marriages, each spouse must somehow redefine the relationship with the ex-spouse. They have to figure out how to continue to work together as partners in raising their children. Because parenting creates more stress than anything else in marriages, it creates major challenges for divorced parents. They have to sort out how to work together as co-parents at the same time they are both forging new marital bonds and also working out ways that the new couple will handle two sets of children in a new family unit. Patrick and Tess have experienced these challenges and worked through them, but it has not been easy. They have been working to build their marriage at the same time that they have struggled into new coparenting roles with former spouses. And they have learned that if there is conflict in a marriage that leads to divorce, that conflict may be even harder to deal with around the issues of continuing to parent together, even if both parents are really trying and willing to call a truce on all the other battlegrounds of the former marriage.

Patrick told me how they have become a family together:

My image of us as a family is a video the children made many years ago for my parents' anniversary. For six minutes, they talked about being "almost a family" to my parents, although there were what we jokingly call "real" and "unreal" kids. My parents treat them all as grandchildren. There was just a lot of humor and love and togetherness in that video. We replay it occasionally, and we all laugh so hard because the children are so young, and their humor is so great, and the animals are all involved. Being a blended family, it's very difficult to move beyond those roles that are assigned to you.

A couple of Christmases ago, my stepdaughter, Jennifer, was a freshman, and she had to do a paper for college, and that paper became a gift. We were opening Christmas presents, and everyone was laughing, and we'd been to church and having our usual fun and silliness. When Jennifer gave me my special Christmas present from her, I opened it up and I started to read; it was that paper. I started to cry, and then Jennifer started to cry, and the whole family was saying, "What is going on? We don't understand." Jennifer had written a paper entitled "My Dad," and it was written to me and about me. It said, "You're my dad. You may not be my biological father, but for all intents and purposes you are what a father is." And it went on to say how she hated me when I took her mom away and how we grew through the years and how she couldn't have done it without me. So that was the Christmas gift. She got an A from her professor on the paper, and I felt like she gave me an A for being a father.

This family has used self-made gifts to one another—a video for grandparents and a college paper for the stepdad—to tell one another, "We're family." Humor in the stories softened and also underlined some of what Patrick calls "things that you struggle with," demonstrated in the children calling themselves "real" and "unreal" kids.

The terms *blended family* and *stepfamily* both imply that the legal act of marriage creates a family almost instantly: throw the ingredients in a blender, give it a whirl, and out comes a "smoothie" family. As any stepfamily can testify, however, there is nothing instant about the process of becoming a family. Trust, respect, and entitlement to be in one another's lives only develop with time and hard work. *Blending,* on the other hand, is a term that implies an ongoing process. Like Bill's relationship with his friend Bob's widow, sometimes people in blending families struggle, often for years, with completely accepting one another as full-fledged family.

John and Nell, Anglo-Americans, described their blending process, which took more than fifteen years. They are actively involved in their Methodist church in the nearby city where they used to live, commuting thirty minutes each way to attend. Nell was married before to a farmer who died when their daughter, Amy, was twelve years old. Nell sold the farm and moved into the city. Six years later, she married John, who had never been married before. Amy had great difficulty accepting John after being her mother's primary focus since her father's death. Amy and John's relationship gradually changed over time, however, especially after Amy married and had children of her own. John and Nell, who took early retirement a few years ago from their government jobs, provide care for Amy's children before and after school. In addition, Amy and her husband and children have dinner almost daily with Nell and John; Nell cooks for all of them. Clearly, although they live in two households, they are one family.

John considered what this new family cost him: "When my oldest granddaughter [his step-granddaughter], Agatha, turned five and was going to start to kindergarten, Nell and I talked about keeping her in the afternoon. I wasn't against it, but I had a lot of thought about whether or not I wanted to be pinned down like that. But it's the best thing we ever did. It was the best thing that ever happened to us."

Amy added, "Up until then, my dad [stepdad] and I pretty much tolerated each other, but once Agatha was born, it provided us with a bond, and it really changed our relationship. It gave me some credentials." She is now mother of his grandchildren and therefore his daughter. *Step-* has dropped out of their vocabulary.

These shifts in family definitions often come when some change alters the family's boundaries in some way. For Bill and Peggy and their neighbors—business partners, the loss of their own parents in some way pushed them to bridge their conflict and reclaim one another in a new way that they recognized as—maybe—family. At a very different stage of family life, the addition of children, Amy and John found themselves also looking at one another differently. As they said, they no longer call one another "my mother's new husband" and "my wife's daughter"; instead, they have become "my dad" and "my daughter." In both cases, it seems, the needs of the family pushed them to open the boundary enough to call one another family. Peggy, Bill, and Mary find themselves increasingly alone in the world, with the death of Mary's husband and all of their parents. Amy and her husband find themselves needing and valuing the support of grandparents in providing care for their daughters after school. Although these needs may have prompted this redefinition of family, these are clearly not just utilitarian relationships. The caring and support are genuine and mutual.

As Patrick and Tess's family experienced, when divorce ruptures families, the relationship between ex-spouses also must be redefined.

Relationships with former spouses may be family-like or not. Some remarried couples I talked to continued to relate to an ex-spouse or an ex-spouse's relatives as family, even with all the difficulties that continued closeness created for them and the lack of social support for such an arrangement. Renee, the mother in the story of a sick dog and a sad boy in Chapter One, let her husband move back into separate quarters in the household to help handle a crisis. Karen, the divorced mother with a preschooler and an exchange student, is still living the fiction for her son—and perhaps for herself—that her ex-husband is only away working in another city.

All of these stories about family membership are about families that have relationships that vary in some way or another from the of-course family, and there is a reason for that! Of-course families do not need stories to say, "This is who our members are." They often tell stories about becoming family, stories of courtship and marriage or the birthing of children. But they do not *have* to tell a story to explain who they are. They can simply recite a list: "Of course, there is my mom and dad, and my brother in Cincinnati and his wife," or "Well, of course, there is my wife and me, and we have three kids; one of them is away at college." These families always have stories to tell about the people on that list. Other kinds of family relationships, however, really need stories to say, "This is how we got to be family to one another."

Beyond Households

Many families live in different spaces and places but are still family for one another. Spouses may live in different cities during the work-week. A single woman raising her nieces and nephews is also, with the assistance of a sister-in-law, providing daily care for her mother, who lives a few houses away: taking her to the doctor, taking care of her house, and paying her bills. Grandparents Nell and John provide daily care for their grandchildren, and toys and other paraphernalia reflect the presence of children in their house, even though, technically, the children live somewhere else.

Some families experience stress because their lives across households run counter to social norms. Shamika, age twenty-four, was raised by her widowed African American mother, Sheryl. They have continued to have a very close relationship, even after Shamika's marriage to Charlie, who is Anglo-American, last year. But that relationship is not without its ups and downs.

As Shamika describes it,

> My mom is very insecure about all the time she spends with Charlie and me because she has friends that she works with who have children that are around our age, and their kids don't want them around at all. They always tell her, "Oh, Charlie's just letting you go because he feels sorry for you being all alone like you are. You're fifty-five years old. A couple of twenty-four-year-olds don't want you around." So sometimes when we're going somewhere and want her to come, she says, "Oh, it's OK. I don't have to go," and then Charlie says, "You're going." So he just drives over there and sits in the car and blows the horn, and she says, "What are you doing?" and he says, "Well, the movie starts in fifteen minutes, and if you don't get in the car soon, we're going to miss it." He wants her to see that it's not that we feel sorry for her.

According to Shamika, her mother has misgivings about the close relationship with her married daughter, fueled by well-meaning friends, in spite of Shamika and Charlie's encouragement that they want her in their lives. Cultural expectations about how mothers are related to their daughters and sons-in-law cause her to worry that she is undermining her daughter's marriage in some way.

Special Family Relationships

When family relationships take on functions that are different from the norms for our culture, they need stories to define for the family and for others what makes these relationships special or "like family." For example, as I learned from talking to all these families, grown brothers and sisters function in a wide range of ways for one another. In particular, siblings are especially central family figures for many single adults. Respondents often mentioned a particular sibling with whom they had a strong bond because they were closest in birth order, because life circumstances pushed them together in some way (for example, one "raised" the other), or because they shared similar interests and enjoyed one another's company.

Maurina, an African American businesswoman in her forties, describes her relationship with her sister, Annalea, as being very close: "We do everything together. We do a lot of traveling together. There's times when I even talk to God and say, 'If one of us has to go, take me. Don't leave me here to have to try to deal without her. Take me first.' We're like the Delany sisters. I don't know if I could ever live knowing my sister's not here because she's all I've ever known. When I had no money, she paid my rent. When I was at my worst and ill, she took care of me."

In addition to other dimensions of her close relationship with her sister, Maurina lives only a few blocks away from their aging parents, as does Annalea. Together, the two sisters are caring for their parents, in addition to traveling together, being best friends, and providing one another with emotional and material support. Their relationship has deepened over the more than twenty years since they were children and teenagers in the same household, becoming qualitatively different, closer than their relationship with two other siblings. Maurina uses the story of the Delany sisters to describe her feelings about her sister. (The book *Having Our Say: The Delany Sisters' First 100 Years* describes the life of two sisters who lived together for over a century.)

The term *sisters* can range in meaning from the closest of family, like Maurina and Annalea, to two women who occasionally see one another at family gatherings. Even if the relationship goes years without being acted on, when a parent becomes ill or another family crisis comes up, sisters are expected to be able to call on and help one another. The same is true for other of-course family relationships of parent-child and brothers.

Like Family

What about special relationships that have no underlying family relationship to hang their name on? If Bill and Peggy decide that next-door neighbor Mary really is family, how will they name her, call her by a family title? How will it change their relationship with her? Family relationships that are not overlays of existing marriage or kinship relationships often use kinship names to communicate, "We are family." They may use the term *sister* with a qualifier such as *like:* like sisters.

Irene, an Anglo-American widow in her seventies, has lived for forty years next door to Doris, also now widowed. They take daily walks together. While they walk, they talk about all manner of life issues in ways they cannot talk to their grown children. Irene says,

> We're more like sisters than neighbors, really. If she needs anything, I can do it; and if I need anything, she does it. I hate to think about moving away at any time, but I know we'll have to sometime. Eventually, I'll probably have to get closer to my son when it gets to the place where I need more help. My daughter and I went two or three months ago to take care of my mother-in-law. She is ninety-eight years old and had fallen and had to be put in the hospital. We finally went down and put her into a nursing home because we couldn't get her to move into assisted living or anything. She was depending on neighbors, and it was getting very hard on them.

Irene calls her relationship with Doris "like sisters." She is more than just a neighbor. Yet Irene makes an interesting distinction between being like sisters and really being family. When ill health makes independent living difficult, Irene suggests that family will trump the people who are like family. She will move nearer her son, just as she, as family, stepped in, took over from the neighbors, and provided the decision making for her mother-in-law's care. Of course, for others, those who are like family do step in, often in the absence of the of-course family. When Maurina and Annalea's brother married a woman who developed terminal cancer just months after their marriage, her own children wanted to put her in a nursing home because they were unable to give her the intensive caregiving that she needed. It was Maurina and Annalea and their parents who became family for their brother's/son's new wife, providing daily care for the last months of her life.

Despite this ultimate distinction between real family and "like family," clearly these "like family" relationships nudge the boundary of family, even if they are not, when push comes to shove, really family as our culture defines it. Naming another as family may even move the relationship into being "really family." Some families use the old terms *godparent* and *godchild* to name family members. The concept of godparentage developed in the twelfth century as a way of establishing spiritual kinship between families unrelated by blood or marriage. In American culture, godparents may be either family members (often siblings) or close friends who agree to be a child's guardian, should the parents die. In some faith traditions, godparents agree to care for the child's spiritual well-being. Clearly it is a relationship that carries both obligations and entitlements. When our closest friends asked us to be godparents to their boys and we accepted, I found myself much more likely to give the boys advice, hug them, and discipline them when they needed it, more like a parent than a friend. After all, I thought, *I might end up parenting them!* In turn, they felt entitled to relate to my husband and me more like parents than friends of their parents, making themselves at home in our home: opening the refrigerator without asking when they were hungry, not having to be on their best behavior, and even living with us for short periods of time. There is much more to our relationship than friendship; we are family.

When I asked Anne, a single, never-married African American woman completing a medical internship, to tell me who her family was, she said, "My family is my mother, my father, my two sisters, my one brother, and my niece and nephew, my sister-in-law, my brother-in-law, and my godmother and her family. That's my family." Without prompting, she followed that list with a story about her godmother, whom she had met as a patient at the clinic where Anne works. The other family relationships don't need a story to be believable, but since "godmother" is not a usual character in our culture's families, Anne needed a story to explain. Out of their professional work together, a friendship blossomed, which then became like family. Anne and her godmother are members of the same church.

The Challenge of Being Family

During illness, they take care of one another. Her godmother is the only one besides her parents that she trusts enough to have a key to her house. Anne told me later that her new phone has a speed-dial feature, and after she entered five phone numbers of her parents and siblings, the sixth and last number she entered was her godmother's. Family means being able to speed-dial one another.

THE IMPORTANCE OF CARING FOR FAMILY

Relationships are frequently organized by caregiving across the generations, most often in the grooves of traditional gender roles. Grandmothers and aunts provide child care; older sisters step in to parent younger siblings; sisters and daughters provide emotional support and cooking and cleaning; and sons provide household maintenance. Anne's sister Hope, younger by seven years, lived with her for five years because their parents moved to another city and Anne could provide Hope with stability in school. Hope was sixteen years old when she came to live with Anne, herself in her early twenties at the time. "I had her at the height of the teenage years. So that was a challenge. An absolute challenge. She is like my child. She and my older sister have that sisterly relationship, but she and I have always had more of a mother-daughter relationship."

Caregiving appears both to intensify relationships and to symbolize and define the relationship as family. In fact, family is fundamentally all about caregiving. To be family, we don't have to talk much, share the same values and opinions, live together, or even like one another, but we rely on one another for care when we need it. When that care is not there, our cultural expectations of family are offended. Maurina, the single woman who described her relationship with her sister as "like the Delany sisters," told me more about the family tragedy that had mobilized her siblings and parents, the terminal illness of the new sister-in-law. As Maurina explained,

> I think God made the decision. I think that's the only
> reason he brought her into my brother's life. He brought

her there so she would have somewhere to die, because her family is a mess. That girl would have been by herself. Her daughters barely came over and saw her. They were talking at one time that if my brother didn't know what he was going to do, they were going to put her in a nursing home. God brought her into our lives so that she would have family to love her while she was dying. That was our sole purpose, to spend that time with her to give her as much as we could of our lives and love so that when she took her last breath she could do it, because she had a family. I even told my mother that, and my mom said, "That's what I believe too."

Maurina judges the daughters who did not visit, who considered placing their mother in nursing care. As a consequence, she and her siblings and parents became the "family to love her." Maurina and her mother talked about the meaning of life and death together as they tried to handle this crisis. As a consequence, caregiving intensified her relationship not only with her sister-in-law but also with all her family as they rallied around to provide the continuous care the sister-in-law needed.

Caregiving sometimes involves extraordinary effort. Anne, the single young adult woman who had provided a home and mothering for her younger sister, Hope, described a time that she was working during the day and going to school at night. Her parents lived more than a hundred miles away in another city. She told me,

We know that no matter what happens, we are family. We're going to stick together. You can't shun each other when you're going through problems. That's the time that you've really got to open up to each other and let each other know about your weaknesses and your fears. Then you can draw upon one another for strength. We had a problem in our family ten years ago, and I put thirty-seven thousand miles on my car driving from here to home that year. No place else, here to home. I would leave school at 9:30 at night after having worked all day, and I would get there at 11:00 or so at night. I'd leave there at 4:00 in the morning, and I would drive straight in off the interstate and go to work, and I did that for a year. I don't regret it. I'd do it all over again if I had to.

In 1992 I had to have emergency surgery, and I spent seven days in the hospital, eight months in a cast, couldn't walk, couldn't do anything. My mother came down here and stayed with me for six months. We do stand by each other, and we lift each other up.

In cases of emergency or a caregiving crisis, these families taught me that defining a family by who lives in the same household is often short-sighted. Anne may have been living a hundred miles from her parents at the time, but she made the trip more than 150 times, about twice a week, just to have a few hours with them during a family crisis. Likewise, her mother moved in with her for six months when Anne needed physical care.

Family Caregiving in Jesus' Teaching

Jesus teaches that discipleship costs everything; even our families should come second. "Whoever comes to me cannot be my disciple unless he loves me more than he loves his father and his mother, his wife and his children, his brothers and his sisters, and himself as well" (Luke 14:26 GNB). Jesus is building on the ancient theme that love and obedience to God must always come first, even when it divides families (Matthew 10:34–36). For example, Deuteronomy 21:18–21 commands the death of a stubborn and rebellious son in order to purge evil from the midst of Israel. God tests Abraham by telling him to sacrifice his only son, Isaac (Genesis 22).

Nevertheless, Jesus makes it clear that obedience to God is virtually the only justification for not providing care for family. When a man interrupts Jesus' teaching with a demand that Jesus force his elder brother to share his inheritance, Jesus responds, "Friend, who set me to be a judge or arbitrator over you?" Jesus is shaming him for arguing with his brother over their inheritance and goes on to tell the parable of the rich fool (Luke 12:13–21 NRSV). The property is nothing compared to the risk this man is running of losing his brother. Anne and Maurina's care for their families, sometimes at considerable cost in their own lives, are modern parables of the role and importance of family in our lives.

WHEN CAREGIVING ISN'T MUTUAL —AND THE GOOD NEWS

For some, caregiving is not mutual. Or at least it does not seem so. Patricia, a divorced African American mother of three children, is currently raising a three-year-old grandson and a seven-year-old niece. She is also a significant leader of the youth program in her church and has taken in children from the congregation when they needed a temporary home. As a child, she and her siblings suffered from neglect and abuse by their alcoholic parents. She has provided care through the years for many of her large family, including ten siblings and several of their children, her nieces and nephews. It has been difficult; all of her own children have been involved with drugs, and one son is now in prison. Her life revolves around her church and the care of the two children (the grandson and niece) she is now raising. She told me that she sometimes feels very lonely, especially late at night. She watches religious programming on television as a means of support. She wonders who will take care of her after she has taken care of so many others.

"You know what hurts?" she told me. "All I have is God. I care for me, and God cares for me. I'm sure the people at church care for me. That's what God says that you have to do. I feel a lot of genuine love in the church. Yeah, they love me. They would take care of me. I'm closer to them now than I am to the family."

Ultimately, Patricia depends on the church. They were the ones who took up a collection and helped find housing when she was homeless, she told me later. Different church members have come in to help her when she was sick. She can call on several women in the church for impromptu child care when she needs it. She began talking to me about her family by expressing feelings of loneliness and lack of support: "All I have is God." Only as she mused about the church's care for her did the recognition dawn that she did indeed feel loved and supported by her community of faith.

The genealogy in Matthew and the final scene at the cross in John serve as bookends, the beginning and the end of Jesus' life as told in the Gospels. From his unusual parentage to his last act of redefining family for the disciple and his mother before dying on the cross, Jesus transformed the basic defining factor of family for believers from biology to adoption, just as he transformed water into wine at Cana. Marriage is fundamentally adoption; a man and a woman leave their parents to adopt one another as "one flesh" (Genesis 2:24, NRSV and NIV). Likewise, the new model of family is not biological kinship but adoption. Sometimes death, desertion, or betrayals rob us of family. Jesus has proclaimed that we shall have a new family, created by bonds of shared faith and commitment. The work of the church, then, is to be sure that all in the community of faith find themselves wrapped in family bonds, that all are adopted. Even kinfolk, related by blood and marriage, when transformed by this good news, become adoptive families, choosing and covenanting with one another by giving themselves to following Christ. A person's biological birth is no longer all there is to defining family, nor is it even enough. We must be born again (John 3:3 NIV), and this second birth also means a new family.

The story of the Ethiopian eunuch in Acts 8 provides a powerful witness to this transformative good news. A eunuch in ancient Hebrew culture would by definition not only be childless and thus without family, but also shut out even from worshipping with the community (Deuteronomy 23:1). He was not a person with a disability; he *was* the disability—a eunuch. Nevertheless, he was searching for a place for himself, reading aloud from the prophet Isaiah. An angel sent Philip, who explained the passage the man was reading aloud, "He was like a sheep that is taken to be slaughtered, like a lamb that makes no sound when its wool is cut off. He did not say a word. He was humiliated, and justice was denied him. No one will be able to tell about his descendants, because his life on earth has come to an end" (Acts 8:32 GNB).

Starting with this passage, Philip explained the good news about Jesus, the one without descendants, like the eunuch himself. Through Jesus, however, he now had family. The beautiful promise in Isaiah 56:3–5 (NIV) that follows two chapters later resonates this promise: "Let no foreigner who has bound himself to the LORD say, 'The LORD will surely exclude me from his people.' And let not any eunuch complain, 'I am only a dry tree.' For this is what the LORD says: 'To the eunuchs who keep my Sabbaths, who choose what pleases me and hold fast to my covenant—to them I will give within my temple and its walls a memorial and a name better than sons and daughters; I will give them an everlasting name that will not be cut off.'"

In Jesus Christ, the eunuch has not only an everlasting name but also the promise of family in the community of faith. It is the mission of the church to fulfill that promise, to be sure that Patricia, who has given her life to raising her own and other people's children and worries that no one will care for her, indeed finds herself embedded in a family created by shared faith and commitment to one another. It is the melody carrying all these stories of how people become family, a melody of choosing one another, of making covenants. These can be called faith families, family relationships in which people mutually commit themselves to be family for one another, to take care of one another over a lifetime, to share their material and emotional resources with one another.

FAITH FAMILIES

A community of faith is not simply one big family. Within the band of disciples, Jesus had a few that were special to him, that formed an inner circle; one was even identified in the Gospels as "the beloved disciple" (John 19:26 NRSV). Jesus' relationship with Mary, Martha, and Lazarus was also familial in nature. Mary and Martha both spoke their minds and made demands on Jesus that have a family flavor to them much more than the relationship one would expect from a follower of a revered teacher. When Jesus was teaching someplace a journey away, they sent for him, saying, "Come as soon as possible;

The Challenge of Being Family

Lazarus is dying." He delayed, however, and when he finally came, it was too late, at least from Mary and Martha's perspective: Lazarus had already died. Neither Martha nor Mary minced any words: they told Jesus just what they thought, as members of families do. Both of them, at different times, said, "If you had been here, my brother would not have died" (John 11:21, 32). This sounds like the frustration, with even a tinge of accusation and anger, one would expect in the conversation of family members, not of disciples with a revered teacher, with the son of God.

The scripture says, "Jesus loved Martha and her sister and Lazarus" (John 11:4). Why does the writer of John note that one disciple was "beloved," when these three also were loved? The love we have for family is qualitatively different from our love of neighbors and friends. These were Jesus' family. We are to love neighbors as ourselves, Jesus taught, regardless of the response. Love for neighbor and for the community of faith does not depend on mutuality, on any commitment others make to us. Family love, on the other hand, is rooted in mutual commitment, at least over the long haul. There are times, of course, when it appears to be all one way, as Patricia feels in raising her own and other people's babies. Yet the assumption is that babies become children and then adults who do love us, who are there when we need them. At least that is the expectation.

Jesus said, "Whoever does the will of my Father in heaven is my brother and sister and mother" (Matthew 12:50 NRSV). How realistic is this ideal? Do his followers find parents and siblings anew within the community of faith? How realistic is Patricia's expectation that the church be family for her? Do Christians find faith mothers and faith siblings in the community of faith, or do we simply call one another brother and sister at church as a form of pseudocloseness or perhaps even because we have not bothered to learn one another's names?

Ginger and Allen are African Americans in their late twenties who have been married four years. They live in a small rental house in a sunny subdivision on a quiet street in a southern town. Allen has a doctorate in sociology and is currently teaching at a university and doing research. Ginger is a businesswoman and volunteers as youth minister in their National Baptist congregation. The house and its

SACRED STORIES OF ORDINARY FAMILIES

furnishings and their established careers seemed more settled than those of most young couples not yet thirty. I soon learned that they are not as settled as they seemed; they are on the move, following a sense of calling in their lives.

Allen's father died several years ago, and his mother and sister have moved to another state. Ginger had a rough childhood; her father has a severe mental illness. She believes this nurtured in her a real compassion for teenagers in troubled families. Both Ginger and Allen are planning to go to seminary to do additional graduate work. Allen feels called to be a pastor; Ginger wants to found a group home for teenagers. Teenagers are in and out of their home now. In fact, two teenagers were in the kitchen talking and laughing while we met in the living room. Allen defined family for me in this way,

> Family means really wanting to be in somebody's life, like Ginger and her kids—or our kids rather. They're constantly calling for something. Some people look at that in a negative way, but that's just part of it. Before I married Ginger, that wasn't really how my family operated. We had friends and whatever, but they weren't as close as Ginger and her family were with other people outside of the family. I learned that purely by marrying her.

> It took some time getting used to it. She's got youth that are in some terrible situations. People have no earthly idea what kids go through these days, and I didn't either until I got involved with her and the youth group. Being family means getting up at two or three in the morning and going to get somebody and all that other stuff. I found that hard. But she showed me that if you really say you love people and you want to be a part of their life, that you've got to go all the way.

For Ginger and Allen, being family for African American teenagers who otherwise might end up on the streets has become not only their personal passion but their vocational calling. They are liv-

The Challenge of Being Family

ing this calling around and in addition to demanding careers. For them, that is simply how Christians ought to think about and live out being family. As Allen says, being family means providing the kind of care that they are together giving to "our kids." Caring means worrying about them, getting them out of trouble in the middle of the night, providing a safe place for them. Allen described how their kids often live with them for periods of time. "Going all the way" with people means taking their problems on as one's own problems, caring for them in whatever way they need. Is there a limit to this caregiving? These youngsters are not likely to remain a daily part of Ginger and Allen's lives when they move elsewhere to attend graduate school. On the other hand, perhaps they will. And Ginger's dream is to come back and open a home that will be even more able to provide teenagers the care they need.

Jonelle, a single African American woman about the same age as Ginger and Allen, told me about the church where she found solace and home as a teenager. She and her mother and siblings had fled with only the clothes on their backs to settle in a city several hundred miles away. They were running from Jonelle's father, who evidently suffered from posttraumatic stress related to his service in the Vietnam War. His wife and children became targets for his violent rage, and Jonelle is convinced he would have killed them if they had stayed. He has since died from what she believes was exposure to chemicals during the war. Jonelle's mother is an alcoholic and has depended on Jonelle, who serves as the emotional support for the family.

Jonelle has always lived in poverty, but she has completed college and is working on a master's degree. Currently, her younger brother lives with her in the small walk-up apartment in an industrial part of the city, an area that is not safe to walk in at night. Another brother is in prison on drug-related charges. When I asked Jonelle to tell me how the church has helped to nurture her faith, she told me about her pastor, a man in his late fifties, and then about the older women in the church, often halting as tears made it hard for her to talk.

> Pastor really tried to be the father I never had. At first, I
> was really bitter with him for that. He would say, "My
> daughter," and I would get angry. I loved him, but I

could not stand it when he made those references. He'd
take me shopping, and he'd say, "I wish I had had you
when you were a child," and I'd just make a smart
remark, "So I'd grow up shopping at Macy's?" But at
the same time, he was doing something for me. Now I
want a man just like him. From him I even learned
more womanly things. For instance, my mother never
put a lot of emphasis on your undergarments. It didn't
matter if your underwear had holes. Not that he's ever
seen my undergarments, but he just knew it. He just
said one day in the mall, "You need new underwear,
don't you?" He knew I didn't have any money. He gave
me some money, and then he went outside the store and
waited while I bought some things. He protected my
privacy. I can't tell the saints at church that he bought
me underwear. People would not understand. He just
made sure that I had decent things."

He would ask me, "Are you hungry?" My stomach
would be growling, but I'd say no. He'd say, "Well, I'm
hungry. Come on." And he just kind of dragged me
along. He is a very wise man because it really takes the
guidance of God to know how far you can go with
someone before you push someone away or before you
do too much. He helped me when I had my estate
money [when her father died]. I bought my mother a
car first. He went shopping with me to make sure I
didn't get ripped off, and then I bought myself a car
with what was left. He walked me through that whole
process and tried to teach me little things. That is just
the greatest thing the church has done.

Then there are the older mothers. I always wanted
grandmothers. I had no old people in my life. For the
most part, my church has made me a star. I know
they're proud of me because they always tell me. Just
the hugs and the "How are you doing?" I think it was

literally just the love of God shining through them, because they didn't know the psychological effects of those hugs. I always say "my church family," but I guess if I think about it, they *are* my family. That's why I'm crying. Every program I ever put on, they would say, "You're doing a great job!" Just being there and supporting me. Not to say that my mother is not a woman of faith, because she really has those principles. She was very depressed and going through a lot, but she gave me that seed of faith so that I could come and get proper faith.

Jonelle does not want to detract from the role her mother has played in her life. Yet she also identifies the church as a significant extension of her family. The pastor has cared for her in ways that she knows might raise eyebrows. A pastor giving a young woman money to buy underwear does sound very inappropriate. In his mind, however, he was claiming the role of father, not pastor, and was therefore entitled to step over the lines of politeness, the way families do—urging her to accept the gifts of clothing she needed but protecting her privacy at the same time. He pushed her to eat when she was hungry, to let him advise her in buying a car. He and the older women in the church gave her a sense of blessing, that she is special, which is also what strong families do for children.

Christine, an Anglo-American, is also single and just a few years older than Jonelle, but her life journey has been one of growing up in a stable middle-class family where she felt loved and safe, a family that had money to send her to college and then on to graduate school. Now she is a college teacher. She lives in a lovely home she bought herself and shares with a roommate, Pam, a friend since childhood. Pam recently married a man in another city and has continued to live with Christine so that she can keep her job during the week. Pam drives the more than two hundred miles to Chicago each weekend to be with her new husband. "Pam and I are really close, but I don't really think of her as family," Christine told me. "Going to see my parents, that still feels like going home." But like Jonelle, Christine also finds family in her church. She described what it was like to move from Chicago, where she had lived with and near her parents all her life, to a city where she knew no one.

Finding a church was important to her:

A big reason I go to church is that it's like a family to me. It's my place to find family when my family's not around. I know that my church in Chicago felt like family. A lot of time at churches, they try to get single people together and the families together separately. As for me, I want to spend time with the families—adults and children. I guess the singles bar–type setup would probably help me more at finding a husband! But I would actually rather meet somebody in the situation of being with a family. I was worried about it when I first moved here.

A family from my church in Chicago had moved down here, and they said they didn't have any potluck dinners at their church. I thought, *Oh no! I hope that's not something about churches in this area!* I love potluck dinners. I think because it's a time to gather with the whole church and the families. So I was really delighted when I got down here and went to this church, and one of the first things I saw was that they were having a potluck dinner. This is where I want to be!

High-powered singles programs cannot replace the fellowship and belonging—and potential for faith families to form—that exist when people of all ages and life circumstances experience community together. The dinner table with home-cooked food shared potluck style serves as a powerful symbol of the potential for congregational life to support the development of faith families. In Chapter Three, we will look more at the powerful shaping that sharing meals has for family life, including faith families.

———

When the 2000 U.S. census data first began coming out, front pages of local newspapers carried headlines about the decline of the so-called traditional family and the dramatic increase in single-parent and single-adult families. When family is defined as household, there is no question that more adults are living alone and many children are growing up in single-parent households. One reporter asked me, "Does this mean the church has failed to make an impact on our culture?" I have pondered the assumption of that question. Is it the responsibility of the church to ensure that people live in traditional families? As we lead congregations to find ways to respond to their concerns about what is happening in family life today, what is the good news of the Christian gospel for our culture with regard to families?

My assessment of the church's responsibility is quite different from that of the reporter's, based on what I learned from these families and all the others I visited. To understand the family life of Christians, one has to look further than household membership. One has to ask, "Who is your family?" Then, the diversity of many of these congregational families begins to unfurl. The melodies of caregiving and covenant give meaning to the stories of caring for a sick sister-in-law, taking in teenagers in distress, making room for an exchange student, agreeing that more than thirty years of working together and raising one another's children may mean that neighbors have become family. The adoptive promise of the psalmist is being lived: "God sets the lonely in families" (Psalm 68:5 6a NIV). Beloved disciples are informally adopting one another into the fold of family (John 19:25–27 NRSV). Isn't that good news?

Chapter 3

BINDING FAMILIES TOGETHER

You met Jonelle in the last chapter; with her mother and siblings, she had fled from her abusive father and found a new family in the care of a pastor and the elderly women of the church. Her father's violence and her mother's alcoholism have certainly influenced Jonelle's life. The pastor who claimed her as daughter and the elderly church-women of the small National Baptist congregation located in a cin-der-block building in an industrial and poverty-ridden inner city have provided a very different experience of family for her. They have named and celebrated her gifts. They have fed her and clothed her. Some of the women, themselves living in poverty, pressed money in her hand week by week while she was in college. She, in turn, loves them, works as a volunteer in the church, and does chores and errands to help them. The family she found in this congregation sings the melodic theme of God's adoptive promise.

You also met Maurina, the single adult woman with a success-ful career and a strong relationship with her sister, Annalea. Their re-lationship, which they characterize as being like that of the Delany sisters, is embedded in a larger family, a family so close and support-ive that they provided the primary care for a terminally ill sister-in-law. Jonelle and Maurina's family experiences have been dramatically different. Clearly they both need their families; they don't know who they would be without them. And they also find much joy in their family relationships. Jonelle doesn't just need her pastor and the older women in the church to be family for her; she also likes them and enjoys being with them. She admires them; she wants to marry a man just like her pastor. Maurina is close to her sister not only because they take care of one another and others in the family, but also because they love to travel together and enjoy one another's company. Both women spoke of their families with pride.

How do close family relationships develop so that they bring joy and company in life's journey? What is it that binds people to one another, that holds them together through the rough patches that come in every family's journey? How does religious faith figure into the lives and identities of these families, or does it? How do families shape their lives together in ways that say to one another and to the world around them, "This is who we are"?

FAMILIES DEVELOP RITUALS

Christine is the college teacher who had lived all her life in Chicago until a university in another midwestern city offered her a teaching position. When I asked her to describe her family for me, she talked about her of-course family, a family that has expanded to include her nephews:

> We go on vacations sometimes, and we like to read. We like all sitting in the same room and reading. With my nephews now, we're also big into having family football games and family baseball games and things like that because they're big on sports. There is a big field by my parents' house where we play football. We also play cards together. We have a family card game that we've actually been playing together since my oldest brother was in high school. A couple of years ago, we started keeping a file of all of our score sheets, because we'd always get in these arguments every time we played about who had won most before. So we finally said, "We'd better start keeping records, so we can refer back to them." My old-

est brother always does the score keeping. We can't play if he's not there, because nobody wants to keep score. He's very creative, always making little side comments on the score sheets. A couple of years ago, we started keeping statistics about who won the most times during that week or who had the highest overall score.

Over time, Christine's family has woven this rather elaborate play ritual with one another around a simple card game peppered with good-humored rivalry and conversation. Carrying the game from one time to the next keeps them connected and gives a sense of continuity and connection with one another, even though their households and daily lives are now scattered across half the country. Their ritualized ways of playing—"My older brother always does the score keeping"—gives everyone a sense of belonging. Though they might have been apart for long stretches of time, the game, with its set roles and banter and even score sheet from the last game they played however long ago, allows them to slide back together as though nothing separated them. On the other hand, they are open to changing their ways of playing together. Their game and their love of reading together have been balanced by the addition of rough and tumble sports with the new members of the family, her nephews.

Every family has rituals or ways we go about both the everyday and the special tasks of life. Rituals are the dance steps that the family knows, the rhythms we can count on to mark our days with pattern. Doing things the same way communicates to family members that they belong. Small children in particular love rituals because they provide the security of knowing what is going to happen next. Rituals can be as simple as the time supper is eaten each evening, who reads the bedtime story, or where people sit in the car. Family rituals are the rhythms, the musical rules of family life. By themselves, they don't mean much. Does it really seem all that important who sits where at the table or who keeps score in a family card game? But it is important. These rituals organize life in ways so that the meaning of shared experiences comes through.

Family celebrations are often full of rituals. The foods we eat on certain days, the games we play at holiday gatherings, whether family

59

members greet one another with a handshake or hugs and kisses—these are all family rituals. Rituals often carry the melodic themes of family life. They not only communicate belonging for family members, but they may also be times new family members—the new son-in-law or foster child—may feel on the fringe, perhaps longing for their "old" families. They don't know the melodies. Family rituals also make us feel keenly the family members we have lost, because of the part they played in the past. No one is there to sing their part. What would happen to the family card game if Christine's brother died? It is those little—and not so little—ritualized roles of family life that make us feel connected and that often cut so surprisingly deeply when someone is no longer in the accustomed place at the family table.

Daily family activities also become ritualized: time at home together watching television, doing chores, sharing meals. Many of these families—and not just families with children—still play board games, dominoes, and cards with one another on a regular basis. Or they find other ways to build a rhythm of playfulness into their life together.

Married for ten years, Aaron and Christy are an Anglo-American couple living in a lovely new home in a beautiful wooded subdivision on the outskirts of the city. Aaron is a lawyer; Christy is a nurse but is currently home full-time taking care of their sons, ages six and three, and expecting a third child in three months. One of the prompts I began with to help me understand how each family sees itself was "Describe to me a picture of your family doing something together that would help an outsider understand who this family is."

Aaron pondered just a moment and then began, "A typical Saturday morning, when I don't have to go in to the office or anything, we go out for breakfast or just go get doughnuts or bagels or something, and just drive around the city with the boys in the car listening to music or singing songs. We go out to lunch. And then Saturday night, we might go to the mall and take the boys to the arcade. We go to the bookstore. We're kind of easily amused."

Christy added, "We're boring. We just like to try to be together."

"We're boring," "we're not exciting," "something that may not seem all that important"—families often included these phrases in describing themselves. Simple family rituals seem somewhat out of step and odd in our high-paced, high-tech culture. Yet I suspect that these seemingly simple activities—rides in the car, a shared breakfast every Saturday morning, playing games at the arcade—are really quite powerful ways this family is building connections with one another that will hold them together in the challenges they will undoubtedly face in the years ahead.

Watching Television—Together

Amy is the young mother whose father died and whose mother, Nell, took John as a second husband when Amy was a teenager. The relationship between and Amy and John had been pretty rocky until after Amy was grown, married, and had children of her own. John and Nell now provide a lot of care for Amy's two daughters while she and her husband, Don, work in the city thirty miles away. When I asked Amy to paint a verbal picture of their family doing something that tells who they are, Amy said:

> Believe it or not, this might not seem like the time that you'd think there was a lot of family connecting going on, but when we watch TV together. If we all happen to be sitting watching the same thing at the same time, that always ends up being really nice. We were all into *Lois and Clark* there for a while. So every Sunday night, we were watching *Lois and Clark* together, and we'd make sure we got everything done so that at 8:00 we could sit down. We have three televisions; the main one is in the family room. The other two are upstairs, and nobody wants to go off to another room and watch TV alone. So maybe it isn't the best medium for a family, but somehow it ends up good. And every time people talk about how bad TV is for you I think, *Gosh, sometimes those are our best times.* We're all sitting there yucking it up over something on TV.

There is a tinge of worry or apology in Amy's voice when she describes watching television together as one of the best times in her family's life. Warnings abound concerning the dangers of television, especially for children. But as Amy has observed in her own family, television can actually be good for family life, depending on how much and what is watched, and whether or not it is shared. Like playing a card game or going out for breakfast on Saturday morning, watching television together may give the family a way to relax and laugh and talk together. In *Families and Time,* research on the ways that families watch television, Kerry Daly reported that people talk to one another almost one-fourth of the time they are watching television. The frequent pauses for commercials provide opportunity for conversation, whether about what is being watched or something else altogether. In many ways, watching television together is much like the family rituals of meals, of Christine's family card game, or Aaron and Christy's Saturday car outings. Family members are in the same space—in front of the television or in the car or around the table playing a game, where talking about important issues is not demanded, but conversation can drift, can be playful, and sometimes turn into one of those serendipitous times of deep sharing.

Choosing what to watch on television together and making rules about what and how much family members are allowed to watch alone influence what families weave into their traditions and memories about life together.

Amy mentioned the three televisions in their home. My husband and I recently toured a builders' home show. I was astounded at the numbers of televisions in many of these new homes—in the kitchen, the family room, every bedroom, exercise rooms, bathrooms. Even a bathtub in one home had a television set embedded in it. Obviously, television can bring family members together, as it does for Amy's family, or encourage them to isolate themselves from one another.

Watching Children Play—Together

Many children are heavily involved in a variety of activities, and their parents provide the transportation, coaching, and other forms of support for those activities. When I asked respondents to finish the statement, "If I took a snapshot of this family doing something together that says who you are," one parent responded, "You'd need high-speed photography" and laughed. Another parent said that the picture would be of parents with car keys in their hands. Yet the dependence of children on their parents for transportation and involvement means that these activities actually become family activities. Parents often go to extraordinary lengths to be present at their children's sporting, arts, and other activities and events, often serving as coaches and leaders.

After talking about watching television together, Amy's husband, Don, began talking about the ways they are involved with their children: "We focus on our children. For example, I make sure Pamela [age eight] gets her piano lessons. I sit with her and practice piano with her. Or we do something on the computer together. My wife does spend more time with them than I do in terms of reading books to them. She is so patient. We each put a different thing into the whole."

Amy continued,

> I think maybe what you could say is that we are very much dedicated and devoted to the kids. They're definitely the center of our lives. Don gets very interested when our daughter is practicing piano. He's right there listening, or he's sitting down with her. And while she might moan and groan about it, I know it's great for her. She doesn't get mad that he gets involved. I think it tells her that he's interested, and that is very important. And the computer too. He spends a lot of time with them, and they're just so happy about it. [When something goes wrong, they'll] say, "Daddy, what happened?" He doesn't say, "I don't know. Figure it out on your own." He tries to help them.

It takes time and self-discipline to sit consistently with an eight-year-old practicing the piano, to figure out and explain the mysterious workings of a computer, to read books with children. Amy describes Don and herself as "dedicated and devoted" parents. One might choose those same words, *dedicated* and *devoted,* to describe the very different activity of Maurina and her mother: sitting by the bed of the terminally ill sister-in-law. These are also church words, used to describe how we are to relate ourselves to God, with dedication and devotion. Is there something about the way these people go about being family with one another, even as they watch television or go out for Saturday morning breakfast together or sit with a child practicing the piano, that is somehow related to their faith? Is their faith, their devotion to God, somehow sung in the small acts of faithfulness and devotion in these ordinary family activities?

Irene is the widow who has lived forty years next door to Doris, her closest friend, musing that although they feel like sisters, when her health fails her, she'll probably have to move closer to her son. She is the part-time volunteer secretary in her church and describes this as her ministry. She quit working in order to be able to take this on as her responsibility. She also serves on a number of church committees and is a congregational leader. She cried as she told me about her husband's death, "I know when my husband died, my son was in California on a business trip, and my husband would not die until his son got home. And our family shares every aspect of our lives with one another. My kids share their joys with me and with each other." Her children and grandchildren talk to each other a lot. "I have a nineteen-year-old grandson, and he's been involved in basketball, football, baseball, and not just my son and his wife and I go, but all of his aunts and uncles go to his ballgames."

In her mind, this moment of such crisis—her husband holding on to life until their son could get there—connected to other very ordinary ways this family supports one another with their presence. They talk to one another and to her, and they find ways to be together. These are all busy people, yet they make time to go sit and watch children play sports. Like rides in the car together, children's sporting events give them a context for being together, for talking if they choose to. It seems that the sports arena replaced the front porch of generations past, conjuring up memories of childhood when parents and grandparents gathered on summer evenings to escape the heat of the house, oversee children playing in the streets and yards, and share conversation. Family members who make time to watch children play—whether in the front yard or a sports arena—are family members that can also be counted on to be present in times of great crisis.

Irene's son made it, leaving his business meeting immediately to catch the next plane from California back to Louisiana. He was there with his father when he died.

Involvement in Outside Activities—Together

Kathryn is Anglo-American and has four children from her first marriage. Her husband, Darren, is African American and has three children from his first marriage. All of those children are grown and more than ten years older than Kathryn and Darren's fifteen-year-old son, Nathan.

Darren described their family this way: "We're always together. We do almost everything together. If he goes up to the high school game and he's there with his friends, we're at the high school game too. It's a lot of togetherness, and I guess that's the way it's always been even when he was small."

Kathryn added, "We don't go to places he can't go."

Darren emphasized what she said. "We just feel like if he can't go, we can't go. It's the same when we go to someone's house. If he can't go when we get an invitation, then we don't go. We are one."

I was wondering what it's like for a fifteen-year-old boy to be "one" with his parents, when Nathan seemed to read my mind and chimed into the conversation, "It's OK with me."

Then Darren went on to explain, "Of course, I think we more or less present a united front because of being interracial. Problems and things don't divide us. We band together and get stronger."

Kathryn confirmed Darren's analysis with an illustration. "Just last night, we talked for about two hours just sitting here, discussing things, working out solutions to things and so forth—all three of us. We include him in everything, so he'll know what's going on."

For this family, physical presence signifies support and unity in the world that can sometimes be hostile toward them because they are biracial. Nathan didn't roll his eyes or look disgusted, which is what we might expect from a teenager whose parents talk enthusiastically about how they like to be around whatever he is doing. In fact, over and over, not only children but also teenagers in many of the families I met (not just biracial families) told me that they enjoyed doing things with their families. They liked having their parents involved in their lives!

At first blush, there seemed little connection between religious faith and these families' stories about going to high school football games or sitting around the kitchen table for two hours discussing things, much less playing a card game every holiday season or going out for Saturday morning breakfast. Yet these were the stories that these families chose to tell me about who they are, knowing that I wanted to learn about how their faith related to their family life. Somehow, these families were trying to tell me about their faith with these stories. In fact, they are stories that are carried by the melodies of dedication and devotion, of being faithful to one another in the daily moments of their lives, of weaving daily rituals that hold them together and give security to individual family members. These stories are ordinary yet shot through with the sacred values of faithfulness and devotion and self-giving love. They are stories that sing of family faith. That faith may not look very religious—card games with their rules, bagels on Saturday morning, and sitting with a child practicing the piano are quite different from worship with its order, the church communion table, and teaching children Bible stories. But one can hear the familiar melodies of belonging communicated by ordered worship and play, of the communion table and breakfast, of faithfulness to "be there" with one another.

Eating Meals—Together

Families talked about eating meals, more than any other activity, as the dominant defining experience of their life together. Many kinds of meals were described to me as the picture of "us at our best" that came to the minds of family members: the daily supper meal, summer cookouts, holiday feasts. These daily and special times are defined by rituals: who sits where, whether or not there is a blessing and who is in charge of it, who serves and who cleans up, and the various rules of conversation.

Anglo-Americans David and Darlene have been married for ten years and have lived all of those years in a southern town where David is a medical doctor and Darlene is a social worker. They each brought a son and a different religious tradition to their marriage. David has continued to be involved in the Catholic Church with his son, Pete, age fourteen. Darlene is a member of the session (the governing body) of her Presbyterian congregation. Darlene's son Paul, age eleven, is involved with her in the Presbyterian Church.

When I asked them to relate to me a picture of their family doing something together that really says who they are as a family, David began: "Having dinner together is important to us. We might not plan on it or talk about the fact that it is important, but it is, and we make it happen."

"Sometimes, it's impossible with Pete's basketball," his wife added. "The games start at 6:00. But we generally really try to eat together. We have so much fun when we eat at night; their friends come over and just sit there going . . ."

Paul interrupted his mother, "They think we're crazy. The TV is off. . . ."

Pete interrupted Paul, "The family is more entertaining than the TV anyway."

Outside activities pull these family members away from the family dinner. But they work at making their dinner table a place to gather, where friends are welcome. The very telling of this story illustrates that this is not just significant to parents but to teenagers as well, as Paul interrupts his mother, helping to build the story of how their friends see their family as "crazy," and Pete in turn interrupts his stepbrother and builds on his words. The boys have a sense of pride in their family; they are quite willing to invite friends in and expose them to their "crazy" family that actually turns the television off during dinner. Mealtime is often the only time the whole family is gathered in one place. As a teenager in another family said, "The dinner table is the place where you find out what's going on."

Family meals are important for Virginia's family too. To know their significance, one has to know something about Virginia's story. As an African American going to high school in the late 1950s, Virginia was barred from taking college preparatory courses. She finally found a two-year junior college nursing program that would admit her, and she finished her degree in nursing before marrying. Soon after the marriage, the babies started coming, and she didn't work for a few years. But one day, her husband announced he had met another woman and was leaving, and he did, leaving her with five children to support. She began working not just one but two full-time jobs. At times she had to take on a third part-time job, just to keep the bills paid and food on the table. She was also determined to save money to ensure that her own children had the financial support they needed to attend college and get the education she had dreamed about as a girl. All her children are now grown, and she is raising her granddaughter.

For many of those years, Virginia slept only two or three hours after putting the children to bed before she was off to her night job. Determined to get the education she values so much, she also took college classes part-time for years. In fact, when I talked with her, she was about to graduate with a degree from a state university and was making plans to go on to graduate school. Virginia described to me how she arranged her work schedule when the children were home so that she could prepare dinner and eat with them before she went to her late-night job. Although the children are now grown and scattered, those that live in the same city still come home to gather at the table for supper one or more days each week.

> I think it's very important. And many times we have breakfast together on the weekends. They know I'm either making coffee cakes or we have grits and eggs and bacon and biscuits, and they look forward to that. They really do. They know I cook every day. My granddaughter had a little friend come over to spend the night. The next morning, I said, "You want a cup of tea or something while I'm fixing breakfast?" and she said, "What are you cooking?" and I said, "I'm making a cherry coffee cake." She said, "Oh, man! My mom never cooks." She ran out that door when her dad came over and she said, "Dad, you won't believe this!"

For many years Virginia's major focus was simply surviving, getting from one day to the next, trying to stay ahead of the bills. There were times she couldn't pay the electric bill, so she kept their food in a picnic cooler, and she heated bathwater and cooked on the wood-burning stove. The meals were simple, but the family ate together. Sometimes they threw a blanket on the floor and had a "winter picnic," roasting marshmallows in the open door of the woodstove. As Virginia said, "That may not seem important, but it didn't cost anything. I just think it's important to have family time together." Like the family who said "we're boring" and "we're easily amused," Virginia assumes that others might think that her winter picnics on the living room floor don't seem important.

Virginia's children had many strikes against them, growing up abandoned by their father, their mother having to be gone most days and nights, working to support them much of the time and exhausted the rest, living in poverty, African American in a racist society. Yet Virginia believed in cherry coffee cakes, roasting marshmallows together, and eating together every day.

When I asked her what kept her going, she responded, "I just kept going. I don't know what else to tell you. The Lord did it. I know I didn't do it." She believes God gave her the strength to endure. She believes that the strength she found year after year to keep on keeping on with the grueling work schedule, to heat bathwater on the stove for five children and keep them fed, reflects God at work in her and through her in the lives of her children. All of the children finished college; one son is now enrolled in medical school in one of the finest programs in the country. And Virginia is about to start graduate school herself.

Patrick and Tess's life differs radically from Virginia's. You met them in Chapter Two, the blending family living in their custom-built home in a rural wooded area, with a wood stove for ambiance, not heating bath water. Their family began with two children each from previous marriages and wove themselves into family. They expressed their identity by making a video about themselves and with a college term paper Patrick's stepdaughter wrote titled "My Dad." When I asked them to "tell me a story or draw me a picture with words of this family at its best," Tess began: "It's just like a warm blanket, when we're all together at the dinner table. We try to sit down as a family most every night. I think just sharing the day or just being together. We get crazy. The kids are usually hanging out with friends. Patrick works long hours. So we're in a lot of different directions, and I think it's a focus time for us to sit down and try to pry into what's going on when they let us in."

Patrick continued the description, "I love summer evenings because the family loves to cook out, and I love coming home, and we catch fireflies, and everybody sits down. Even the kids. The kids would rather be out most of the time, but it's still OK to barbecue as a family. Whether they enjoy it, I don't know, but they do it."

And fifteen-year-old Ben chimed in, "I like it!"

Again, a teenager confirms that he too values this family time around the table. This blending family told me other stories that indicated that they have had more than their share of stress, both externally with jobs and ex-spouses and in the strained relationships that often come when trying to blend two different families of children and parents. But those "warm blanket" moments give them a sense of identity that runs more deeply than the daily squabbles and even more serious conflicts with which they have had to contend. This same family told me later that, at Ben's urging, they keep a stack of army blankets in the back of their sports utility vehicle in the wintertime. On cold nights, the father and the teenage boys drive the streets, giving blankets to homeless persons to keep them warm. The image of the warm blanket serves not only to describe their relationships with one another but also one of the ways they seek to care for others beyond their own boundaries.

Throughout the Bible, eating a meal together has special significance. Much more happens than physical hunger being satisfied. Intimacy develops between people who share food together. Jesus used his last meal with his disciples to symbolize his continuing relationship with them, even after his death. He fed them after his resurrection, and with the bread and fish came the opportunity to talk together (John 21:9–23). It was only when Jesus fed them that the two disciples on the road to Emmaus finally recognized him: "their eyes were opened" (Luke 24:30–31 NRSV).

For many families, supper is the only time the family assembles in one place. If families choose to make mealtime together a shared priority, it can be an enriching experience, a time to nourish not only physical bodies but also the family body. To share a meal says that we care for one another, that we want to have our eyes opened to knowing one another anew. Tess called this "prying into what's going on." To enable this to happen takes considerable planning, compromise, and continuing adjustment.

"Prying into what's going on" gives a hint that these family dinners are not always warm, intimate gatherings, however. A snapshot of most families having dinner together would include arguments and disagreements. Studying family dinners by audiotaping them, sociologist Samuel Vuchinich reported in "Starting and Stopping Spontaneous Family Conflicts" that the American family spends anywhere from fifteen minutes to more than an hour eating together, and during that time, family members have an average of more than three arguments. Family dinners are the time when we share conversation and information, and also when family members air disagreements. Conflict too is a significant and inevitable aspect of family life.

Corrine is the mother of Kyle, age twelve, and Kurt, age ten. They are Anglo-American. She is a homemaker; her husband, Brent, is a prominent businessman. Their large suburban home, with its carefully and expensively decorated rooms, reflects his financial success. She described a winter trip to the family's cabin, where her husband loves to go but which means a significant amount of work for her as the mom and family cook:

> You know how you have your ups and downs in a family? Nobody's ever happy at once. I remember one January in the dead of winter, and it was miserable, and everybody had colds and whatever. I was in a snitty kind of mood like I was doing this great thing for him, to drag the kids and the groceries and open up that cold cabin. It never does warm up there, because there's no heat in the bedrooms.
>
> It turned out to be a beautiful January day, springy-like and mild temperatures, and there was a beautiful sunset as only these winter sunsets are. We built a fire on the beach, and the boys toasted hot dogs and marshmallows. I just felt a sense of contentment that just comes so few

times. I thought, *I'm just so happy and content at this moment in my life.* That's just one moment that kind of stands out for me. They go for excitement; I go for peace and contentment.

Cooking and eating together are activities that transcend socioeconomic differences. This family toasted marshmallows on the beach of their vacation home; Virginia's family toasted them over the woodstove they use as the only source of heat in their small home when she couldn't pay the electric bill. Different experiences, but the same melody of eating connects them.

Praying—Together

Many families find ways to make prayer a part of their family life on a regular basis, although it's not easy. Those families who do pray together told me that praying is a key to their commitment and strength as a family. Most often family prayer takes place at family meals. If families don't eat together regularly, they don't pray together either. That does not mean that family meals are the only time families pray together. Many families observe the ritual of saying grace or singing together at meals, but they also pray at other times.

A Mother's Morning Prayer　On a warm spring evening, Margaret welcomed me into her home, a small bungalow in a southern inner-city neighborhood. A shy, soft-spoken woman, she had settled her nine-year-old twin daughters, Dianne and Deborah, to doing their homework at the kitchen table so that we could talk in the living room, with an aquarium gurgling in the corner. Margaret has been living with Joe for more than a decade. She works as a bookkeeper; Joe does construction work. Margaret is very active as one of the few African Americans in an aging, predominantly Anglo-American United Methodist congregation downtown; it hasn't been able to reach many in the African American neighborhood around it and so is shrinking with each funeral. Joe doesn't go to church, and Margaret tries not to nag him about it. She told me she likes the quiet, reverent worship of the Methodist Church, different from the faith tradition in which she grew up, where the loud music and preaching style intimidated her.

Margaret worries a lot about the safety and well-being of her daughters. The violence of the inner city and the racism in her larger community frighten her for her girls. She tries to spend as much time as she can with them, nurturing and protecting them. She also prays a lot for them and for herself. She told me that she not only prays *for* them, but she also prays *with* them every morning before she sends them off to school:

> We usually pray about ten minutes before the bus comes. I pray and ask God to bless their school and to bless their teachers. I call their teachers' names out, and I call the bus driver's name out. I ask God to bless my girls, to help them have a good day, to help them to follow their teacher's instructions, to help them be good and do good in school. If it's Monday, I always thank Him for a good weekend, and then we end, "In Jesus' name we pray, we can do all things in Christ who strengthens us, amen."

Every parent knows the frantic, pressured morning time of getting children out the door to the school bus. Nevertheless, Margaret has found a way to carve out time for a prayer that blesses her daughters and sends them into God's care for the day. It is simple yet powerful. The prayer to help them "be good and do good" communicates that she wants her daughters to be righteous and good in themselves and also to work for justice and goodness in the world around them. Her prayer not only blesses Dianne and Deborah, but it also helps their mother deal with sending her daughters out beyond her watchful care, two little African American girls in a violent and racist inner city. This is a prayer for all of them. The simple words petition for courage for both generations: "we can do all things in Christ who strengthens us."

Carrying on a Praying Tradition   Allen and Ginger are the young couple who are planning to go to seminary, he to become a pastor and she to found a group home for African American adolescents. Their home is already a second home for the teenagers in her church, whom she serves as volunteer youth minister. They told me how prayer and Bible study have been vital ingredients in their life together, even before they were married. Ginger began,

> One of the things we're focusing on is praying together as a couple. We teach in Sunday school, and sometimes when you're always in positions of service, you miss that nurturing yourself. It's something we're working on. Actually just setting aside time and saying, "OK, we're not going to do all of this other stuff. This is our time." We did that a lot when we were dating, just pray, pray, pray about everything. And sometimes you get so busy that you lose that, but now we're setting aside time for family prayer. We talk all the time about things I don't understand or he doesn't understand in the Bible, or things we may have different opinions about. And we talk when we're preparing for Sunday school.

Allen continued, "So we don't have like an everyday pattern that we go by. Sometimes we wake up, and we are in a rush to get to work, and when we come home we're dog tired. We just want to sit and watch *Mad About You* and go to bed."

Ginger agreed and then went on, "We're not consistent now, but that's what we're working toward. We pray together in the evenings. At bedtime. Every time we're heading somewhere."

"That's a tradition from my family," Allen explained. "Every time we go somewhere and we are about to leave, everybody gets together and says a prayer. It started with my grandmother. I told Ginger that my grandmother could pray for two hours. Two hours! One time when we went to visit my grandfather's family, just about the whole family was there, and my grandmother prayed for everybody in the room. I know we were standing there for an hour."

Prayer not only connects them and gives them strength for their demanding lives, but it also connects them to the larger family identity. Allen told Ginger how his grandmother prays. And Ginger is the one who says that they pray together "every time we're heading some-where," following the tradition of Allen's family. They are also now working to develop traditions of their own. The struggle to maintain prayer and devotional reading is an ongoing one for many families. As one father of a family of teenagers said, "It seems like we do it for a while, and then we get off track."

An Evening Ritual Kathryn and Darren have faced a lot of obsta-cles as a biracial couple, both in a second marriage, wrapping family closely around their son, Nathan, to try to protect him from racism. Darren told me that prayer has helped.

> About the time we go to bed, we have our Bible study and our prayer time together. Very seldom do we miss. A lot of turmoil and heartaches have brought us closer together in a day-to-day Bible study and prayer time in the evening. So our lives revolve very much around where our strength comes from. In the last couple of years, we have been using the concordance, and we've done a word study. We started alphabetically taking a look at words like *faith* and *integrity.* Then of course we have our Sunday school books and preparation for Sunday school.

These families are working hard to make time to talk about, read about, and pray over their daily activities and struggles and the deepest questions of life. As they do, they are weaving a story of fam-ily and faith with one another.

FAMILIES SERVE—TOGETHER

These busy families also find ways to spend time together in service to their congregations and communities. Many parents and grand-parents serve as volunteers in programs that include their children: room parents and tutors in their children's schools, coaches and canteen organizers for community sports leagues, and Sunday school teachers and choir leaders in church programs.

Teaching

Nobody asked them to serve as a family; they are creating their own ways to serve others that also bind them together. Sadly, many parents worry that such family involvement may do some sort of damage to their children. Apart from Kathryn and Darren's example of involvement in their teenage son's life, many other parents told me that they sometimes worry that they might embarrass their children or even somehow hurt them. Sheryl, the widowed mother of Shamika, still worries about being too close to her daughter, even though Shamika is grown now. Her friends tell her that she spends too much time with Shamika and her husband, that her involvement will somehow damage their young marriage, even though Shamika and Charlie want her in their lives.

Ironically, not a single child or teenager I interviewed complained about parents being too involved. Paul and Pete both go to Sunday school at the Presbyterian church where Darlene, Paul's mom and Pete's stepmom, serves as their Sunday school teacher. David said, "Even though Pete's Catholic, he goes to that church for Sunday school because I want him to go."

Pete told me: "The people that I've talked to don't want their parents around when they are doing stuff with their friends. But then they never had their parents around. I don't mind for my parents to be there, and I've had them there, so I guess that's . . ."

Darlene interrupted her stepson, "Well, one of the things that I've always tried to be real conscious of was not treating them differently than I would treat any of the other kids, either playing favorites or coming down harder on him than I would someone else. It wouldn't be fair to them."

"It gives me something to do, and my friends are there," Pete continued. "I kind of enjoy it because Mom's teaching it. She does a good job too. Last Sunday we had this little worksheet on right decisions to make that we filled out and talked about. That was pretty good."

David added to his son's affirmation: "She's real good with kids."

Pete encourages his stepmother's involvement, volunteering that he actually enjoys having her as a Sunday school teacher, saying, "She's pretty good, too." I learned later that David also coaches the school basketball teams on which both boys play. I had the sense that Pete, like many children and teenagers with whom I talked, was proud and pleased at his parents' involvement. At least for the youngsters with whom I talked, our culture's unwritten rule that parents really should not be involved in their children's peer relationships not only doesn't make much sense but creates parental uncertainty about one of the most important ways they can be effective parents.

Volunteering

Families find other ways to be together, often by redefining individual volunteer jobs as family activities: when one family member takes on a responsibility, others in the family become involved as well. Couples teach Sunday school as a team or serve as coleaders of a choir. In one small congregation, families together take weekly turns cleaning the small church building. Parents in another blending family of four children told me that they have responsibility for a monthly dinner for the senior adults in the church. Together with other young families, they prepare a meal at church, serve the senior adults, and plan and lead a short program.

Singing

Jacob and Kate are a busy young African American couple, both working and raising Dillon, age nine, and Shane, age seven. They are members of a small but rapidly growing midwestern Baptist congregation with a rich diversity of families: African American, Anglo-American, a few Latino, and several biracial families. When I asked my question about a picture of their family doing something that says, "This is who we are," Jacob answered, "Singing."

And Kate explained, "At 6:00 every Sunday evening, we codirect the children's choir at church, and our kids are in the children's choir."

"That's why I say singing," explained Jacob.

Kate continued, "We sing around the house. I try to figure out what song the choir is going to learn next, and the kids learn it. Jacob directs the choir if I'm playing the piano. I write too. We do like music as a family together, and we do like the church music, gospel music. I write gospel. I'm just a beginner at it, but I really do enjoy it."

Being the Church Family

For some, church service was a way of finding or creating family-like relationships, especially when they had experienced losses of family members. Irene is the widow whose husband waited to die until his son could fly home from California and whose whole family attends the sporting events of grandsons and nephews. She described for me her work for her Methodist congregation:

> I'm up at the church most of the time anyway, so they asked me if I would volunteer on Mondays and let the office manager have that day off. Then I'm there on Wednesdays. I'm the bazaar chairman. And I'm also in charge of the jewelry at the cottage industry we do there to make money for missions. And then I do all the garden work. I plant the flowers and trim all the bushes. The men do the mowing of the grass and the trimming, but I trim all the bushes.
>
> I retired at age sixty because I had a dream to be able to do what I'm doing for my church. I wanted to be in fellowship with Christian people, doing the work I thought the Lord had called me to do. And that's why I spend as much time as I do up there. The people, and not just the women, it's the men too, have formed great friendships. It has been my salvation since my husband died, to have this group of Christian friends around me all the time. Some of my secular friends don't under-

stand why I spend so much time over there. But it's where I feel good. I'm on the finance committee; I'm on the vision team; I'm president of the United Methodist Women. I was in charge of the rummage sale we had Saturday. I am a worker; I'm a doer. I think the Lord has led me to do these things. He wants me there doing these things. Our church was in turmoil the last five years until Pastor came. And I helped hold our church together. There were several of us that did that. We've worked very hard at it because we knew the Lord felt that this was a good working church, and we needed to keep things together. And we did; we worked very hard. Sometimes, it would have been much, much easier to give up.

Clearly Irene has found a sense of purpose, personal identity, and community in the significant commitment of time she has made to her congregation. The church has been her "salvation" since her husband died. She has found family-like companionship and support there. At the same time, her congregation is like a family in that it has also been the source at times of great turmoil. A controversy in the church nearly split the fellowship. She told me how at times she was actually physically ill over the stress the congregational conflict created for her. Families and family-like relationships provide identity and fulfillment and also stress and strain, often at the same time.

Working Toward Dreams and Goals

Another clue to what binds families to one another in good times and bad is that their dreams and goals, their plans for the future, and the reasons they are working so hard are often shared. In American culture, family life often focuses on preparing for the success of the next generation, whatever success in the family means. Adults parenting children almost always answered questions about meaning and

79

purpose in their lives by talking about their dreams and goals for the children. Virginia worked two and three jobs to be sure that her five children could go to college. Children too focused on what they wished for in their own lives.

Dreams for Children

Later in the conversation with Darlene and David and their sons, the Presbyterian-Catholic blending family, I asked them about their goals and dreams for the future.

Fourteen-year-old Pete had a quick answer, "Going to the NBA."

David, his dad and basketball coach, laughed and then took the discussion in a different direction: "My energy is going toward making sure they go to college."

And Darlene went in yet another direction, "Mine is that they grow up to be good people, happy people, and I'd prefer them to be well-educated people. I just want them to know how fortunate they are, how unfortunate some people are, and to be the champion of less fortunate people. That's what I would like."

"And not grow up to be spoiled brats, which some of the kids that go to their school are," David added.

Darlene elaborated, "They go to a private school, and you always have to fight against that. Both of them have won a Christian student award, and that's something I'm real proud of."

Pete agreed, "In both grades, in [the] same year. Pretty cool."

And Darlene emphasized again, "I just want them to be really good folks and happy."

Pete went on, "Probably to spend a lot of time with each other because, you know, I'm going to be gone in four years when I go off to college. My mom says she's going with me."

David picked up this theme: "I remember when I went to college, my brother was a year behind me, so my mother was telling me how quiet it was when I left, and then when my brother left, I can imagine how difficult it was. We've all been so involved as a family that it's going to be quiet around here. Time flies. We've been so involved with our kids, probably much more than most parents. I've always coached the boys since they played T-ball."

This family conversation provides a fascinating picture of weaving individual goals and dreams into a sense of family purpose. In the beginning, Pete launched this discussion with his dream of being a professional basketball player. No one in the family picked up on that, and David said he was more interested in education. But when Darlene said she wanted them to be "good" and "happy" people, David built on what she was saying—"and not grow to be spoiled brats." Here is an agreed-on goal. She came back to the theme by talking about the award they each had won, and that was affirmed by her stepson, who described how "cool" it was that they both received the award "in the same year." Darlene added the emphasis, "I just want them to be really good folks and happy," not mentioning either the NBA (her stepson's goal) or college (her husband's goal). Her stepson then tied this family goal for him to his own and his father's assumption that he is going to college. He went on to say that spending time together is important because they won't always be together. And his dad picked that up and told a fragment of a story from the previous generation, when he left a brother behind to go off to college. In this family story, everyone weaves together experiences: the school awards, the parents working hard to ensure their sons have the resources to go to college in the future (and attend private school now), and their projections about what it will be like when the first son leaves home. Stories about goals are still being formed; the family is in the midst of shaping paths down which they are only beginning to see.

Financial Security

For many of the single parents I interviewed, the goal was simply surviving and doing the best they could for their children, keeping them housed, fed, and feeling secure. Renee, the recently divorced mother in the story about the sick dog and the sad boy in Chapter One, said that her main goal is "to maintain whatever cohesiveness we have left." Faced with trying to provide for her children with only sporadic support payments from their father, her most immediate concern is trying to pay the rent on the family home so that she can keep the children in their familiar school and neighborhood. Karen, the divorced mother of a preschooler who is also providing a home for a South American exchange student, said, "I don't know. I just keep going. Knowing that I'm a single parent and I've got to provide. I've always worked full-time. There's no point in wallowing around in self-pity, so I just try not to think about all I have to do. I just do whatever needs doing. Because if I don't, if there's something that needs to be done, that's not going to get done unless I do it. Even if I ask the boys to do something, I have to be the motivator."

Families often talked about goals that involve financial security, but they always couched those goals in what they want to be able to do or to purchase that financial success will enable. They want to be able to send children to college, to travel when they retire, to buy a new house or a new car. Shamika, the young wife raised by a single African American mother after her father's murder, said that she and her husband, Charlie, want to be "economically successful" and then went on to describe what she means:

> I want a new car. A simple thing. I want a new house. I guess I just want a mixture of it. When we have children, I want them to be strong, but I don't want them to have to go through the kinds of things that my mother and I did. I don't want them to have to know what it's like to be evicted. To not know if you're going to be able to go back to school in the fall because I don't have the $200, and that was all it came down to one semester. I didn't have the $200, and if my aunt hadn't helped me out, they wouldn't have let me come back. Some people look at that and think it's not important. It *is* important when all you've got in your bank account is $3.24. We hope we can be a family that cares for each other. We are planning to have kids.

Shamika has known poverty, and as a consequence, financial security is at the top of her list of goals. But she puts this within the framework of family: she wants to provide a secure future for children yet to be born.

Communicating Love and Safety
in One Another

Wrapped around all the goals these families talked about was the expectation that they will go on loving one another. Parents talked with longing in their voices about wanting their children to love each other enough that they will continue to be close after they are grown.

Patrick, the architect whose stepdaughter wrote the college paper titled "My Dad" and gave it to him for Christmas, spoke what seemed to be important to many families,

> If there is a sense of purpose, it is to keep a tightness even though certain threads or certain strings are going to loosen up at times. It's still going to be a common thread that will always keep us bound. That is it for me. Of all the things that could happen in the family, I hope that they will always want to be together. Really the common denominator of all this is that ten, fifteen, twenty years from now, I want everybody to say at Thanksgiving, "I cannot wait for all of us to get together" versus "I've got to go through this again." My goal is mutual genuine love and liking for one another. That's not always easy to do.

Patrick wants his children and stepchildren to feel like Christine does, the single college professor who looks forward to the family football games in the open field next to her parents' house and the everlasting card game with her brothers.

Perhaps stepfamilies like Patrick's know best the challenge that establishing this kind of "genuine love and liking" can be. Nevertheless, many families told me that, indeed, they feel this kind of love for one another. In fact, they see glimpses in their lives that they can count on that family love no matter what. Catherine, a divorced Anglo-American mother of a preschooler, describes the response of her family when, as a teenager, she had to tell her parents and grand-mother (whom she calls Nanny) that she was pregnant. "I thought, *This is going to be a stroke for Nanny when she finds out I'm pregnant.* But she just gave me the biggest hug and she said, 'I love you.' They love me regardless of what I do, what stupid things I do. They're al-ways there for me." Obviously, this no-matter-what love is what all of us yearn for from our families; sometimes, when we experience it so fully, we mark it in our memory, as Catherine and others who talked with me did. Perhaps they have forgotten the times when that kind of love was missing. What family can love like that all the time? Perhaps for some families, the more common theme may be one of shame and rejection than unconditional love. Even so, the melodies these families wanted to share, to hold on to, were those that carried stories of no-matter-what love. Pete, the fourteen-year-old who has an eleven-year-old stepbrother, defined family as "Somebody to argue with so you don't lose any friends." His stepmother, Darlene, ex-panded on his statement. "Having these children, I understood for the first time how much my mother loved me. It's a different kind of love. Family will always be there, no matter what. You can depend on them. They are people you can be the meanest to, and they will still love you."

Shamika echoed this same thought and then made the connec-tion that this experience of unconditional love helps her to understand experientially what God is like. "My family makes me realize that no matter what happens to me, they'll always be there for me. They're not going to leave me out or let me down. If I stray, they'll always help me back. I think God is the same way. Your family is definitely more fallible but kind of an extension of God's love, of my faith. Something physical. My family makes me realize I'm not alone."

Perhaps no characteristic of God is more fundamental than that God is love. Jesus taught that our relationships with one another are to reflect that love (1 John 4:16–21). All through the scriptures, God's love is portrayed in family relationships. The Old Testament prophet Hosea loved Gomer, his wife, who kept running off into prostitution. He kept taking her back and used his troubled family to illustrate God's love for the people of God, however unfaithful. In the parable of the prodigal son, the father took the wayward son back and also

SACRED STORIES OF ORDINARY FAMILIES

loved the grumpy elder brother, looking for him too and inviting him to the party. So God folds us into parental arms of love. The endurance of family love points to the endurance of God's love: "love never ends" (1 Corinthians 13:8 NRSV).

The love Jesus is describing here is reciprocal. Although love certainly involves sacrifice of self, even to the point of giving one's life, such self-giving is not the ultimate aim but rather a means to the end of mutual love. Even Jesus' ultimate sacrifice of his life for unrepentant sinners was aimed at restoring us to relationship with God, to mutual love. Parents love infants, who cannot yet focus their eyes or recognize the parents as separate entities, much less reciprocate that love. But over time there is the expectation that children will learn to love their parents in return. And parents dream and hope that their children, drawing lines to divide the territory of the car backseat as eight- and ten-year-olds, will grow up to want to spend Thanksgiving together, to be friends as well as siblings, to come from being scattered across the country to play football together with grandchildren and nephews and nieces in the empty field next to the house.

God's grace sustains us as we stumble through life together, making mistakes, losing our tempers, becoming weary and sloppy in our relationships with one another. We experience God's grace in grown children who turn out to be wonderful people, in grandmothers who stand by us during difficult times, in parents who have become friends despite the hell we put them through as teenagers, in friends who have become family despite all our imperfections.

Not only do we experience grace ourselves, but we model grace for others. Others see in us the evidence of God's grace and of our hope that God can continue to work with us and through us even though we sometimes make a muck of things. Families teach us that God truly does work a process of miracles in our lives. Sometimes we surprise ourselves that we can be better than we thought we were. We find ourselves staying up through the night by the bed of a sick child or frail parent, giving money to brothers or children or parents who need financial help, loving a family member who lets us down time and time again. We learn through the experiences of family life the truth of Jesus' promise that those who sacrifice their lives will truly find life.

We are sometimes graceful without realizing it. These families I met are successfully swimming against the currents of our culture. They are making time together in very simple and yet remarkable ways: playing cards, taking rides in the car on Saturday morning, singing together in church choirs, cooking for the senior adults in their church, praying together, taking trips to visit grandparents. They argue and bicker with one another because they know they can and still be loved; they hug one another and encourage one another when they mess up. In the process, they are quietly and sometimes unconsciously modeling the no-matter-what love of God.

SACRED STORIES OF ORDINARY FAMILIES

Chapter 4

FAITH THAT SUSTAINS US

❧

Lydia must have been remarkable in her male-dominated Roman world of the first century (Acts 16:13–15). She was a householder and businesswoman in a culture that reserved household and public leadership roles for men. I wonder if that role in that world must have felt lonely at times. Perhaps that is why, despite her status, she sought the company of other women at the river where they washed clothes and fetched water for their homes and shared and prayed together. When Paul and Silas showed up and preached where the women in town had gathered by the river, Lydia was there and experienced God "opening her heart." She had the apostles baptize her whole household. Paul and Silas ate in her home and stayed with her family.

Some time later, Paul and Silas were arrested. While they were in prison, singing hymns and praying through the night, a violent earthquake shook the foundations of the prison and opened all the prison doors. The jailer, afraid that all the prisoners had escaped, prepared to run himself through with his sword, but Paul stopped him, shouting, "Don't harm yourself! We are all here!" (Acts 16:25–34 NRSV). In response, the jailer asked what he must do to be saved. Paul's response was "Believe in the Lord Jesus, and you will be saved—you and your household." In response, the jailer and his family were baptized "immediately." The story concludes, like the story of Lydia, with Paul and Silas going home with the jailer for a meal with the family, the jailer "filled with joy because he had come to believe in God—he and his whole family." And at another time, when Stephanas decided to be baptized and join the church, Paul tells us that he baptized "the household" (1 Corinthians 1:16).

All three of these stories indicate that in the early church, when the head of the household became a Christian, so did the rest of the household. In contrast, deciding to be a Christian in our culture is largely a personal choice. If a husband or wife makes a decision to become a Christian, we don't usually round up the spouse, children, sisters, brothers, and anybody else living in the household and dip them in or sprinkle them with baptismal waters. Did Lydia's family take a vote about whether or not they wanted to be baptized? The jailer's wife hadn't been at the prison to hear Paul and Silas's impromptu prayer meeting. Did her husband even ask her first if she wanted to be baptized? What is more, Paul told the jailer that if *he* believed in the Lord Jesus, he *and his household* would be saved.

It was a different time and place, of course. In the patriarchal Roman culture of the early church, householders controlled the religious expression of the household. Households had their own gods and their own altars, and joining a household meant joining that household's religious practices. Christians adopted this household model for the early churches. Churches did not have land and buildings; they met in private houses. The earliest missionaries tried to win over one household, which then became the base for reaching out to other households in the community. We do not have any way of knowing the extent to which all members of the household understood, much less chose, the faith they were adopting. I wonder, though, if it is too easy to dismiss the concept of faith belonging to the household or family as a first-century cultural artifact. As I heard families twenty centuries later in a very different cultural context talk to me about their faith, I recognized that we may have something to learn about the faith of families from these first-century households. In this chapter we will hear families explain what faith means to them and the ways in which family life has been a crucible for the shaping of their faith. In addition to seeing families as a context for individual faith development, we will see that they also have a dimension of faith that belongs to the family itself. We begin by considering the meaning of the word *faith*.

What Is Faith?

Darlene is the mother and stepmother, respectively, of Paul (age eleven) and Pete (age fourteen), whom you met in Chapter Three. When I asked Darlene's family what faith means to them, she answered, "I guess faith is the belief that Jesus was here and real and died for us, and we have new life through him." For Darlene, faith is belief about who God is and how God relates to persons. Faith has to do with the answers we have come to as we have wondered about the big questions of our lives. Faith is something that involves our minds, our thinking, our pondering and deciding on what we believe to be the truth.

Belief leads to trust, a second facet of faith. Another word for trust is confidence. The beliefs we hold increase our trust, our confidence that we can face life's challenges. Shamika is the young wife and only child of her widowed African American mother and her deceased Anglo-American father. When I asked her to define faith, she said,

> It seems like faith is so much a part of me, but it's not
> conscious. It's inside me. It's like a thread in fabric that
> runs all the way through. You can't see it, but if you pull
> it out, all the other threads fall out. Even though you
> don't really see it, you know it's there, holding it togeth-
> er. My faith doesn't really hold my family together, but I
> think it definitely holds me together. I rely on it, and
> then I don't worry so much about things that I can't
> control. I believe in God—that He loves me; that I can't
> control everything. I can't do everything by myself. I
> think my faith makes me stronger for the rest of my
> family.

Like Darlene, Shamika talks about her belief in God, but she goes further. She believes that God loves her and acts on that love by making her strong. She trusts God to hold her together. Her faith does not keep her from worrying, but it keeps her from worrying "so much."

And it prepares her for the demands of family life. If belief has to do with our thoughts and minds, then trust has to do with our emotions, our heart.

You met Nell in Chapter Two; she is the mother of Amy, now grown and married with two daughters of her own. After her first husband died, Nell married John, when Amy was a child. John and Nell are providing after-school care for Amy's daughters.

Despite a busy life with her husband of juggling careers and parenting, Amy volunteers as the children's program coordinator in the small Methodist church she has attended all her life. She is carrying on what she has watched her mother and stepfather and her father before his death do all her life, work in the church.

As Nell said, "Most of our activities have been in the church; that's where we've met people and had friends." They have done renovation of the church building, carpentry, and painting. And they have been leaders in various programs of their Methodist congregation, teaching adult Sunday school classes and leading children's groups.

Amy said, "I can't remember ever a time in my life that the church was not there and a very active part of my life and our family's life."

Currently, however, her mother is discouraged and angry over a conflict in their congregation and has not been attending. "It's the most traumatic experience I've ever been through," she told me. Even so, they are still busy serving. Nell and John are running a food drive for an ecumenical community ministries agency. John repairs bicycles for the church to give to poor children. And they volunteer to deliver food in the Meals on Wheels program.

Here is how Nell defined faith for me:

Two things best describe my faith in God. One of them is a story about a little boy and little girl. They are late for school, and the little boy says, "Let's stop and pray," and the little girl says, "Let's run and pray." That's kind of my faith. I've got faith that God is there. I talk to Him. I pray for the guidance. "Just show me, guide me, and help me be aware that you are guiding me." The other thing is that I guess my faith is too simple. On Sunday mornings, you can hear radio preachers painting a picture of what heaven is like. Like if you had a choice you aren't going? To me there are just two verses in the Bible that are really important: "Love your neighbor as yourself" and "God so loved the world, He gave His only son." Oh, and a third one is where Jesus said, "In my father's house are many mansions. I go to prepare a place for you." That's good enough for me.

Nell says her faith is "too simple," but it is really quite complex, with at least three facets. Like Darlene and Shamika, she believes that God is there and listens to her prayers. Like Shamika, she trusts God and doesn't have to worry; heaven will be there for her. But she actually begins her definition of faith with action; she believes in running while she is praying. She does not simply leave it to God to work out problems. The three scriptures she refers to touch on these three aspects of faith: belief ("God so loved the world"), trust ("I go to prepare a place for you"), and action ("Love your neighbor as yourself").

RELIGION, SPIRITUALITY, AND FAITH

The Christian scriptures say, "faith, if it has no works, is dead" (James 2:17 NAS). Faith is about doing, not just believing and trusting. Faith means striking out in a new direction, one we couldn't have made for ourselves but that God makes possible. The concept of faith originates in the Hebrew scriptures, from a root word that has to do with reliability and trustworthiness. It is the same root for the affirmation *amen*. Bible stories of faith tell about humans responding to God's promises. For Abraham faith was the active, creative force that pushed him to be bold and take great risks.

Faithful action flows from belief about what is real and what is important. Jesus taught us to be active, storing up treasures for ourselves in heaven, not on earth, where moth and rust destroy. "For where your treasure is, there your heart will be also" (Matthew 6:21

NRSV). We treasure that which we think has value. That treasure is what we give our hearts to, what we trust. Action not only grows out of our faith, but action also turns around and shapes our faith. Sometimes our actions confirm our beliefs, and sometimes they pull those beliefs into question. What happens if we believe that God answers prayers and so we pray believing that God will bring healing if we ask, and still the sick child for whom we are praying so fervently and confidently dies? Sometimes the outcomes of our attempts to live faithfully deepen and confirm our faith. But other times, our faith is shaken and changed.

Christian faith is not a set of intellectual stages that we can somehow tackle and master, leading us to ever more mature beliefs. Jesus gave a child's faith as an example for how we are to have faith (Mark 10:14–15). The focus of Christian faith is living faithfully— faith fully. To truly understand persons' faith, we need to know more than a summary statement of beliefs or even what those persons value and trust. We need to know this third aspect of faith, how they are living their faith day by day in response to who God is and what they believe God is doing. We need to know the stories of how they came to their beliefs, their experiences in learning to trust those beliefs and act on them, and the stories of how their faith has been shaped as a consequence. So what is the relationship between faith, understood this way, and family life?

FAMILY AS THE CRUCIBLE FOR OUR PERSONAL FAITH

Family life provides a crucible for individuals to learn faith, both as children and as adults. Family experiences test, shape, and deepen our faith. A stepmother described faith to me this way:

> I don't know if I can express this, but I think this is real-
> ly weird. Real issues of living a Christian life are more
> difficult in an intimate relationship with your family
> than they are with anybody else. I mean, people can go

out and serve food in a soup kitchen and think they're doing this Christian deed and then not understand how to nurture or help somebody in their family who is starving for some other thing. Right now I am not getting along with my stepdaughter. Last Sunday I sat in church and listened to the sermon, and I just kept thinking about what it meant in my own life. I thought, *This is horrible; I am not treating her in the way I would think of myself as a Christian.* It tortured me to try to figure that out. I didn't get any further than that. A lot of people are looking for very simplistic guidance instead of having to suffer the pain of wrestling with things. The family represents a working path to get there.

Figure 4.1. The Cycle of Developing Faith

Faith is believing something to be true and then trusting that truth. We act based on what we trust to be true. The outcomes of those actions based on our beliefs and trust in turn shape our beliefs.

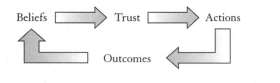

Families are not the only contexts in which we live and have experiences that shape our faith, of course. As individuals, we represent a mosaic of stories from different contexts that we somehow put together to shape our identity, our beliefs, our commitments, and our ways of living our faith.

Families Shape Personal Beliefs

When Shamika's parents met and married, she told me, her father worked at an automobile factory. She was born a year and a half later. By Shamika's description, because he was Anglo-American and married to a African American woman, other men at the plant harassed him, and this continued month after month for two years. Sometimes, she told me, he ignored the taunts and threats, but when they got to him, he would lash back. Shamika's father ended up dead, his murder still unsolved, leaving Shamika fatherless before her second birthday. Obviously her grandmother or mother had told her this story, because it all happened before she was born and while she was just a baby. This, then, is a family story—one they share with one another—as well as being Shamika's story. Shamika went on:

> You would never think that someone would be that
> prejudiced and narrow-minded that they would actually
> want to take another person's life. But it does happen.
> And it had happened in that town before. They knew of
> other cases where black men got together and killed a
> white person because they felt like "You don't need to be
> with our women," or white men did it. It went both
> ways. When I was thirteen or fourteen, I was looking
> through my photo albums one day. I don't know why,
> but I just couldn't handle it anymore. I felt so alone and
> so by myself. I was really depressed for a while, and my
> mom asked, "What's wrong?" I finally just broke down
> and started sobbing, and she said, "You're not by your-
> self. Remember how I used to tell you when you were
> little that he's still watching you up there. He knows
> what's going on with you." She also told me that my dad
> was such a good person that he was just too good for the
> world. When I got married, the depression came back
> again because I thought, *Why can't I have my dad walk
> me down the aisle?* There are questions that come up that
> there are no answers for. There's no why. It's not some-
> thing I can stop myself from asking, and it's very diffi-
> cult for me.

Shamika went on to say that faith has meant believing that she can leave justice in God's hands, as her grandmother taught:

> My grandmother was one of those nice old ladies that
> always had those little sayings. She always used to tell

my mother, "What goes around comes around. Don't worry about it. God sees it." Instead of thinking about revenge, she believed that the Lord will take care of people who don't do what they're supposed to do. It's not up to me to decide it or find them or try and bring justice. That's not my job. God takes care of people who do things right and who do things wrong, and I have to believe that. I have to let my hands not touch that one. It's almost evil, hating like I hate them for killing my father. I shouldn't be this angry. It's something I have to work through, and I have to let it go, and it's very hard. I think if I didn't have my faith, if I didn't believe in God, I don't think I would come out of it.

Growing up with the story of her father's murder has created significant challenges for Shamika's beliefs about God and justice. The family has not been just the context for the challenge, however; it has also provided ways of thinking about it and emotional support for dealing with the challenge. Her mother was there, sensitive enough to see through the moods of an adolescent and later a blossoming young woman that something was wrong; she then offered presence and comfort and suggested the image of her father's continuing presence in her life. Her grandmother offered a belief system that there will be justice, that Shamika can put her trust in God for that.

Families Teach People to Trust—and Mistrust

Families also provide a context for persons, both children and adults, to learn to trust or to mistrust. As we learn to trust one another, we learn to trust God. Christy and Aaron are the parents of two youngsters and another on the way, the family that likes to go out for breakfast together on Saturdays. According to Christy, "You just have to have faith that it's going to work out the way it was meant to be and that our vision is so limited, our scope is so small compared to God's. It's similar to being a parent. I have to have faith that I'm doing the right thing for our children, that I'm feeding them the right thing and teaching them the right thing. They really don't have a whole lot of

Faith That Sustains Us

choices, and so it's a trust issue. And to me, it's the same relationship that you have with Christ."

Christy believes her children are learning faith by experiencing her faithfully taking care of them. She connects their trust of her with her own trust that God is guiding her in "doing the right thing" for her children. In other words, their faith in her underscores for her the role of faith in her own life. The awesome responsibility of parenting drives her to trust God for guidance. She and her husband had left the church as young adults but came back because they wanted to rear their children well. The challenges of parenting led them into an active religious life.

In contrast, when family relationships are not trustworthy, then faith in God may also be shaken, for adults as well as for children. Developmental psychologist Erik Erikson describes the first task of human beings as the establishment of basic trust. We learn basic trust in others—or mistrust. Theologian Sharon Parks has pointed out that this learning of trust and mistrust does not happen, if at all, merely once and for all. We repeatedly find our anchors of trust shaken loose and then reestablished, often and especially in family relationships.

You met Jacob and Kate in Chapter Three, the busy African American couple, parents of two sons, Dillon (age nine) and Shane (age seven). Twenty years ago, Jacob and Kate met in college, fell in love, and married when they graduated. Now they sing together in their church choir. Jacob directs and Kate plays the piano for the children's choir in which Dillon and Shane sing enthusiastically. Sometimes Kate writes the music for the children to sing. They all go to Sunday school and worship every Sunday. It all sounds so "John and Mary Churchfamily," until they talk about the tragedy that has shaped their life together and their understanding of God's ways.

Kate grew up Catholic, and Jacob grew up in a National Baptist church. Their different faith traditions weren't important when they met and married, though, because church wasn't important to either of them. As Kate said, "I really didn't want to be committed to any church or to a certain set of rules." Kate remembers being one of only two African American families in the church of her childhood and how uncomfortable and unwelcome she felt there.

Jacob became disillusioned with the church when his pastor's daughter became pregnant, and because of the pregnancy, the pastor refused to allow her a church wedding. "I thought to myself, *Here you're teaching us forgiveness. Are you really learning any of what you're telling us?* After a while I just found myself saying the heck with it. We'd read the paper in bed on Sunday mornings instead of getting up and going to church."

Their first son, Mark, was born when they had been married three years. Their lives revolved around him, a happy child, the first grandchild for both sets of grandparents. When Mark was three years old, Kate began having nightmares that something terrible was going to happen. *Does God send dreams?* she still wonders.

Jacob describes what began as an average day, with Kate rushing to take Mark to the babysitter on her way to work. "I remember the expression on Mark's face. He had his coat on, and he looked at me and said, 'Bye!' and he had this expression on his face like, 'See ya. Everything's fine.' I often wonder if children communicate with God more than adults do. He came back and gave me a kiss good-bye. He hadn't done that in a while. I still remember."

While they were both working, a fire swept through the babysitter's home. Kate told me, "He died from acute carbon monoxide poisoning. The flames didn't get him."

Jacob interrupted, "Smoke inhalation. He was asleep at the time. They said that it was painless. He probably just took a deep breath and never woke up. Our pain never stops." The meaning behind Jacob's words seemed to be, "At least he didn't suffer," the only source of comfort they could find as they reeled in pain with the catastrophe of losing their son.

Their world fell apart. Both of them were angry—at God, at one another, at the world in general—because the loss was so terribly painful. Jacob said that he woke up every morning thinking, *Well, there's a plan out there. Nobody consulted me when He thought it up, but there must be a plan out there for something like this to happen.* But how could God come up with such a terrible plan? They struggled to hold on to one another. Two more sons were born. But they were growing apart in their search for meaning in the senselessness of Mark's death.

Kate was desperate: "I went to see spiritualists, and they said, 'You need to pray more.' They gave me some suggestions, and I went to the library, and I was looking at different books. I came across the

Faith That Sustains Us

dream books, and I came across meditation, and one thing just led to another. I was into searching, so I looked at a lot of different things. Channeling and all that. What is everything about? This was my thing. Strictly my thing. I tried to share it a little bit with Jacob, but he wasn't into it. I didn't want to impose."

As Jacob said, "We just took different paths." They occasionally visited churches together, because Jacob was looking for more traditional answers to his grief. No place felt right, and they never attended the same church twice. Seven years after their son's death, the pastor of a little Baptist church in their community came to visit them and said something they had never heard a church leader say before, "Is there anything we can do for you?" He held their hands and prayed with them, and they went to church with him to find a delightful mix of Anglo-American, African American, and biracial families worshiping together. They felt at home. The congregation didn't try to salve their grief or tell them why their son had died but gave them a safe place to grieve and struggle together. It had been almost ten years since their son's death, and the tears still rolled down their faces as they told me about their lost son and the grief that will be a part of their story all their lives.

They still don't agree on what Mark's death means. Jacob believes that somehow God needed his son: "He was three. At every family gathering, he'd dance. And I just believe that there must be somebody out there that needed whatever that spirit could provide more than us. I have to think that there's a reason why. Somebody else must have been going through some serious deprivation in their life, and it was time for them to feel good too. I think I'm a much better parent now."

Kate disagrees. "I don't have the same feelings about God taking him for someone else. I just don't believe that. I do think everybody is part of a plan. His death pushed me to grow spiritually. I don't know if he was still here if we would be going to church. I really don't know."

Jacob added, "I've never thought about that, but it's true."

"I like to think I would have," Kate continued. "God doesn't give you burdens that you can't bear. It was really traumatic when that happened. We survived it. We've moved on. We've progressed. We did not go backwards."

Clearly, their faith has been shaped by their shared experience, and they both think they have grown spiritually as a consequence. The account of their son's death—the terrible fire, getting the news, finding each other, and sharing their initial grief—is a family story. They told it to me in typical tag-team family storytelling style, interrupting one another, adding details the other omitted, shifting the storytelling back and forth between them. But then the family storytelling stopped. They were not just helping one another tell a familiar story to an outsider; they were listening to one another, because they moved into a new conversation. They had not talked much before about their attempts to understand the meaning of their son's death, indicated when Jacob said, "I've never thought about that." As they talked, they found that they agreed about trusting that God allowed this tragedy to occur for a reason, though they did not agree on what that reason is. They both described the resulting spiritual growth they have experienced, but they use the word *me,* not *we.* Sharing this terrible family experience has been a crucible for shaping their personal faith, but it is not exactly a faith that they yet share—although our conversation may actually have become a beginning of shared faith for them. They do agree: God was in this somehow.

In spite of arriving at different answers, putting their lives together afterward has clearly been a shared experience. As Kate said, "We survived it. We did not go backwards." *Me* has become *we* again. With all their unanswered questions and even fundamental differences in understanding God's role in Mark's death, they celebrate their survival. They had lived in their current home three months when Mark died. For Jacob the house has come to symbolize their life since their child's death:

> I think this house pictures the way that things have been
> with us. It looks great now. But if you had seen what it
> was like before we got hold of it, you wouldn't have
> believed it. I put the floor down. Kate and I patched and
> sanded and primed and painted those walls. I put the
> moldings up. Whatever you see here is because we did
> it. Sometimes people come in those rooms and say, "Oh,

this is beautiful," and I feel like saying, "Do you want to see the scars? Do you want to see how it got to look beautiful?"

Their family is "beautiful" because they have survived. They may never agree on the meaning of their son's death, and many in their church community probably would not agree with either one of them. Does God cause the death of children because their spirits are needed elsewhere? Or to shake their parents into a spiritual journey? Or do senseless, evil things happen outside of God's control, and God grieves with us as we grieve? If God does not cause such things to happen, then is God not in control? Why do bad things happen?

No one who loves others is spared such questions. Every family has or will someday face faith-shaking tragedy. Perhaps it won't be Kate and Jacob's or Shamika's kind of tragedy, but it will be a tragedy nevertheless. In family life we confront the most fundamental issues of life and death and faith. We learn faith here, and we are shattered here, and we struggle—whether together or in isolation—to make sense of it all here. For Kate and Jacob, theirs has been a lonely path because they found different answers. And yet they did so in one another's arms and finally in the arms of a community of faith. They held on to one another, gave one another room to struggle, and at the same time did not leave one another alone in the struggle. They remodeled their house—together. Now they sing, their two sons in the children's choir, Jacob directing, Kate playing the new music she has written.

Living Personal Faith in Family Life

Not only are families the places where beliefs and trust are shaped, but they are the places where we act on our faith, day in and day out. Beliefs and trust take on living action in the crucible of family life.

Catherine, the divorced young mother who worried about telling her grandmother of her pregnancy, lives just a few blocks from her parents, Beverly and Art. Beverly told me how she and Art had moved to another state shortly after Catherine was born, more than twenty years before. Their marriage was rocky, and Beverly was miserable:

Finally I left. I went back to my mother's. But down deep inside, I knew I had learned one thing, that if you ever did get married, that you were not to be apart. I knew that I could not leave him permanently. When I was home with Catherine at my mother's house that week, I said, "Well, Lord, I know I've got to go back." But I said to God, "You're going to have to take it, and you're going to have to shape it and mold it because I can't do it." And I did go back. And that's not to say we didn't have conflicts later on.

For Beverly faith meant acting on the marriage commitment she had made and believing that God would be at work changing her world in ways she could not.

Sometimes faith-based action is the quiet heroism of simply caring for one another in difficult circumstances. Virginia raised five children by working two and sometimes three jobs, managing to find time to entertain her children with winter picnics in front of the woodstove. I asked her how she had been able to do what seems impossible in the telling. She answered simply, "The Lord did it. I know I didn't do it." Families repeated this theme over and over, often giving emphasis by quoting a favorite Bible verse: I can do all things through Christ who strengthens me.

Children shape the faith of parents just as parents shape the faith of children. The adults in these families often talked about their sense of responsibility for guiding their children toward faith. As they wrestle with this responsibility, they find themselves growing spiritually, seeking out a faith community for the sake of children, and making decisions about the behavior and faith they want to model. Their lifestyles and behavior change.

Aaron, the dad in the family that goes out for breakfast on Saturday mornings, told me that responsibility for their children led him and Christy to seek out a community of faith. "I always had too many bad habits to make a real commitment to Christ. Then I finally realized that I couldn't wait until I was perfect, that I was going to have to leave it to Christ and then let Him make the changes. I finally figured that out. He finally showed me that. I think He used the boys. I knew

Faith That Sustains Us

that I was responsible for bringing the boys up in the ways of the Lord, and so we both gradually committed our lives to God."

Christy added, "I feel that the Lord is with our children. They will say certain things that I know is a part of us teaching, but I also think it is God working in their little minds. I know God has answered prayers for us. There is no other way that certain things could have happened unless He did it. I was telling Aaron the other night and I don't think I had ever told him before. . . . Probably a year ago or more I would notice that the kids would do something, and we would yell at them. And we would find ourselves constantly just going, 'Stop doing that!'"

"Mainly me," Aaron interrupted. "I just rubbed off on her."

Christy went on,

> Instead of telling them to stop, we would just yell at them and yell at them. I got so tired of being that way, and I prayed a lot for God to give us patience and understanding. The other night, I said to myself, *Did you notice you have not yelled at these kids in probably two months?* And like I told Aaron, it's not something I made a conscious effort to wake up every morning and say, "OK, I'm not going to yell at the kids. I'm going to take time out and play with them and listen to them and read to them." It's not something I've done on my own. It just happened. It's been a big change.

Daily parenting challenges every bit of energy and strength Aaron and Christy have but also is the ground on which their faith and understanding of God's working in their lives is growing. Note too that this is the subject of conversation between them. She began the story by saying, "I was telling Aaron the other night. . . ." Families often wrestle with faith issues in the corners and along the ways of their days as a part of the daily conversation. Faith conversations are not limited to designated family devotional and prayer time; they happen along the path, day after day, and we sort out the meaning of our lives as we go.

Family as the Context for Faith Crises

Families provide many experiences for faith crises, when the outcomes of family members' faith-based action are not what they believed and trusted would happen. Corrine is the mother and homemaker who described her reluctant trip with her sons and husband to the family cabin on a January day, only to find the day warm and the campfire on the beach a serendipitous moment of great contentment and joy. In contrast with that experience, she also told of the crisis of faith she experienced that began with a routine surgery on one of her sons shortly after her conversion:

> I had my newborn faith. I felt like I had been born
> again. As I think about it now, I was trying to be a little
> bit too rigid in my behavior. At the time I was thinking,
> *I'm not going to cuss, and I'm not going to think bad
> thoughts.* I had my little checklist and thought if I did all
> these things I would be OK with God. And I prayed
> every day for forty-five minutes for all these people on
> my list. I thought if I did this, I would be okay with
> God. Kurt [the younger son] had all these warts on his
> hand. They said they could remove them with laser
> surgery and just give him a general anesthesia. That's
> pretty traumatic to give a little seven-year-old. I was so
> relieved when it was over. While Kurt was in recovery, I
> looked across the street, and I saw a cross on a church. I
> started praying. I said, "God, I know that this is a sign
> that everything is going to be just fine. Thank you,
> Lord, that you protected my child just like I had been
> praying so hard for. And thank you for the doctor saying he's going to be OK."

Everything was not fine, however. Kurt developed a rare infection from the surgery and almost died. That infection led to other major problems that have continued to threaten his health and challenge his mother's faith:

Some churches teach that if you pray those prayers of protection and if you do everything right, things will be right in your life. And I thought, *So why didn't God protect him?* I even went to a Bible study called Trusting God. My next-door neighbor took me. She said, "I think this will help you." It left me even more spiritually devastated because I felt like they were pointing a finger at me: "This must have happened for a reason. Did God do this to you to bring you closer to Him?" And I thought, *He would not use a child! These things don't happen to bring me or my husband to the Lord.* I will never go back to that kind of thinking. I don't try to fit theology in little neat boxes anymore. I just say that I don't understand. We're just supposed to help each other through it. I will never go back to those churches again. I love my church because they comfort, but they weren't pushy like we had to get in and solve this today. They were just there.

This family experience challenged her basic beliefs about God. In fact, she rejected her old system of beliefs and those of her church community. In the resulting crisis of faith, she sought out and joined a new faith community and in the process redefined her beliefs about God and suffering. When the results of being faithful are not what we expect, our beliefs often change. Thus, the spiral of belief, trust, action, and its outcomes continues, ever changing through our shared experiences of both the joys and the tragedies of life.

Things Work Out   Some family members told me that they believe that "things work out for the best when you have faith." Many persons told how they believe their fervent prayers caused God to act. Successful prayers included everything from praying for the healing of a sick child to praying that God would send money or would cause someone to buy a house for sale. Several families living on the brink of poverty talked about God providing ways for them to buy or repair the car they needed, or checks they didn't expect coming in the mail, enabling them to buy groceries to feed their children. Soon after Virginia's husband left her with five children and no money, she found herself in dire straits. The electricity was off, and she was frantically trying to keep the rent paid and to provide enough food to keep them nourished. "I knew God was in control," said Virginia. "There were days. . . ." Tears rolled out of her eyes, and she stopped speaking for a few moments.

> I'd come home, and there would be bags of stuff on the porch, everything from toilet paper to canned meats. Sometimes I'd know who it came from, sometimes not. I remember the first Christmas that I didn't have much money. I shop on Christmas Eve; that's the way I've always done it, because if I don't have the rent money, then we do without Christmas presents. I had all the kids in the car, and we were getting ready to go shopping. I didn't have the money but for maybe some stuffed animals and some things for their hair. I was upset because I couldn't get my kids a tree. My children said they thought it was OK; they were trying to make me feel better. We were in the car getting ready to go to the shopping center, and the mailman was coming, so we waited a minute for him to hand me the mail. There was a red envelope in there with "Santa Claus" in the corner, but it was addressed to me. I opened it up, and a $100 bill fell out of that envelope. I still today don't know where that came from. But I know who's in control if you have faith.

Some people told me that God only works things out for those who have faith, who pray, who tithe. An adult daughter landed a job because her parents prayed. Critically ill children live because their devout grandmothers, parents, and congregations prayed for healing.

When Things Don't Work Out   The belief that things work out for the faithful leads to disillusionment and doubt when life events do not seem to make sense. That was certainly true for Corrine as she struggled with the life-threatening illness of her son after what was supposed to be routine outpatient surgery. And it is true for many others.

Dorothy is a widow in her late sixties, living with her adult daughter and her frail elderly mother in a southern city's suburb of tall trees and lovely new middle-class homes, not far from the Baptist church where they are members. Like Dorothy's family, most of the families in the neighborhood are middle-class professional African Americans. A few years before I talked with her, Dorothy had moved with her husband from a northern city several states away, following his job as a company executive. They didn't know when they agreed to the move that he had cancer, but he became ill and died only a couple of years after their move. Now she finds herself hundreds of miles from her closest friends. Things have definitely not "worked out" for Dorothy. She didn't want to make the move in the first place, and when she prayed for God to heal her husband, he died anyway.

She expressed restlessness and a wish that God would hurry up and do something in her life. She seemed to imply that she meant meeting a man. When I asked if that was what she meant, she said, "Well, it's not my goal, no." She hesitated. "But I'm hoping that's in the plan of the Lord. I would hate for Him to take my husband for nothing. I know all the widows feel the same way. I just feel that, 'Why take him? I prayed hard for you to heal this cancer. You wouldn't do it. You took him. Now what are you going to do for me? Give me a replacement?'

"Isn't that horrible to think that way about the Lord?" she continued.

> I'm like Job. There have been times when I thought, "Lord, I know you know all things, but have you forgotten I'm sitting in this little town in Louisiana?" Sometimes I think, *Well, He doesn't know I'm around anymore,* but I know better in my heart. That's Satan putting those silly thoughts in my mind. I feel like I've been forgotten, and I feel like . . . nobody really cares for me anymore, especially a male. I keep praying that the Lord will send me a nice Christian man because I need someone. I get tired of cutting grass and hammering

and fixing. And I also miss the companionship. The worst thing in the world about being alone is making decisions alone. I really miss him because we used to sit down and talk about every little thing and plan it out, and I don't have that any more. Now when I make my decisions, if they turn out bad, I don't have anybody to blame. So I pray a lot. "Lord, you guide me and show me what I should be doing." And so far, so good.

As mad as she is at God for depriving her of a man, as abandoned as she feels, she finds herself now relying on God to replace the man in her life and to help her, and she admits, albeit unhappily, "so far, so good." But she is not yet ready to sing about it. She is struggling to understand why she trusted God and prayed and did everything she could, but God didn't heal her husband. She is experiencing a crisis in her faith, in what it means to believe in and trust in God. The themes of our faith, the melodies that anchor our daily songs, take on different words and stories as life carries us on together as families. In times of great crisis and loss, the melodies themselves seem to change or even to be lost for a time, as they were for Jacob and Kate in the death of their baby, as they were for Corrine in the scary illness of her son, as they are now for Dorothy as she wonders why she is left a widow, abandoned far from the place she considers home.

God Works Through Whatever Happens   Other families told me that they believe that God is working goodness through whatever happens, even in bad times. Catherine is the young mother who became pregnant as a teenager, dreaded telling her family, and remembers with gratitude the blessing of her grandmother. Two decades before her baby was born, Catherine was herself the baby daughter Beverly carried "back home" to her family, only to realize she was committed to her marriage and so returned to her husband. Catherine and her baby's father, Doug, married before the baby was born, and he is now in prison, convicted of fraud and of drug possession. She still loves Doug, but she felt she had to divorce him to protect herself and her son financially from responsibility for his enormous debts. Talking about the rough patches of life she has experienced, she says that she does not exactly believe that God caused them, although she seems not to have finished working this out in her mind: "God may not have caused the bad things to happen, but I believe that He puts things in your life that you can learn from if you trust in Him. Maybe there's a reason that Doug got put in prison; maybe that was his ticket out of the lifestyle he had chosen and how he can turn his life around." "Maybe," she says. But she is not sure. The story will go on.

FAMILY FAITH

Up to this point, we have been looking at ways that family life is a crucible for shaping, challenging, and reshaping our faith as individuals. So far in this chapter, you have heard family members reflecting on their individual understanding of family experiences and sharing their personal faith, formed in and tested by family life. They shared their reflections with me and with one another; for some, our conversation appeared to be the first time they had talked about these experiences together in light of their faith.

In addition, however, families have sacred stories that tell about their shared understanding of their experiences as a family. Social scientist Hamilton McCubbin and his research colleagues have studied how families cope with crises and catastrophes such as surviving floods and tornadoes that wipe out their homes, living through chronic illness and unemployment that wipe out their financial security and ability to manage the very basics of life, and even having a family member reported missing in action in wartime. These researchers learned that the families that are most resilient in the face of crisis or catastrophe have a shared set of beliefs and values that provide them with a common understanding of what their experience means and what they can do in response. When families told me stories in the informal tag-team storytelling that characterizes many families' conversations, the meaning those stories had for them as a family stood out.

When James and Marianne married, they brought three children from their previous marriages. James's young adult son, Corey, has severe developmental and physical challenges and uses a wheelchair; he works part-time at a sheltered workshop. Marianne has two daughters, Sasha (sixteen) and Sandi (eleven). Last year, the "ours" baby, Ariah, was born. The family lives just beyond poverty. It is literally around the corner from them. They are African American, living in a predominantly African American inner-city neighborhood that is a mixture of apartments and old homes, many rented rather than owned by residents, just a few blocks from the most violent, physically decaying, and gang-infested public housing in the city. James works in that public housing as a maintenance man. Marianne works as a secretary downtown, and together they are excited both about their life together now and planning for the future for their children. They are proud to own their two-story house. Although their house is just around the block from poverty, it is located on a quiet street, and several other families have also bought homes there. Like one or two other houses on the street, the cheerful new coat of paint and flowers planted by the front fence anchor James and Marianne's house as a home that aims to change its community.

Their life has not always been so full of promise, however. Shortly after their marriage five years ago, James lost his job, and the only other work he could find was as a bartender. Discouraged, he slipped into alcohol and drug abuse, sometimes not coming home at night. Marianne hung on, praying for God to help her husband. Now James is recovering and has had a profound religious conversion. He loves their Baptist congregation and their pastor, and he is in training to become a deacon. They spend much of their free time involved in church activities with their children and helping with the church's many programs designed to stabilize the community and tackle the complex problems of poverty, violence, and hopelessness.

As we talked about their faith, Marianne told me that she thinks she is a bit like Moses' wife:

> She just stuck with him being gone up to the mountain, waiting for him to come back down. That's how I look at myself. I'm there for my husband through thick and thin. I came close to giving up because I kept thinking when we were going through it, *I'm just going to tell him*

to get out, to leave. And then I thought, *No, because if I tell him that, he'll really do it. If I tell him to leave, he won't come home.* Through all of what was happening, I kept praying and praying and praying. It just made me stronger. I needed that experience to increase my faith and to make me strong. One of my nieces told me one day, "You just think you are the perfect family, don't you?" No, we're not.

She chuckled deeply and then laughed out loud at the thought of being a perfect family. "But we made a pact," she continued. "We never go to bed mad. We try to agree to disagree or whatever. That's what makes me know who sent it to me because we always just seem to work it out."

James added,

I'm just so glad she prayed. I like to think that while I was out there in all that trouble, the Lord knew that I wasn't ready, and He was preparing me for something. He gave me a new testimony that I can go back out on the street and I can witness to someone about what it was like for me to be out there in the streets. Even when we first got married, I smoked a little marijuana, and I drank a little beer, but then when I got out there in the streets I started doing everything under the sun. It was like that bar was all I lived for. It's just amazing what we put ourselves through when we don't know the Lord. I draw strength from the testimony that I have now; I have a lot of hope about the work I can accomplish through God in the future. Because you know sometimes if you haven't been through something you tend to look down your nose at someone with that uppity attitude. Some people I work with haven't been through some of the things that the people in public housing are going through, and they talk to them as if they were children and can't understand. But I know. I've been there.

SACRED STORIES OF ORDINARY FAMILIES

Eleven-year-old Sandi wanted to get in on the conversation and picked up on her mother's earlier statement of identifying with Moses' wife. "I know who I'm like. I'm like David, because he fought Goliath with only five stones. And Goliath had a sword and shield, and David killed him with just one stone. I think I'm as strong as David, and I can do anything with Christ."

James and Marianne told me a story of strength, and Sandi echoed the strength she has seen in parents who have "been through it" and persevered. Sandi voices the family theme: "we do all things through Christ who strengthens us," based on Philippians 4:13. Mom lived through her husband's days of drug abuse and not supporting his family and not even coming home. Dad found his way through the alcohol and drugs, sustained by his wife's prayers. And the children learned that they too can slay the giants that threaten them. Their stories echo the themes of great Bible stories: Moses and his wife, David and Goliath. They are singing the same songs of the ancient biblical heroes and heroines. Given all they have been through, Marianne laughed at the thought of being called perfect. But it was not just a laugh of disbelief. Her laugh was also tinged with belief that her niece just might have hit on an element of truth, that there is a process of perfection at work here. No, she says, in many ways they are not perfect. But if perfection is not about being problem-free, if perfection is about allowing and celebrating God's work through them, if it is the mark at which they are shooting, then perhaps *perfect* is a word worth pondering. According to the Apostle Paul, the Lord says: "My grace is sufficient for you, for my power is made perfect in weakness." And Paul goes on to say, "Therefore I will boast all the more gladly about my weaknesses, so that Christ's power may rest on me. That is why, for Christ's sake, I delight in weaknesses, in insults, in hardships, in persecutions, in difficulties. For when I am weak, then I am strong" (2 Corinthians 12:9 NIV). Paul boasts; Marianne laughs. God makes weakness and struggles into "perfection."

Family Belief and Trust

The cycle of faith begins with what we believe and trust. For families, that belief and trust is often shared, giving direction for their

Faith That Sustains Us

decisions and challenging them to make sense of the joys, struggles, and tragedies of life. Even experiences that to others may seem like senseless chaos or unexplainable suffering may, in the frame of family beliefs and trust, have meaning and deepen their melodies of faith.

A Son Lost in a Storm   Peggy and Bill are one of the first families I introduced to you, the senior adult couple who lived all their lives in friendship and real estate business with Mary and Bob. Since Bob's death and the death of parents, they are realizing that Mary is like family. Peggy and Bill raised four sons, and the story of their life that overshadows all others is that of losing one of those sons, Chris. Chris was in the military, stationed in the Philippines. They knew that Chris and his wife were having marital troubles, but they didn't know how serious those troubles were. Chris became depressed. As they told the story to me, they interrupted and verbally tumbled over one another, both of them with tears in their eyes through most of the story. First, they received a call that Chris was missing in action from his military unit. During those same days, Bill's elderly mother became ill and died. Her funeral occurred in the terrible, anxious days as they waited for some word about Chris. They soon learned that he had killed himself.

As Bill began to relate how one of their grown sons and his wife came to stay for his grandmother's funeral and a few days afterward, Peggy interrupted. "Let me tell this," she said. "The Lord just takes care of you, because Grant [their oldest son] was here. The day that they came to tell us that Chris's body had washed ashore, Grant and his wife were here because of Mom's funeral."

Bill picked up the story again:

> It was about this time in the afternoon. Grant came to me and said, "We have some folks here that want to see you. Are you up to seeing them?" I said, "Sure, I want to see them." He said, "They're from the military." I said, "Are they here to tell me they found Chris's body?" He said, "Yes, sir." I don't believe there is any way I could have made it through something like this without the Lord. For three days, knowing our son was missing

and not knowing where he was. All I did was pray and talk to God about it every waking minute. And then there they are; the military folks are on your front porch, and you know.

Peggy picked up the story, "Earlier that day, we were just beside ourselves. We just didn't know what to do. Thousands of miles away, and he's missing. So each one, Bill and all three of our other sons had gone to see their pastors."

Bill explained, "I went to talk to Brother Tim and said, 'Preacher, I don't know how to take it.' I just told him about Chris being missing, and I just talked to him about thirty minutes. Well, I didn't know that Grant called his preacher that day, Marty in [another town] talked to his preacher that day, and Bart over in [another state] went and talked to his preacher that day. All four of us talked to our preachers that day."

"A kind of peace came over me," Peggy said. "I just sort of relaxed, and when they came and told us the news, I stayed calm. I didn't go to pieces or anything. I guess we had been prepared. Bill told me that when he talked to the preacher, they mostly prayed for me. So I felt like that's what happened."

"A peace comes over you that is unexplainable," Bill agreed. "Those four days, I spent a lot of time out in the swing in the back-yard. I wasn't working because I had just had a heart attack, and I'd just sit around and mope and dread and cry my heart out and talk to the Lord. I told the Lord that day if he'd help me find Chris . . ." He paused, choking on tears, "I'd try to live my life to suit him. And I'm trying to do it."

Peggy went on with the story: "The lady that came from the base to talk with us told us that if a storm had not come up, his body would never have washed ashore."

The details of Peggy and Bill's story turn what seems like a senseless tragedy into a story of God at work in their lives during this terrible time. Because of his grandmother's death, their oldest son was with them when the news came of his brother's body being found. Peggy cited this detail as evidence that "the Lord takes care of you"; Grant was there to support and comfort them. They credit Peggy's

Faith That Sustains Us

sense of peace to the fact that the three remaining sons and Bill all independently consulted their pastors on the same day and prayed for her. The father had prayed for searchers to find his son, presumed dead by that point. He pledged to live a more suitable life if God would just help the searchers find Chris. When Bill, tears rolling down his face, added that he was "trying to do it," his wife explained that a storm washed their son's body ashore, or Chris would never have been found. She implied that God sent the storm as an answer to the father's prayer.

Peggy and Bill have suffered tremendous grief. But the story is one that communicates not chaos and meaningless but quite the opposite. Through the presence of others orchestrated by God, and through a storm many miles away, they trace orderliness and experience these events as God's care for them. Telling the story confirms the meaning they have found together in these events. One can almost hear the melody, although a somber one, that carries the story of seeing evidence that God is with them, carrying them in the darkest moments of their lives. This belief in God's care and active presence in their lives is a family theme, a theme that supports but is more than just an independent reporting of their individual beliefs and trust.

Wet Paper and Mama's Jewelry Box   Darlene and David are the Catholic and Presbyterian couple raising their sons from previous marriages, his son, Pete (age fourteen), and her son, Paul (age eleven). When we were talking about what faith means to them, Paul volunteered that for him,

> Faith means living the life that I think God would want
> me to live and believing that He is our creator, and
> nothing happens without God having a plan. I was talk-
> ing to my mom about it in the car just a few days ago
> about how every bad thing ends up with a good thing.
> When my mom moved down South here from New
> York, she probably thought it was going to be the end of
> the world because she didn't know anybody or about
> anything that goes on down here in Mississippi. But if
> she hadn't done that, she wouldn't have met my dad.

And chances are she wouldn't have had me. And another example is if my mom hadn't gotten divorced, I wouldn't have Pete or my [step]dad.

Paul took two crises in his mother's life, her move with her family as a teenager to Mississippi and her divorce, and traced how God used them for good. These must be family stories he had been told, because all of this happened before he was born or could remember. He did not simply tell the story but further developed it, pointing out that without the move, she would not have met his father (and had him!), and without the divorce, he would not have his stepfather and stepbrother. Notice too that he had this conversation with his mother "in the car just a few days ago," as he tried to sort out in his eleven-year-old mind how bad experiences have really had good results. Conversation about faith and other matters of importance often come when we are on our way somewhere else, not when we plan for them.

Paul's stepfather continued the discussion of faith: "I really don't think about faith a whole lot. I think something good is going to come out of everything no matter how bad it is, and I always feel like you're not going to have too much thrown on you that you can't handle. Especially when I was going through the divorce and I was taking care of Pete who was very young. I said, 'There's got to be a reason I'm going through this.' After going through that, I can handle anything."

Following his stepson's comments, David described difficult experiences in his own life that he perceived God has used for good. He focused more on trusting the bearable limits of trials ("You're not going to have too much thrown on you that you can't handle") rather than the goodness of even bad circumstances. Like his stepson, however, he believes there is a purpose in what he has experienced ("There's got to be a reason I'm going through this") and that he is better for what he has experienced.

Family stories were not all sweetness and good feelings, however. Later in our conversation, I asked the family if they had ever experienced a time when God seemed absent. Paul began hesitantly, casting his eyes at his parents, "I don't know if I should say this because it was a real bad time."

"What is it? Go ahead; it's OK," his mother reassured him.

And so Paul plunged in, still watching his parents' faces as he launched into the story, "Well, I know God wasn't absent, but I remember one time my mom had accidentally put some of my dad's file papers next to the sink. I think I might have bumped them into the sink and . . ." He looked his stepfather full in the face, continuing, "You got real mad because your meeting was the next day. The ink went all over, and you couldn't read anything. You thought Mama did it, and she didn't." He began talking faster, "And I kept trying to tell you that. But you were so mad that you got Mama's jewelry box and threw it out the back door."

Quickly, Darlene inserted, "I don't remember this."

But Pete came to his stepbrother's defense, "I remember that. I don't know if it was papers, though." He remembers the jewelry box part; it stands out in the children's minds, an incident forgotten, or repressed, by parents.

David reinforced his wife's lack of memory with his own: "I don't remember this," he repeated, laughing nervously. He tried to remember, "Was this in our old house, before we moved here?"

Darlene also laughed and said again with a note of puzzlement, "I don't remember this." Notice that they didn't say that it didn't happen but just that they didn't remember it.

Paul answered his stepfather, "Yeah, it was before we moved." Pete added his agreement, and everyone was talking at once, trying to remember when and where this happened.

Undaunted by the stir his story was creating, Paul pushed on, talking louder to be heard over the conversation about where and when and "I don't remember." Still looking at his stepfather, he said, "I felt like, 'God, why didn't you . . .' I tried to tell you that, but you were too busy yelling at Mom."

The parents agreed in not remembering this incident and seemed to be considerably embarrassed at the telling of it, and yet they did not discount the story or say that it wasn't true. It was a poignant scene as the older stepbrother powerfully sided with the younger child by affirming that he also remembered this event his parents had forgotten, yet at the same time softening the tension of the moment just a bit by questioning one of the details of the story (whether or not it was papers that got wet).

Paul framed his story as a time when he felt God's absence, even though he "knew" God was still there. His trust was shaken, even though his belief did not change. He had been through the divorce of his parents, although he didn't remember it because he was a baby. But here was his stepfather, and the man he knew as Dad, throwing his mother's belongings out the back door, perhaps in Paul's own mind sending a frightening signal that his mom and he might also be thrown out of the family.

It is doubtful that the parents ever considered this to be a faith-shaping experience for their children, whether they actually remembered it or not. But now they could not escape it, because the story had been told, affirmed by the older boy, and told in the context of the younger boy's understanding of God. The story is now a part of the family's narrative about God and faith and themselves.

Stories often take on a life and develop meanings that were not apparent when they actually happened. In fact, they are continuing to "actually happen" as the family tells the story as an illustration of their life together. The story of the angry stepfather is such a recollection. The story "happens" all over again as the eleven-year-old links this memory to his understanding of God, bringing the past into the present as they process it together and frame it as a story of faith. As frightening as this event is, it is a story of faith and trust. The stepson felt secure and trusting to be able to tell the story, with his mother's encouragement, his eyes fixed on his dad, waiting to see the reaction. The storytelling itself became a family event, a testing of the strength of family relationships. And the trust was warranted. The parents did not dismiss the story; they just wished, I suspect, that their sons had not remembered it. They survived the storytelling, as uncomfortable as it was, just as they had survived the family uproar over wet papers and a mother's jewelry being thrown out the door, experiences at the time that may have also been a scary test of the strength of their family bonds. Imagine a stepson watching his stepfather throw his mother's precious belongings out the door. What else, or who else, might be cast out? Was the family about to be torn apart? But the bonds held. In the same way, the storyteller seems to say, God is there even when God feels absent and we are afraid. God was there. And this family is here, still a family. The ruined papers are no longer important, except as reminders of forgiveness and restoration. The jewelry box has been reclaimed. This stepson can look his stepfather full in the face and trust that he will be there for him, to listen to him even when there are troubles, just as God is there, even when we wonder where "there" is.

Family Faith as Action

In one sense, Paul put the faith of the family into action by risking telling that story to them and to me. Daily, families make decisions like the one Paul made to take belief and trust the next step, into the decisions they make about how to live life together.

Bring Your Church Clothes   Darren and Kathryn are the biracial couple you met in Chapter Three who have grown children from previous marriages and now are protectively raising fifteen-year-old Nathan. They are deeply involved in the leadership of their Southern Baptist congregation, the same congregation where Jacob and Kate found home and began finally to put their life back together after the death of their infant son a decade before. Darren is a deacon, and he and Kathryn teach Sunday school together. Despite their heavy involvement in congregational activities, Darren also serves as a volunteer baseball and soccer coach. I asked them to tell me how their faith shapes their life together.

Kathryn began,

> When Nathan has overnight company on Saturday, they
> know that they must bring church clothes, because in
> the morning they're going with us. One boy has joined
> church with us. He had never been in a church before.
> We encourage all of Nathan's friends to attend church.
> We're not to the point where we turn the kids off. One
> of the stipulations they all know, though, is that if they
> don't go to church another time in their life, if they
> come here and spend Saturday night, Sunday morning
> we're going to church. And I think this is important to
> them.

"I think some of them look forward to it," agreed Darren. "Being a coach is an expression of faith because I try to be a role model for the kids to see what I'm doing and how I am in my daily walks of life."

"He doesn't ever berate a child," Kathryn added. "He never uses profanity."

For Darren and Kathryn, the hospitality to teenagers, involving them in their faith community, and Darren's positive style of coaching are expressions of faith. It shapes their life together and their life with others in the community.

Giving It Over to God When We've Done All We Can Families told many stories together of how things work out, or not, as a result of faith. Jan and Harold, Anglo-Americans, live a very large old home in a downtown neighborhood in a southern city. Their divorced daughter and their two grandsons live upstairs. They are not totally happy about this arrangement, but they are trying to help their daughter through some difficult times. They have a large sitting area and living space in their bedroom, located at the back of the house, behind the kitchen. Their bedroom is their only private area; they share the rest of the house with their daughter and two grandsons. Harold is semiretired; Jan is a schoolteacher. The two of them take care of their grandsons after school. They also have three other grown children and several other grandchildren. Their son Martin has been a particular source of challenge and grief, having been involved with using and selling drugs for almost a decade. Their relationship with their son has been the most significant context in which their shared faith has been tested and shaped. Harold said,

> I figured if I set him down and tried to talk to him the way you and I are talking, I could convince him. You can't do it. The drugs are stronger. Lying upstairs, I said my prayers. I said, "All right, God, he's yours. I've done all I can do." God intervened. I had taken out a $40-a-month insurance policy on him, kept it for a year, and it paid $12,000 for treatment. That took care of the whole thing for a while, but then he got back into the drugs,

and he disappeared. God intervened again. He went to the beach, found a friend, and the friend said, "If you stay drug-free, you can live with me until you get on your feet." He met his wife, and she straightened him out. God has come in so many times.

Jan added, "That's the only time we ever had results. It was when we told God that he was no longer ours anymore."

Harold went on to say that he learned that their son had sold drugs to an elementary school child, right on the school grounds where Jan teaches. "I wanted him in a pine box in the ground. I wanted him dead. We got to the point that, although we didn't plan the funeral, we knew we would be all right if we lost him. But when I turned him over to God, that night you cannot imagine the doors that started opening."

This story began as Harold's but quickly became a family story of faith as Jan added her thoughts. When Harold said, "I said my prayers. I said, 'All right God, he's yours,'" Jan responded, "It was when *we* told God that he was no longer ours anymore." She broadened the story and its underlying meaning; this was no longer simply the story of a grief-stricken father. This was their story. He was not alone in it. And he affirmed what she had just said, by continuing, "We know . . ." Undoubtedly they have talked over these experiences many times before. Each of them has thought about them, trying to make sense of them. But they have also talked them over together, constructing this shared understanding of their experiences. Even so, Harold ended this segment by returning to his private prayer, "And when I turned him over to God that night . . ." The individual's faith experience is not lost in the family's experience. Rather, the two interact with one another. Together and apart they have struggled with what they believe, with what they trust, and with what they ought to do. Ultimately they have come to sing together the deep and somber melody of trust in God, even if it means losing their son.

Every family provides a context in which faith develops and is challenged. Family life may provide the context for the individual's faith experience, such as Shamika's struggle to trust God to deal justly with those who murdered her father. Both children and adults have their faith shaped in the crucible of family life, as so many of these family stories testify. The family's life offers multiple crises that challenge or affirm the faith of family members. In turn, as these stories are told and retold, they become family stories, stories in which individuals participate in a story of faith that belongs to the family group, such as the story of Jan and Harold's wrestling with the darkness and despair over their son's drug addiction.

Belief and trust lead to actions based on faith, and those actions have consequences. In turn, the consequences give us more to ponder, confirming, challenging, and sometimes modifying beliefs and trust. When Corrine's prayers for her son's safety during minor surgery were met instead with life-threatening illness that is still affecting his health, her beliefs and trust were thrown into disarray. When their infant son died in a fire, Jacob and Kate spent years struggling to find answers for themselves. Family life can be a safe haven, but it can also present faith-threatening challenges. Almost never in the midst of these challenges but only as we look back can we say with Marianne: "It just made me stronger. I needed that experience to increase my faith and to make me strong."

Chapter 5

THE CHALLENGING PRACTICES OF LIVING FAITH

❧

Jake and Jana painted their thirty-year-old house a sunny yellow and have surrounded it with well-tended flowerbeds that provide a bright spot in their shady, middle-class neighborhood in Indianapolis. Not only is the outside warm and inviting, but the inside of the house has been remodeled into a large living and kitchen area that communicates welcome. A rabbit, a turtle, a hedgehog, and two cats also are part of the household. Jake is one of those people everyone likes, with a delightful sense of humor and an ease about him that encourages others to relax and slow down. Jake and Jana are Anglo-American in their early forties; Jake looks like he just stepped out of 1968, wearing faded jeans and his hair in a long ponytail. He describes himself as a recovering alcoholic, recently celebrating his twenty-year membership in Alcoholics Anonymous (AA), in which he still serves as a sponsor for a number of people. He works as a chef for a large local hotel and also volunteers his services as the chief cook for their Presbyterian congregation. Jana has been the primary earner in the family for much of their marriage; she has a highly demanding career as a business analyst that requires her to travel most of every week.

Jake has been employed at the hotel for only six months. For the six years before that, he stayed home to be what he called a "domestic engineer" and primary parent for Luke (now age fourteen) and Stephen (age eleven). In addition to Luke and Stephen, Jake has a seventeen-year-old son, Dustin, who lives in Washington with his

mother and spends summers with Jake and his family. Jake says about
those six years,

> I was here to get the boys on the school bus in the morn-
> ing, do the field trips with them at school, do the bake
> sales, and that got me into being the Halloween were-
> wolf at the elementary school the last six years. I haven't
> had a child in that school in three years, but we still go
> back so I can be the Halloween werewolf. The boys and
> I have been in their school variety show for four years.
> They volunteer; they give time back. So the three of us
> will go back each year, helping out with the Halloween
> party and doing other things they need.

He laughed, reflecting on the years he had been a domestic engineer. "There was a lot of resistance from other kids' mothers to my
being around. They would say, 'Well, what do you do?' and I'd say,
'Well, I do the same thing you do.' They said, 'Well, my husband
works.' And so I answered, 'Well, my wife works.' It was not a proud
position. But the benefit was amazing for the guys."

"Yeah, it was good," said Luke. "I mean, we've never had a
babysitter. Not like day care. We don't go to somebody's house every
day after school. We are basically full-time with our parents, so that
was kind of neat. I liked it. But as we grow up, we still need them, but
we don't need them to have them there before and after school."

Service as the perennial Halloween werewolf for the elementary
school and the expectation that the boys "give time back" to their elementary school provide a clue to the important melody of service for
this family, modeled by Jake's volunteering as the church cook and
serving as an AA sponsor.

I was guessing that all this community involvement might be
tied, in their minds, to their faith. So I asked, "How does faith figure
into your lives as a family?"

Fourteen-year-old Luke continued, "Sunday is the only for-sure
day that my mom's going to be home, so it's the only night we know
we're going to have dinner together. So basically we talk about what
we are going to be doing this week, and who's staying after school and

who's not, and what days Mom is going to be out of town. We don't really have Bible study at home as much. I go to a Sunday school class that my dad teaches, and so does my brother, so we get our Bible study during the week at church."

"We say prayers at meals, and we say prayers before bed," Jana added. "We still say the same prayer we said when they were growing up. We nurture our faith just in conversation and the way we treat each other. And some days, as with anything, we live it less than we could."

Jake picked up the conversation,

I think by reaching out in the community as a family . . . and nurturing other kids that, as I see it, don't have it so well. Broken homes. Stuff like that. And the boys ask, "Can so-and-so spend the night?" At first, I think, *Oh, man. Don't we get a night to ourselves?* But then we say, "That's the way it is. They need this too. Let's not be selfish." Other parents will say, "Oh, that's a real bad kid." So my response is, "Oh, good, come be on my baseball team." They're my favorites. I got one this year. They gave me this kid and said, "He's a real trouble-maker." Well, good, that's the kind I want. He's a child of God, and he's going to know that when he's on my team. He'll get tired of hearing it. I guess because I feel we have so much, I want to share with others. We're really lucky. To watch our sons interact with younger kids. On the phone the other day, Stephen told a boy, "No, I can't come play with you because I have this commitment to this other friend." He could have blown off the other friends and gone down to this one's, which I knew he really wanted to do. But instead he chose to live his commitment.

I think one of our purposes is volunteering and giving back to the community. Luke cooks on Wednesday night for the fellowship meal at church. Stephen has helped out whenever he's needed with the church. We get out there. I do dance chaperones for the junior high, and that's kind of fun. One person signs up, and every-body ends up going. And soccer courts. We do soccer courts, painting the lines, for the whole district. It kind of makes you feel connected. I think a lot of purpose and meaning is putting back in the community. It's not something we just talk. I think we show it.

Like Jacob and Kate, who lead their sons' church choir, Jake and his family have transformed the activities that could pull them apart into shared family activities: "One person signs up, and everybody ends up going." In addition to being the boys' Sunday school teacher, coaching Stephen's baseball team, chaperoning Luke's dances, and in-cluding the whole family in cooking for the church and marking soccer fields, Jake also serves as scoutmaster for both boys' troops.

Not only does this family seek ways to be together, but they also have a home and family time open to other community children, es-pecially children who are in trouble or at risk of trouble. It isn't al-ways easy; Jake pointed out that sometimes they just want time to themselves. But he also points out the payoff. With pride in his voice, he told the story of Stephen choosing to "live his commitment." Jake explained that perhaps he learned the importance of service from his own father, who also was a scoutmaster and who welcomed lots of children into their home.

This conversation began with my asking how they try to live their faith as a family. And like most families with whom I talked, they began by talking about Bible study and prayer. Luke described their Sunday dinnertime, the only time they can count on being to-gether as a family. He implied that this could be a time of Bible study and prayer for them, but it is really more of a strategy session about how they are going to get through the next week. Bible study, he said, is something they get at church—from their dad! Even so, their faith is lived more in the ways they relate to one another at church, at home, and in their service in the community than in a structured time of family prayer, study, or worship at home.

Praying together at meals and at bedtime, attending worship services and Bible studies together, "the way we treat each other," serving their community, offering hospitality to children: all of these are family faith practices. Faith practices are those activities that individuals and families engage in because they help us to know God and make us aware of God's presence in our lives. Practices also give us ways to participate in what we perceive God is doing in our world and calling us to do. Faith practices can open a family to an awareness of God's presence in its midst in the daily round of routines and activities and pressures.

Faith practices are for the soul what physical exercise is for the body: a means of strengthening and conditioning. They can also be enjoyed for their own sake. Walking, swimming, lifting weights, and riding bicycles do not ensure that we will be healthy, stay free of cancer, or live longer. But they do provide some of the right conditions for us to be healthier and live longer than if we did none of these things, and we find that when they become a part of our lives, they often bring satisfaction in themselves. Faith practices are God's way of making our souls strong and flexible, more receptive to God's presence and God's work with us and through us. They are God's means of grace, through which God can bless us.

Although we work at it and make ourselves receptive to it, faith is not something we ourselves can develop; faith is a gift from God. "For by grace you have been saved through faith, and this is not your own doing, it is the gift of God—not the result of works, so that no one may boast" (Ephesians 2:8 NRSV).

In some respects, then, health continues to be a somewhat imperfect metaphor for faith. We can make ourselves receptive to good health by taking care of ourselves, eating wisely, exercising, and resting appropriately, but ultimately health is a gift. People who eat wisely and take care of themselves do get sick or disabled. And some people who are couch potatoes, eating too much or all the wrong things, live disease-free lives to a ripe old age. Health too is ultimately a gift, even though there are many ways we can make ourselves more able to receive good health.

Faith practices make us receptive to that gift of faith; they tune our ears and hearts to hear and feel what we might otherwise miss. I found that families did not often name "things we do to practice our faith" so much as they used stories to talk about their faith practices—

127

Jake's story of encouraging their boys to invite other children into their home, even when they would like an "evening to ourselves"; the story of drawing soccer court lines and serving as coach and Sunday school teacher and school dance chaperone. On one level Jake says these are ways they are giving back to the community. But on a layer underneath simple reciprocity, underneath the virtue of being a good community member, Jake says, these are ways they are living their commitment. They are participating somehow in what God is doing; they are living their commitment, their calling to be about God's work. Living our commitment is a familiar melody in this family, with lots of verses. That theme can be heard underneath stories that otherwise might seem completely unconnected to faith at all: donning a werewolf costume for the elementary school party, drawing soccer courts for the community, Stephen deciding to keep a promise to play with one friend when he really would have preferred to be somewhere else with someone he enjoyed more. Yet the theme of these stories, living our commitment, is really the faith practice of serving others as a means of serving God.

Faith practices like prayer, Bible study, or welcoming a child into our home are good for us, even when our prayers are not answered in the way we had hoped, or we have more questions than answers after studying the Bible, or the child continues to be an ungrateful delinquent. We engage in these practices because we need to do them, because they make us aware both of God's presence and of God's transcendence, and because they are what we are called to do as Christians. They do have benefits, however, to those of us who engage in them, as well as to our communities. Our knowledge of ourselves and of God is deepened and transformed. And sometimes our prayers are answered; we find the answers we seek; and that child's life is turned around because somebody like Jake said, "Come play on my baseball team."

Other than family prayer and Bible study, our Western brand of Christianity with our culture's emphasis on individualism has emphasized faith practices we engage in as individuals. In fact, some faith practices—meditation and solitary prayer, for example—pull us away from family, although the fruit of such practices may benefit family life. A parent who has carved out a time for meditation and prayer may come back more patient, better able to provide guidance and discipline that are sensitive to the child's needs. But carving out that time for solitary meditation and prayer is quite a challenge, especially for parents of preschoolers.

For two thousand years, some Christians in every generation have decided to live their faith by leaving families for a solitary life, where they can devote themselves to meditation and prayer. A chasm has developed, placing this ascetic life of prayer and devotion on the spiritual side and a life in the mainstream of family and community as mundane and of this world. Parents who struggle unsuccessfully to find even ten minutes to pray and read a Bible passage at the beginning or end of their day feel guilty and unspiritual. Without discounting the value of time alone for meditation and prayer, therefore, it is important to recognize that family life can also be a significant context for practicing faith. The following twelve faith practices have been adapted from the work of Craig Dykstra and others currently writing about faith practices. These can be a part of the lives of families as well as of individuals and the larger community of faith.

> Worshiping God together; giving thanks for God's work in the world; hearing the word of God in scripture and sermon; singing and speaking words of praise, of petition, of confession; and receiving the sacraments given to us in Christ

> Telling and reading the Christian story to one another, from the Bible, from the stories of the church throughout history, and from contemporary stories of God's work in the world

> Sharing with one another our interpretations of the Bible and God's continuing work through history and today, and what it means for us

> Having patience with one another's shortcomings and encouraging one another as we seek to live the life to which God has called us

> Praying together and by ourselves

> Serving others as a means of serving God

> Giving generously our money, time, and other resources for the work of the church and to care for the needs of others

Welcoming others into our homes and to our tables, especially those who are strangers

Listening and talking attentively and empathically with one another about our life experiences, our struggles, and our joys

Seeking to identify and resist the systems and powers that harm people, that weaken human communities, and that destroy God's creation

Working with others to create relationships, communities, and social systems that are in accord with God's will

Confessing our sins to one another, forgiving and restoring our relationships with one another

As you have observed so far, and as you will continue to witness as you read this chapter, all twelve of these faith practices give opportunity for God to shape our life together as families. Most of the time, however, churches have focused primarily on urging families to pray together and read the Bible together. Even fourteen-year-old Luke has picked up this expectation and rather apologetically explains that the only mealtime they can rely on being together needs to be a weekly strategy session, so they get their Bible study at church.

Many of these faith practices are not just one more activity to be slotted onto the family calendar for that one hour at the Sunday dinner table, however. Instead, they are woven throughout our time together and apart. Prayer can be done on a schedule, but it can also be breathed as we slog through the day; it can be sung as we rock a baby at 2:00 in the morning; it can be exclaimed as we say with a toddler putting bare feet in spring grass for the first time, "Thank you, God, for the green grass and the warm sun."

One of the challenges for families is that these practices don't come naturally. They are learned. Jake learned to welcome children and to serve by experiencing his own father's welcome of children and his father's service as a scoutmaster. And he is teaching his own children to serve by taking them along, weaving them into his own service, from their annual involvement with the elementary school Halloween party to cooking on Wednesday nights at the church. Family Bible study was not a part of either Jake or Jana's life growing up, nor perhaps has their church encouraged or taught them how to make this a part of family life. They learned to pray together in saying the mealtime grace and bedtime blessings. They are still saying those prayers, prayers they taught their boys as preschoolers and perhaps learned as children themselves.

Because the church has emphasized faith practices as individual activities, church leaders have not given much guidance to help families make these practices an integral part of family life. Instead of helping parents know how to study the scriptures and other devotional literature together, some churches have communicated that this is something you do at church, which Luke points out. Being resourceful, Jake uses his role as the boys' Sunday school teacher to read the Bible and teach them about faith. He has transformed Bible study, which is something to be done at church, into a shared family activity—at church. Moreover, he has opened his family's boundaries to include other children in what is really his family studying the Bible together!

I did not give families the list of these twelve spiritual disciplines and ask them which ones they practice or how they integrate them into their life. Instead, I simply listened to them tell me about how they live their faith. The rest of this chapter tells a few of the stories of how these families are practicing their faith.

WORSHIPING GOD TOGETHER

When asked how they nurture and live their faith, most families said, "We go to church." Pete, the fourteen-year-old who defended his younger stepbrother in the story of the wet papers and the jewelry box in Chapter Four, explained how his family lives its faith this way: "I would say this family is church based. We've gone to church all of our lives. There has never been a time that we haven't. If we're on vacation somewhere, we usually look for a church to go to, Presbyterian or Catholic. I don't think I would have become a Christian at all if I didn't live in this family. I wouldn't have gone to the church I went to. Stuff just builds up after a while."

"We are church oriented, but we're God based," his dad, David, adds. "It's not like we pray to our church or something, but I know that isn't what you meant."

For Pete, his family's most significant way of living their faith is taking him to church. Church serves as the core of his understanding of faith life. There is something about what he says that is a little disconcerting to his father. Clarifying that they are "church oriented" rather than "church based" somehow moves the church just a little off center. God needs to be in the center. Many families see their primary role as getting everybody involved in the worship and programs of the church, and Pete knows this—almost too well!

Over and over, families told me that participation in the worship and programs of their congregation is the most significant (and sometimes only) way they are intentionally practicing their faith as families. Parents count on the congregation to provide the religious guidance and teaching for their children; and it is the parents' responsibility to get them there. Some parents required their teenagers to be involved not only in worship services but also in other youth activities of the congregation. And some parents even become their children's Sunday school teacher, making sure that not only their children but also other children receive religious instruction at church. What they may not realize is that in doing so, their family is engaged in Bible study together as a family, in the context of their community of faith.

Parents recognize that involvement in the congregation includes more than religious instruction. Pete's stepmother, Darlene, went on, "One thing that we have consciously done throughout their lives is to try to surround them with people of faith whom we trust to be good role models. I've never felt that we had to be their only role models. And so it has been a conscious kind of a thing to get them into situations where they can have positive role models from other adults." Church provides not only worship and faith education; it also provides children with adults besides their parents to be their friends and encouragers. Moreover, it often has a built-in positive peer group, something all parents long for to reinforce the values they want to instill in their children.

Singing songs of faith can be a powerful form of worship, and several families described how important singing is to them. Jacob and Kate, the couple whose first child died in the fire at the babysitter's house, emphasized the significance of singing with their boys at home and also singing together at church, where they serve as their boys' choir leaders. Many other families talked about the importance of singing together in the church choir. Singing is also something families do at home standing around a piano, in the car on trips or even around town. Of course, sometimes families with preschoolers are singing "The Wheels on the Bus Go Round and Round" as they travel, not the great hymns of the faith. Nevertheless, families do sing together, at home and at church, and sometimes that singing is worship.

TELLING AND READING THE CHRISTIAN STORY

Studying the Bible and reading other devotional literature are important ways families recognize for nurturing their faith. Some have routines for study; most feel guilty because they don't. A time to study together and have prayer as a part of a daily ritual is most common in the families of young children, whose parents read them Bible stories and books with religious themes. When the children begin to read, parents listen and help them read the stories themselves. A mother of five children described how she found that, although time for private devotion was nonexistent for her, she could still maintain an active devotional life with her children. She prays and reads the Bible with them rather than trying to carve out a time of solitude for herself. When the children have a scripture verse to memorize for Sunday school, she puts it on the refrigerator and memorizes with them. She has stopped fighting for an hour of solitude for Bible study and prayer for herself, explaining: "[The children] are little such a short time. I can have time on my own for Bible study and prayer when they are a little older. God understands that."

As children grow up and other changes take place over time, the family's ways of sharing the Christian story also change. For example, once children begin reading well on their own, the practice of bedtime Bible stories often stops. A single mother with teenagers described another such change, "We used to do the devotions at the dinner table. When my older daughter left for college, my younger daughter and I quit eating at the table. We took the devotion book with us to the living room coffee table, and over time it just seemed that it was forgotten. So I moved the book to my bedside table. It became more of a personal thing than a family thing." When the two remaining family members gave up sitting at the table together for meals, they also gave up devotional reading and prayer together. Over and over families described the significance of sitting at the table for meals together as the place where Bible study and faith conversations take place, if they happen at all. When this place and time together disappear from family life, so does the opportunity for sharing not only the Christian story with one another but impromptu conversation about life and faith as well.

Parents often provide their children (and sometimes one another) with materials, whether Bibles or other literature, to encourage them to read the Christian story. One wife and mother described her strategy for involving her husband and children in reading faith-related materials: "There are all kinds of materials that come through the church, or we buy at the Bible store, that I share with him. This is my secret; I started just laying it around in the house. I'll leave it on the kitchen table; I'll leave it in the bathroom. That works in this home, even with my children."

One stepfather ruefully described how he had tried to require his family to spend time together in Bible study around the supper table, because he believes he is supposed to be the family's spiritual leader. He has tried hard too. He even spent $300 buying Bible study guides from a door-to-door salesman to help him. As many stepparents can confirm, however, stepchildren often protest, if not verbally then in sullen and silent resistance, a new stepparent who tries to move immediately into a position of authority. And the role of spiritual leader falls into the category of authority. Not surprisingly, then, this stepfather encountered teenagers who communicated clearly that they wanted to be anywhere else but sitting at the table listening to him try to teach them from his Bible study guides. As he said, he learned rapidly that he could not "shove prayer and Bible study down the throats of teenagers." He has therefore resorted to doing Bible study on his own, and the youngest child (his child from a previous marriage) often joins him in that. The whole family goes to church together, and he says, "What I've found now is that they will not accept it from me as well as they will from somebody else they admire at church. So now I try and let them get all their biblical study and knowledge from somebody else."

Although most family members who do engage in Bible study or read other Christian literature do so on their own, they find themselves talking about what they have read and sharing what they read with one another. One woman said that if she reads something especially meaningful, she says to her husband, "You ought to read this!" Or they read the same Sunday school literature independently and then talk about it together. As one man said of his wife, "She does the intense study, and we get the condensed version at the dinner table."

Many family members have also found joining others in group Bible study to be a powerful influence in their family's lives. These groups provide a kind of structure that families otherwise may find difficult to put into their lives. They also provide supportive contact with others in the community. They seem to function much as health clubs do in helping people deal with the discipline of daily exercise.

Jan and Harold are the couple you met in Chapter Four who have agonized over their son's drug use and have tried so hard to "give him over to God." Harold is now semiretired, although he still does some private work as a financial consultant. Jan teaches second grade in an inner-city public school. They are helping their divorced daughter raise their two grandsons, as well as involving themselves deeply in various forms of community service. Some of that service takes place through their church and other community organizations. They also are involved in more informal ways, like their care for Mac and Penny, a frail elderly couple in their neighborhood who no longer can drive. Harold provides all their transportation, negotiates the Medicare system for them, and helps them with paying their bills. Jan ties her involvement in a Bible study group to her desire to be more involved in caring for others: "I'd come home every Tuesday and say, 'Guess what I learned this week?' It was where my faith really began. Since then I have started wanting to do things that I maybe didn't want to do before. Like taking time for Mac and Penny. Well, I might have cared about them before, but I wouldn't have taken the time to really go over and check on them and help with chores they can't do. And then we had a young adult group from church that we met with every Sunday, and we did that for eight years."

Harold added, "We'd usually have eighteen people here."

Jan continued, "We'd have a fun evening. We might go bowling with them or have class, something they were interested in hearing about or discussing. I just wanted to do more. It wasn't a chore. So I think that's where my faith really began. Now, like I say, we go to Sunday school. Harold teaches sometimes. I have to continually be learning." Jan attributes her involvement in Bible study to her becoming much more involved in caring for others and also in their becoming leaders for a young adult group in their church that ended up meeting in their home. Bible study, she believes, led to and continues to be the foundation for their service and caring: "I have to continually be learning."

Sharing Our Thoughts About Faith

Jan goes to her Bible study and then comes home and says to Harold, "Guess what I learned this week?" Many of the family members I met who engage in the study of the Christian faith and scriptures privately or in a Bible study group then talk with their families about what they are learning. In Chapter Four, I quoted eleven-year-old Paul as he defined faith as "living the life that I think God would want me to live and believing that He is our creator, and nothing happens without God having a plan." He went on to explain how he had figured out, talking to his mom about it in the car just a few days before, "how every bad thing ends up with a good thing," and then told the series of troubles that had actually landed them all together as a family. This conversation did not take place as a part of a family devotional; it took place in the car, as he and his mother were on the way to wherever their schedule took them that day. Opportunities to share our experiences and our ponderings about life and about faith are woven into the fabric of family life.

Families frequently talk in the car on the way from church or over the dinner table about the sermon of the day or what they learned in Sunday school, especially if they are studying the same material. In some of the National Baptist churches with which I worked, the pastor leads a whole-church Bible study on a weeknight, for adults and children. Families attend these sessions together and then talk over what they have learned in their comings and goings the rest of the week. I was struck by the shared language of faith this experience gives families. They know and use images from favorite Bible stories in family conversations. They also use language they have learned together at church, such as the verse I often heard quoted, "And we know that in all things God works for the good of those who love God, who have been called according to his purpose" (Romans 8:28 NRSV) and the related faith statement, "God is never late, but God's time is not our time."

David, Paul's stepfather, remembered and shared this story about his stepson, who usually attends the Presbyterian church with his mother: "When Paul was about five, he had gone to the Catholic church with me right before Christmas. We were sitting there, and the minister was speaking, and Paul leaned over and said, 'They say the same thing at my church too.' And I thought how rich for him to know that, yeah, there's a lot of different denominations, but we're talking about one God. And it gave me something to think about." David was sensitive enough to Paul's thoughts and learning to listen to what the child had to say, even though he was talking in the midst of a sermon in a worship service. In fact, this five-year-old had something to say that gave his adult stepfather something to ponder. These moments of sharing thoughts about faith often come when families are busy with something else, even congregational worship.

Not just Bible study and sermons but also music can provide fodder for family talk about faith. Jacob, the dad who leads his sons' children's choir, explained,

The Challenging Practices of Living Faith

It provokes thought in their minds too, those songs do. They have one song, "God's Not Dead, He's Alive." It says, "I feel it in my heart, I feel it in my hands, I feel it in my feet," and Dillon [age nine] looked at me and said, "Well, where is He? He's not upstairs in any room." I said, "He's all over," and we talked about that for about an hour one Saturday morning. I had brought him to my office. We go by McDonald's and get something to eat and take it to the office and eat. I'm working, and they're talking and having a good time. A lot of times, they'll go straight to our break room in our office and turn on some Saturday morning cartoons, and that's it. That particular Saturday, we just talked. I never did do any work. Our conversation kind of ran its course, and I looked at my watch and decided we had done the business we needed to do, so we just went home.

As he often does, Jacob took the boys with him to the office, and then when an important conversation unfolded, he abandoned this work and spent the time talking with Dillon. "A lot of times," he says, the boys watch television while he works. Family life is like that. Most of the time, it is business as usual. For those who try to make ways to live life together rather than separately, and who have ears and eyes to watch for it, however, sometimes these become moments for important conversations. These moments provide faith education for the young and also for those adults privileged to share those moments, if we open ourselves to hearing the melodies that connect themes of faith to daily family life.

That is not to say that families would not benefit from rituals of sharing Bible study and prayer and talking with one another. Most simply have not been taught how to make this a part of their life together. As one mother said, "It's everyday conversations that come up with us. We don't do Bible study and prayer together. I know people who do. I thought about it one day, and I thought I might feel kind of awkward, but I guess that's just because we never have."

SACRED STORIES OF ORDINARY FAMILIES

HAVING PATIENCE
AND ENCOURAGING
ONE ANOTHER

Family faith sustains individuals even when their individual faith wavers. When Maurina, the single woman who described her relationship with her sister as being like that of the Delany sisters (see Chapter Two), was in the midst of a long and complicated illness after surgery, she hit bottom. "That illness took me out so bad," she remembered.

> They thought I was going to be out four months, but I was out nine and a half months. I was filing bankruptcy to try to get back on track. It was a horrible disaster, but in all of it I never lost the faith. And that's because of the family. It's like they force you to keep it, even when I just wanted to be left alone in my misery. I didn't want anybody around me, just feeling sorry for myself. I would get so angry at my sister. I couldn't go to church, so she would bring me all the tapes from the church. I told her, "I'm not going to listen to them." And she'd say, "That's OK; we'll listen to them together." She would put them in my cassette player while she was here. So she would almost say, "I'm not going to let you turn your back on this. I know you're hurting. I know your life is really as low as it's been in a long time. I'm not going to let you give up." And that's what happened. And that's what we do; we all just kind of jump in and hold each other.

Maurina is a strong independent woman and was no doubt a rather challenging patient. But her sister just kept prodding and encouraging. That is what faithful families do; they balance patience with one another with prodding and encouraging change.

PRAYING TOGETHER AND ALONE

Many families pray together at meals. Like the prayers Jake and Jana say with their sons, these may be prayers adults learned as children that they have then carried on in their own families. For some, however, this is a difficult ritual to establish. Several families mentioned the television as a significant barrier to having mealtime prayer. The television is always on, and dinnertime often becomes time to watch the world and local news instead of talking. For busy adults with careers, this may be their only way of keeping up with what is going on in the larger world. They feel unable to turn it off for prayer and conversation. Or perhaps they use it to keep from having to talk with one another.

Parents often pray at bedtime with their children. This practice may sound simple, but keeping at it is hard. Jake explained, "I was going into the boys' rooms every night, and I was teaching them to pray and praying with them. I still do sometimes but not every evening. For about the first month, I did. And that's just my weakness. And every evening when the boys go to bed, it seems like as soon as they're asleep I think to myself, *I wonder if they did it?* I just sit there wondering instead of getting up and going to do what it takes to ensure that they do it."

The teen years present particular challenges. One mother described how she had prayed with her daughters every night at bedtime until they became teenagers, but now, she says, "I can't stay up late enough."

Some parents pray with their children before school. In Chapter Three, you met Margaret, who prays each morning with her two daughters, naming the teachers and the bus driver for God to bless and guide, and asking God to help her daughters "do good and be good," before she sends them to catch the school bus.

Aria is another mother who prays with her child every morning before school. All I knew from her pastor, who gave me Aria's name, was that she is a single parent in his inner-city Baptist church, one of the largest African American churches in the city. Aria's home was located in a suburb of middle-class homes built in the 1960s. Even on a Sunday afternoon with no traffic, the drive from the church to

Aria's front door was almost thirty minutes long. *This family has to work at staying involved in their congregation,* I thought to myself.

A towering six-foot-five-inch young man of sixteen answered the door. He looked puzzled when I explained that I was there for a meeting with his mother to talk about their family. Politely, he said, "I'm her son, Dan. She's not back from lunch with her sisters yet, but if you want to wait for her, I'll be glad to talk to you until she comes." *Surely he knew better than to let a stranger into the house,* I thought to myself. Surely he had better things to do than talk to me. Nevertheless, Dan escorted me to the dining room, and I began to fumble with my microphone and tape recorder as I tried to explain that I wanted to learn more about how families live their faith together. A four-year-old bounced into the room and began checking out my taping equipment. "He's my brother, Joe; I'm babysitting," Dan explained.

As we talked, he clarified for me that Joe is not "really" his brother. Joe's mother, Angelee, is his mother's cousin, but Angelee is mentally ill and in the hospital a lot. Joe has lived with Dan and his mother since he was four months old. Joe and Dan call one another brothers. Dan told me that his mother had a good job in an office, though he wasn't exactly sure what she did. He wants to go to vocational school and become a mechanic when he graduates from high school next year. We talked on for more than an hour, before the garage door opening announced Aria's arrival.

After she apologized for being late and Dan filled her in on what we had been discussing, she told me more about her family. There had been hard times, especially right after Dan was born. She and Dan's father were not married, and Dan's father soon disappeared from their lives. For a few months, she supported her son with welfare, and there were times she had to borrow money for food. She went to business school and then to work. The church became her community, and she poured herself into Bible study and into working in the various ministries of the church, or at least as much as her work schedule and parenting responsibilities would allow.

"It's hard for a mother to raise sons by herself," she said, "but I'm strong, and I have taught them to respect me and to respect themselves." A couple of times, Dan has worried her, not doing as well in

141

The Challenging Practices of Living Faith

school as she thinks he could and hanging out with some friends that she considered a bad influence. Feeling she needed some reinforcements in guiding him, she took him for a "few little talks" with the pastor, and then she started him in karate lessons to teach him self-discipline and to channel his strength in positive ways. Dan hasn't been in any trouble since.

Money is still tight. Yet she is currently arranging for another child from the neighborhood, who will otherwise have to be placed in a foster home, to move in with her. "That child has been mistreated, and I want her to be somewhere she will be loved. And besides, if she lives with me, she can stay in her same school. She's been through enough without having to change schools on top of everything else."

In our conversation before his mother arrived, Dan had told me about Aria's morning prayers: "Back in elementary school, when I was having some problems in school, we used to pray every morning before I left the house. I guess I didn't notice it then. It didn't seem like it made a difference then, but I guess it did. I think that's why some of my problems have stopped. I started realizing what school was all about. I think she was worried about me, and that's why she knelt and prayed." This mother wove a whole network of support for her son: the karate lessons, her pastor's support and guidance, and her on-their-knees morning prayers with him.

SERVING OTHERS

"So faith by itself, if it has no works, is dead" (James 2:17 NRSV). In Acts 7:55–56 it is Stephen who, "full of the Holy Spirit, gazed into heaven and saw the glory of God, and Jesus standing at the right hand of God." As theologian Marianne Sawicki has pointed out, no one in the New Testament grasped the meaning of the resurrection better than this man, whose daily job was running the first church soup kitchen, a feeding program for widows. Families too practice their faith by serving one another and others; often in the midst of that service, they experience God's presence and glory. Sometimes that service is through the programs of their church: from cooking church suppers to leading choirs, classes, mission groups, and committees. Although some of the families I met said that they grew weary with the busy-ness and enjoyed times of respite from serving, the reasons people served were clear; they told me about their church jobs in response to my question, "How do you live your faith?" They serve because that is what their faith calls them to do. Families that perceive faith to be connected to service in the church may also be those serving in the community. That may be painting lines on soccer fields, caring for frail elderly neighbors, taking blankets to homeless people on a cold night, or serving as a school volunteer.

Lynette is Anglo-American, an elementary school teacher. Her husband divorced her ten years ago to marry another woman, leaving her to raise their daughters, Patsy (now age twenty-three) and Helen (age nineteen), alone. She has done so, she says, with the help of her Presbyterian congregation. Patsy is now living with her while she puts her life back together after becoming addicted to cocaine. Lynette shared with me her worries about her daughters and the loneliness of trying to figure out on her own what to do to help Patsy.

Visiting a Prisoner

Lynette told me about her involvement with yet another young woman in trouble, currently incarcerated in a youth detention center, euphemistically called an adjustment center:

> She's an inmate and has been in and out of juvenile
> facilities for over ten years. I started to go see her
> because a friend asked me to. She really didn't have any-
> body. She has family, but nobody ever came to see her. I
> have become very fond of her. I try to express to her
> how God has made a difference in my life and the dif-
> ferent paths that I may have chosen. All through my life,
> I have prayed. I think God has been there for me even
> though I may not have known it and may not have
> always chosen the right way. I'm trying to help, trying to
> help her see that once she gets out and she's finished

with this, then instead of going back to that same lifestyle with those same people, that her life would be different if she asked Jesus to be a part of her life. She had a drinking problem as well, and I can relate to that. Not that I've had a drinking problem, but I've dealt with it with my own daughter. So I think of it as I could be coming to visit my daughter, and I thank God that I'm not. And we've become friends, and I think that has been good for her as well as for me. It just makes me feel more blessed because I know it could be one of my children. I would hate to think that my child was there and nobody came to see her.

Caring for the Sick

Lynette uses her own experiences, her own loneliness and looking for answers, her struggles and worries about her own children as the foundation for her care for this young woman. She is busy; she is working full-time and running the household on her own. Yet she has made time to care for another, someone who "could be one of my children."

Clearly service as an expression of faith often takes place both inside and outside the family. Irene is the widow in her seventies who told me about her morning walks with her lifetime neighbor who is like a sister (see Chapter Two). She answered my question, "How do you live your faith today?" in this way:

I try to reach out to people, especially the people at the nursing home who have AIDS. I try to make sure that I sit with one of them every Sunday. There was one that I used to sit with all the time, Bob, and in fact I had my picture taken with him in the last church directory. But he died in the last year. So now I just try to find one that nobody's sitting with, to reach out to somebody that a lot of people ignore. Just trying to think about other people and not think about me. I had an aunt who was like that. They said she was always giving to somebody, and I guess that's where I learned it.

Alone after her husband's death, Irene has found ways to use her own loneliness as a catalyst to care for others who are lonely. In doing so, she recognizes she is carrying on a faith tradition passed to her by her aunt.

Helping Those in Need

Anglo-Americans living in a rural suburb of a midwestern city, Brad and Lisa recently retired, he as a long-distance trucker and she from her job as a store clerk. Two of their three sons are grown, although twenty-four-year-old Tyler still lives at home and works in a local grocery store. Their other grown son lives with his wife and daughter not far away. Toby, age sixteen, was working a jigsaw puzzle on the coffee table when I arrived. Brad is a vivacious, outgoing man, obviously a much-loved deacon in their small Southern Baptist congregation. Lisa, a warm smiling woman, was evidently a force to be reckoned with as the only woman in a family of four men.

Lisa told me about a recent experience, when she talked her church into helping a family that had experienced a devastating fire:

> This family was burned out right before Thanksgiving. And everybody brought things to the church, but as so often happens, if you suggest it, it kind of gets thrown to you. So here we were, getting trucks, and the boys had to help me carry couches in. I'll never forget one night when we couldn't get a couch in a door. And it was cold. But the boys were down there with me carrying, and they weren't real happy with me sometimes. And I would always say, "I feel like we have to do this. This is our responsibility to help these people. God has given to us, so we have to help these people." I tell them to do it, and I guess out of love they do it for me because they could say no, but they don't.

Toby added, "At least three times in a week, I cut grass for people."

Lisa explained, "He mows grass for women that don't have anybody to mow their grass, and I won't let them pay for it. I won't let him take any money for it because he needs to do that. He doesn't need the money."

And Toby went on, "She got me into something else. I had to cut up this wood and stuff for this lady, and she paints it, and then we try to sell it."

Again, Lisa explained, "This lady in our church is disabled, and she lives on less than $400 a month, and she can paint and do things really well. He got a saw for Christmas, and he likes to cut out wood and shapes. So he cuts them out for her, and she paints them, and we take them to work, and other ladies in the church take them, and we sell them for her. And make her a little bit of extra money. And he's doing pretty well with his woodworking."

Toby laughed, "I get a lot of practice and a lot of exercise with my mom's projects."

Brad summed up, "I think as far as our Christian living, what we practice on Sunday we try to do Monday through Saturday too. I think that's kind of important."

Lisa went on to tell me about Brad's part in all this.

Since he's retired, he takes people to the doctor. He goes and takes them back and forth for treatments or whatever. Usually church members. My husband helps one of the members of our church. Every month he helps her with her utility bill because she's on disability, and they just keep cutting back and cutting back, and she has such limited resources herself. I feel strange telling this because it's so private. But he helped them with medical bills, or he's helped them with insurance. I don't feel that's something you go around telling people. But he's done that any number of times. We felt like the Bible says there are various gifts. And we felt like sharing our money was one of our gifts.

Brad added, "When we moved out here, I fortunately made pretty good money for somebody with just a high school education. Of course, I had to put a lot of time in at work. Lisa quit work while the kids were in school, so she was always here. This was a comfort to them, and they've never forgotten that. When they graduated from high school, she went back to work. She went back to work primarily to support the church financially. Of course, when things crop up, fortunately, the Lord provides us with the ways and means to help people. I've noticed in the last few years with the kids that when somebody is in need, they help out friends if they're in trouble or help them move or something. It's the Lord's leading."

This prompted another story from Lisa:

> Our oldest son heard of a young boy who would come
> in to work, and he had muddy shoes. Our son heard
> that he was living in a little lean-to back here in these
> woods. I guess he had been thrown out at home or
> whatever. So our son went back into the woods and
> looked for this boy and took him home and fixed a place
> for him. He stayed with them for several weeks. I'm
> really very proud of both of them. I hope that Brad and
> I helped to instill some of that in them over the years.

Researchers Eugene Roehlkepartain and Peter Benson have found that service involvement is a key factor in nurturing young people's growth in faith. In fact, it appears to be more powerful than Sunday school, Bible study, or participation in worship. Young people who are involved in service that is connected to their faith are much more likely to be firmly bonded to their churches and much less likely to drop out of school. Some of this service takes place in congregational activities, but the family also is powerful in shaping service as a practice of faith. From his research on the roots of kindness and caring, Robert Wuthnow concludes that caring is not innate but learned, and it is first learned in family life. Parents model for their children, both in their family relationships and in relationships with others in the community, the kindness that youths then emulate in the world around them. In fact, the small acts of kindness of daily family life are probably most significant, showing as they do that caring is not terribly difficult or exceptional but can be a natural part of life.

Wuthnow found that most teenagers who themselves were involved in community service saw their parents as caring people. Caring was just a part of who they were as persons. Many of these families did not describe the ways they serve others as a faith practice. I had to probe to find out if and how they might be involved in their communities. Often their congregations did not know about the ways they were caring for others in the community, outside the congregations' own ministries. As one senior adult said about faith, "We don't talk about our faith. We just do it."

GIVING GENEROUSLY

As Brad and Lisa illustrated, giving our time and energies is one way of serving, and sometimes that includes material resources. In fact, very few of these families talked about serving others without mentioning that it often means financial sacrifice. Serving others and giving generously tend to go hand in hand. Lisa went back to work when her children were grown, primarily, according to Brad, so that they could give even more to their church and to others in need. They both felt awkward describing how they practice their faith by providing out of their financial resources. These acts of kindness are ones that people normally do quietly or even anonymously, attempting to keep from embarrassing those they help or bringing attention to themselves. Lisa and Brad are thrilled, however, to see in their young adult children the practice of generosity.

Dan is the sixteen-year-old African American youth who, when he was sliding into trouble in elementary school, found himself whisked into karate lessons, marched to the church pastor to have a "few little talks," and then prayed over by his single-parent mother, on her knees, every morning before school. He told me more about how he experiences faith practiced in his family:

No matter what happens, my mom always pays her
tithe, and we always try to go to church. She might be
on her last amount of money. I don't know if I could
tithe, but she believes in God a whole lot. And I think
that's why she's so comfortable with being single because
I don't think anybody else could do it the way she does
it. I think my brother and I *are* her social life. She seems
to like working with teenagers a lot. We used to have
this youth ministry at church, and we always had
teenagers over to the house talking about their problems
and stuff. We talked about our problems, and about sex
and AIDS and all kinds of stuff: gangs, violence and
everything. I think it helped some of them out a lot.
None of that really affected me because I always thought
that, outside of my father being gone, I had the perfect
home.

Later, he described seeing his mother reading her Bible every
night in her room with a highlighter pen at the ready. Raising kids
and working full-time is a huge challenge for all parents and especially single parents. There isn't much time for anything else. In some
ways, Aria lives on the edge, an unmarried African American mother
with a clerical job and never quite enough money or time. Yet her son
sees her tithe, sees her commitment to helping kids make good choices
and find a safe place at her house, sees her pour herself into loving
others, including him. The practices of faith are all a part of their life
together: worshiping regularly in their congregation, joining in Bible
study and prayer, sharing their concerns with one another, serving
others, taking in children who need a home, and giving generously.

I talked with Aria four years after our first conversation, two
years after Dan graduated from high school. She happily told me, in
her words, "He made it. A black kid with a single-parent mom, who
almost got into trouble, but he made it. He didn't end up shot or in
detention like so many of our young men. He's in the air force, and
he loves it, and I pray for him every day." I know she does, and so
does Dan.

The Challenging Practices of Living Faith

I remembered Dan's words, "I always thought that, outside of my father being gone, I had the perfect home." I can hear Marianne's deep laugh of recognition when her niece called her family "perfect." What makes the perfect home? Is it about what kind of family structure the family has, a first marriage with children, or is it about being a family that practices its faith, that allows God to work through everyone in the family as they study the Bible and pray and serve and care and tithe and sacrifice and love one another into faith?

WELCOMING OTHERS

Service becomes hospitality when we welcome strangers into the family's space and at the family's table. Christian hospitality is quite different from the connotation the term *hospitality* often carries in our culture. It is not synonymous with social occasions, with cooking longer than usual to prepare a special meal for friends, with using the good dishes in the dining room instead of eating in the kitchen. In fact, Christian hospitality is quite the opposite of our culture's sense of hospitality, which is often synonymous with entertaining. Entertaining refers to a break in a family's routine in order to take care of visitors in special ways, different from ordinary daily life. It means picking the mess up out of the living room and shoving it in a closet, running the vacuum cleaner, changing to nicer clothing, and serving fare that is fancier than the everyday. Too often such special care actually communicates otherness rather than welcome. In contrast, true hospitality means inviting people, strangers, into the heart of the family as a valued representative of Christ's presence. That can be symbolized by pizza over the kitchen table or other ways we truly make others feel at home. This can be by welcoming children's friends to spend the night, newcomers in the neighborhood to a simple meal in our kitchen on moving day, a brother fallen on hard times to use the spare bedroom for a few weeks or months until he gets back on his feet, or making room for a foster child so she can stay in her familiar community and school when abuse or neglect by parents means she can no longer live with them. Christian ethicist Christine Pohl points out that hospitality in the early church and for many centuries thereafter meant offering to strangers the food, shelter, and protection of our homes, following the teachings of Paul, who urged Christians to welcome one another as Christ had welcomed them. The writer of Hebrews urged readers "to show hospitality to strangers, for by doing that some have entertained angels without knowing it" (13:2 NRSV). According to theologian Robert Roberts, hospitality happens when three conditions are met:

> The others have to be outsiders. They cannot be your own children, for example. You can be generous to your children, but not hospitable, because this is their home too.
>
> You must have some territory to share: your living quarters, however elegant or humble.
>
> You must provide outsiders with the benefits of your home territory (food, friends, car, and so on).

Giving $1,000 to a homeless person on the street is generous giving, says Roberts, but to be hospitable, we have to welcome the person into our home.

Hospitality has always been difficult because it makes us vulnerable. That stranger may well disrupt or even harm the family in some way. The new neighbors invited to supper may stay too long and keep us from other activities or prevent us from going to bed at our accustomed time. The troubled youngster we invite to spend the night might actually steal from us or in other ways abuse the privilege of being folded into the family. A foster child who has not resolved previous abusive experiences might in turn abuse the family.

Hospitality is often quickly overwhelmed by need. There are so many who could benefit by our hospitality; how do we draw the line? Christine Pohl describes being a member of a small church in New York that welcomed and resettled hundreds of refugees in a four-year period, compelled by the biblical stories and teachings about hospitality and welcoming strangers. The task was enormous, and the costs were great in time, energy, funds, and innocence. Some of those they helped were not grateful. Sometimes the church felt those they helped took unfair advantage of their generosity. On the other hand, hospitality often brings unpredicted blessings. Some were grateful. Some became friends and joined the faith community. The church learned a great deal about its own gifts and capabilities. Over and over scriptures tell stories of the blessings from strangers to whom hospitality was extended: the widow who fed a stranger her last bit of bread, only to be blessed by unfailing provisions and the restoration of life in her son (1 Kings 17:8–24); the prostitute Rahab who welcomed the spies into her house and gained protection for her whole family (Joshua 2:1–21); the woman at the well who gave a strange rabbi a drink from her own dipper and received in return "living water" (John 4:7–30).

At its extreme, hospitality becomes a paradox. Hospitality's success makes hospitality impossible, because adoption of the guest as a family member makes the outsider an insider. The goal of all Christian hospitality is to be transformed into the fellowship of the kingdom of God, where the distinction between insiders and outsiders, between those who belong and those who don't, is broken down. Hospitality thus points us to the New Testament ideal of adoption as God's good news. It is the beginning of the adoption process.

Being an open-door family to children was a pronounced theme for several of the families I met. One man described his wife as the "Kool-Aid mom"; the young children of the neighborhood seem to collect in their home. Many parents like Jake, the domestic engineer who is the perennial Halloween werewolf at the elementary school, strive to make their home open to their friends' children, particularly those children who have particular need for the temporary shelter their home may offer.

Dan described how his single-parent mother, Aria, became the volunteer youth minister for their church, inviting the youth group into their home for frank discussions about the issues that worry them. In addition, she has permanently welcomed Joe, her cousin's son, into her home as her son and also was making arrangements for a little neighborhood girl who was being placed in foster care to come live with them.

It isn't only children that families fold into their households. Lisa ropes her husband and sons into caring for the community: carrying furniture to the home of a burned-out family, mowing yards for women who live alone, making wooden cut-out figures for a woman who is disabled to paint and sell. She also tends to bring folks into their home on occasion to live with them. After his divorce, her brother lived with them for almost two years. It was often very difficult; he tried to sneak alcohol and women into their home, both against the house rules and not the kind of behavior Brad and Lisa wanted exemplified for their sons. They had to bail him out of jail when he was arrested for driving while intoxicated. Friends and parents have also lived with them for short and not-so-short periods of time. A nephew with a drug problem lived with them for a year. Brad finally built rooms in the basement to accommodate these periodic guests. As Lisa explained, hospitality is far from easy:

> When we took my brother in, it was a thing of "He's desperate, and we've got to do something." I took him in simply because I thought my family was strong enough to be able to really make a difference in his life. And when I did that, I knew the risk I was taking. I might not have known to what extent I was doing it, but I felt like we were strong enough to help him. But when I took my nephew in, I had doubts because I had already gone through it with my brother, and I thought *I just don't know if I'm willing to do this again.* But we did. We didn't reach him, though, and I feel very badly about that. I don't know that we made a difference. Maybe someday it will come through.

According to Brad, even this family has its limits: "I guess it is an expression of faith to reach out and help people. But I don't know that we would take somebody in that we didn't really know."

"I think as Christians we're supposed to reach out to others," Lisa mused. "And I've tried to teach my family that. I've always said to my sons, 'I don't care how well you do in school, but be a decent

The Challenging Practices of Living Faith

person. Be kind; don't laugh at other kids.'" Lisa connects what they do as faith practices with what she hopes she is teaching her children—how to be a "decent person."

Some families express hospitality in relatively undramatic gestures: the "Kool-Aid mom," the family that "adopts" college students who are far from their own homes by bringing them home for dinner every Sunday, the couple who lets the church use their cabin on the lake at no charge. Others are more dramatic: families that adopt children or provide them with foster or respite care, who take in alcoholic brothers, who care for sick friends in their spare bedrooms, who find a place in their home for exchange students, and who even build extra rooms in their basements for guests—a geographic flipping of the custom of the upper room where guests stayed in Jesus' day.

Many of these hospitable families are the same families that serve as leaders in their congregations: deacons, teachers, volunteer staff members. For example, Allen and Ginger are the young couple planning to go to seminary (see Chapter Two). In addition to serving as a volunteer minister to youths, Ginger brings home troubled young people who need a place to stay.

In fact, as I reviewed the transcripts of interviews with these 110 families, I found that twelve families met my definition of *hospitable*; that is, they took people other than their own parents and children into their homes to stay one night or more. Sometimes it was a brother or brother-in-law down on his luck, sometimes a foster child, or sometimes a one- or two-night respite for a teenager who needed a safe harbor during a time of family conflict. Of those twelve hospitable families, only two are not also involved in some form of church leadership—serving on committees, as deacons or elders, as teachers or program directors. These are busy families! Clearly families don't make a choice between hospitality and service to the church. Rather, those who are the busiest with opening their homes to others are also most likely to take on leadership responsibilities. The families that take in children and alcoholic brothers also serve as deacons and Sunday school teachers; they serve their communities as scout leaders and build homes for poor families on Habitat for Humanity work crews; and they serve as informal counselors and mentors.

LISTENING AND TALKING ATTENTIVELY AND EMPATHICALLY

Clarence and Doreen, an Anglo-American couple in their late fifties, told me their wrenching parallel experiences of losing their first spouses to Alzheimer's disease. They have been married for three years, after meeting five years ago in a support group. Their spouses had been much, much younger than most who were struck with this disease. Younger themselves than many caregiving spouses in the group, therefore, they were drawn to one another. With tears welling up and sometimes spilling over, they quietly told about trying to work and raise children while caring for spouses who needed more and more care until they were not able to feed themselves, not able to be left alone, not even able to recognize their own spouse and children. Clarence told about how guilty he felt when he left his first wife just for the few moments to go to the grocery store and how he worried for his children. Talking to one another on the phone for hours helped Clarence and Doreen keep on coping. Soon those talks became stolen moments to meet in a coffee shop, and when Doreen's husband died, their emotional support became physical intimacy. Their children did not know about the affair. A year after Clarence's wife died, they finally felt free to marry. The children all hated the idea of their parents remarrying. Although Doreen's children have adjusted to the idea of the marriage, Clarence's grown children still refuse to accept Doreen as a member of the family.

Trying to find a way to start their lives over, Clarence and Doreen left the congregations they had attended with their first spouses and found themselves in a lively United Methodist congregation full of older adults and young families. When I asked them to tell me about how they practice their faith, they did not know how to respond. But when I asked them to tell me about a Bible story that is especially meaningful for them, Clarence lit up:

> The Easter story—all the suffering, and how they
> ignored what [Jesus] was there for, and how they tore

his clothes off. It kind of makes you think of how some people are treated in life. They're cast aside; they're not worth anything. But they are worth something. Our church until recently has been an older congregation. Just since we have been there, we have seen so many of these people pass away, and their spouses are left. It's mostly the women who are left, the widows, and we always talk about how these people don't need to be by themselves. Somehow if they could be together and just talk about whatever they want . . . They have a lot to say. That's what we would like to do. There's probably about six of us that are going to be visiting shut-ins and nursing homes, hospitals, homes of widows. The pastor is giving us some guidelines and teaching us. There's quite a bit involved. You just can't jump into this. You have to know what you can do and what you can't do and how to do it.

If anyone knows what it is like to feel cast aside and not valued, alone in the world, it is Clarence and Doreen. They have found one another, and they have found a community of faith. They want to hear the stories of these people who "are worth something," who "have a lot to say." They want to communicate interest and empathy. Clarence implies that there is much like Jesus in those he wants to visit; in other words, visiting them is being attentive to the crucified Christ. "Truly I tell you, just as you did it to one of the least of these who are members of my family, you did it to me" (Matthew 25:40 NRSV).

Dorothy is the senior adult widow you met in Chapter Four, who cares for her own frail elderly mother with the help of her daughter. She has raged at God for taking her husband, who died from cancer shortly after a move to a new community where she has no roots, and she has prayed for Him to send her another man. Despite her disappointment that God has not answered that prayer, she has found her experience to be one she can use in listening empathically to others and sharing her own experience with them:

After losing my husband, I knew firsthand how people were feeling, and I could go in and talk to them and relate to them. I could tell them that "Yes, it hurts now, and it's going to hurt for a long time, but you'll be all right." And I can say that with confidence because there's nothing like your own testimony to help people believe that, even though they're going through their trials now, they're going to come out OK on the other side. I felt that was part of being a Christian, sharing my life and my testimony with people. I had a girl whose mother died, and she would call and just say, "I'm on my way." She'd come in the door in tears, and we'd just sit and talk and talk.

Clarence, Doreen, and Dorothy have turned their own life challenges into ways to practice their faith because they can listen with empathy, and they can share their own stories with others. James and Marianne (see Chapter Four) are using James's journey into the hell of drug and alcohol abuse as a way to communicate to others in trouble that they understand, because they've been there. These families have transformed life catastrophes into opportunities for service. For them the concept that "all things work together for good for those who love God, who are called" (Romans 8:28 NRSV) has been a wrenching process of waiting to experience that goodness. Paradoxically they also believe that this goodness has been made manifest through their present ability to care for others; their surviving their own worst experiences becomes a way to encourage others.

FIGHTING AGAINST EVIL SYSTEMS

Lynette is the divorced mother of Patsy and Helen, who has also taken on a friendship with a young woman in a detention center on drug charges. She told me this story:

The Challenging Practices of Living Faith

The high school seniors planned a picnic. There is one black girl in the class, and they conveniently didn't tell her about the picnic. Helen was incensed because they didn't tell this child that they're having a picnic. Therefore, Helen boycotted the picnic and took the girl to lunch instead. Of course, as a mother, I want my daughter to be socially in the middle of things and to have plenty of friends, and I thought, *This is your senior year. It's your last gathering with all of these people in your class.* But I also wondered how they could try and cut out one girl. Helen knew that was wrong. She told the whole class she wasn't going. Helen doesn't always think ahead of time. This time she planned, though, and made her announcement when she knew the girl was not going to be in the room. And I was very proud, very proud. Helen simply knew that she would be devastated if she had been in that girl's place.

Lynette doesn't want her daughter to be hurt nor to miss out on what could be a special occasion, and yet she is proud that her daughter is willing to stand against the systemic evil of racism, expressed in this instance in a southern high school's senior class picnic. Helen has learned courage, and Lynette connects that courage to the nurture of her congregation and the faith she has learned there.

Although most of the time families talked about their faith in daily acts of service in their congregations and communities, there were glimpses that they see themselves involved in their own way, in their own communities in a much larger divine plan to restore God's justice, to resist evil. Some participated in hunger walks together; some were involved in efforts to protect the environment, God's creation, from human abuse. Several conservative families were actively involved in antiabortion legislative campaigns; other families were involved in trying to get legislation passed that would limit gun sales. Most found themselves engaged in the justice work that their congregations supported, but many families also found that the concerns of children and adolescents pulled their families into finding ways they could stand together against what

SACRED STORIES OF ORDINARY FAMILIES

they considered evil, like Helen's bold stand against racism in her high school class.

CREATE RELATIONSHIPS, COMMUNITIES, AND SOCIAL SYSTEMS IN ACCORD WITH GOD'S WILL

Harold and Jan are the couple who provide transportation and care for their frail elderly neighbors (see Chapter Four). But that is not all they do. In addition to working in their congregation, they are involved in many community organizations. Harold serves on the board of Community Youth Services, which provides mental health services in local high schools. He also serves as a volunteer with the Juvenile Court Conference, because of his concern for adolescents who have no one to stand with them in court. He visits them in the detention center and serves as a friend and advocate through the process. Harold says that his faith calls him to help make the world a place where all children have hope and opportunities and someone to care about them. He is trying to create systems that are more just through his volunteer work.

In contrast, James, whom you met in Chapter Four, is doing his work as an employee, a maintenance man in public housing, as his opportunity to create relationships of respect with residents as "the least of these" (Matthew 25:40) who represent Christ. He is working for "the system" and, he hopes, transforming at least his corner of it: "I stretch myself very thin simply because no one else there cares enough to want to serve the people. Being a servant is not just my job; it's a mission for me. Sometimes I've made myself too available, and I've felt used because they were always saying, 'Call James.' If they call at 2:00 in the morning, they know I'm going to get up right away; I'm going to go and do the job. I'm just a diligent worker. And it all carries over from the teachings that I'm getting from my pastor and applying to my daily life." Indeed, fixing wiring and plumbing and making other home repairs for people living in public housing *is* a mission. It is one of the ways James practices his faith, trying to transform in the only way he knows how the very impersonal system of

The Challenging Practices of Living Faith

public housing for the poorest of families in our society. And back home Marianne prays for his safety as he travels those dark inner-city streets, waiting anxiously, like Moses' wife, for his return.

CONFESSING OUR SINS TO ONE ANOTHER, FORGIVING AND RESTORING OUR RELATIONSHIPS

James and Marianne's life has been interwoven with confession, forgiveness, and restoration, as they struggled with the dark valley of James's unemployment, despair, and drug abuse, as Marianne pondered whether or not to throw him out. Without confession, forgiveness, and restoration, no human relationship can last for very long. People hurt one another, sometimes accidentally, sometimes with malice. With confession and forgiveness, however, we can move on from the hurts and failures through reconciliation to a strengthened covenant with one another. In fact, as we forgive one another, we are showing evidence of God's forgiveness for all of us (Ephesians 4:32). When we strike back to hurt and punish the other, we widen the gulf of hurt and anger between us rather than finding ways to heal the relationship. Of course, we need to communicate our hurt or anger as a first step and invitation to resolve the difference between us. But the focus is on inviting the other to a process of reconciliation, not on punishment.

Punishment intends to give the other what he or she deserves for the harm done; whether it hurts or helps is not the issue. According to the New Testament, forgiveness means expressing a willingness *not* to do to the other what the other deserves for the offense, but instead focuses on what the other needs, a blessing rather than a cursing (1 Peter 3:9–12). Forgiveness says, "You have hurt me, but it will not help either of us for me to try to get even. I want to see what we can do to make things right between us." Forgiveness does not even wait for the other to recognize the wrong done and say so. We can forgive another even if the other never confesses what he or she has done to us and even if the relationship cannot be restored. Ultimately this kind of forgiveness does not depend on the partner making amends or swearing never to fail us again.

Forgiveness alone cannot reconcile persons to one another, however. It is a gift that has to be received before reconciliation can begin. Relationships are restored and strengthened when each person owns what he or she has done (confession) and decides not to do that again (repentance). Then reconciliation begins. In this way, our human relationships are like our relationship with God. God invites us into relationship by forgiving us, but we must respond with repentance. God does not overlook or excuse our sin; we are responsible for what we do. In the same way, family members hold one another responsible for what they do. In Jesus' parable of the unforgiving servant (Matthew 18:21–35), a king forgave an enormous debt when the servant pleaded for mercy. The same servant then refused to forgive a fellow servant who begged for mercy over a much smaller debt. When the king heard about it, he became furious. He expected the servant he had forgiven to change his ways, to accept the forgiveness he had been given by changing his relationship with others. Forgiveness frees the other from having to do restitution for harm done, but it also carries the expectation that the future will be different. For example, to forgive infidelity or violence in a family relationship is one thing, but to be reconciled without repentance allows the offender to continue in the sin of unfaithfulness or violence. It is sometimes necessary to say, "I love you, and I forgive you. I will not seek to punish you for what you have done. But you must change your ways before we can be reconciled. Otherwise you will just keeping hurting me and yourself."

Theologian Lewis Smedes says that "forgive and forget" is not a Christian concept, even when there has been true repentance. If we forget how we have been forgiven, by God and by our loved ones, then we lose the very stories that show God at work in our lives. Remembering is the responsibility of the one who has been forgiven, not the forgiver (see Matthew 6:12, 14–15). Smedes suggests that we should replace the concept of forgiving and forgetting with the concept of "redemptive remembering." In the exodus from Egypt, Moses told the people of Israel always to remember what they had experienced: their own sin and God's forgiveness. The prodigal son probably never forgot his father running to meet him on the road home. Because they remembered, they could celebrate their reconciliation.

The Challenging Practices of Living Faith

Marianne and James have learned to celebrate their experience of forgiveness, repentance, and reconciliation. It is a melody they sing in their story, the testimony that James is so ready to share with others: "I've been where you are. I understand. God can help."

I heard the themes of forgiveness, confession, and reconciliation in the stories of many of these families, but none of them framed these processes as ways they practice their faith, even though no family can exist for long without this trio of practices, so they surely had such stories to tell. Perhaps they didn't talk about them because these practices are so much a part of our lives that they don't stand out as "a way we live our faith." In that sense, perhaps they are more ordinary, more the warp and woof of our life's weavings with one another than those that seem more immediately spiritual, such as worship and prayer. Perhaps too we have not talked about them as much in congregations as the ways we practice our faith day in and day out together. We talk a lot about God's forgiveness and our reconciliation with God, but perhaps we are less comfortable revealing in the community of faith the ways in which we fail one another day in and day out, the ways we learn to forgive, the ways we put relationships back together again.

PRACTICING FAITH TOGETHER

A young adult woman, when asked "How has living in your family influenced your faith?" answered: "I inherited it from Mom." Although faith is not passed down biologically from one generation to the next, she is right that one generation teaches it to the next. The transmission, however, is not all one way. Parents deliberately model what they want their children to learn and in so doing perhaps commit themselves to faith practices they would not do otherwise. As a father said of his children: "They motivate me to do a lot of things, even to believe in God." Siblings and spouses and faith-family members model faith for one another, practice tolerance and encouragement with one another, pray for and with one another, and share the inspiration and challenge they find in group and individual Bible study. When beds feel cozy on Sunday morning, family members prod one another out and on to worship together in the community of faith. Parents also learn faith from children: from a high school senior who takes a shunned classmate to lunch rather than participate in a senior picnic, from children who have learned enough about faith from their parents to expect that their friend who is in a bit of trouble at home and needs a safe harbor will be welcomed in their home. In short, families practice their faith together.

Chapter 6

KITCHEN LINOLEUM AS HOLY GROUND

❦

Bible stories often tell about God speaking to people as they go about their ordinary everyday responsibilities. Shepherds taking care of the herd hear angels' greetings (Luke 2). Jesus comes to talk with brothers fishing together to provide for their families (Matthew 4:18–22). A Samaritan woman meets him on her daily trek to draw water for her household (John 4:17–26). Jesus speaks to Martha as she flusters about her kitchen work (Luke 10:38–42). Women performing the family duties of care for the dead meet an angel and become the first witnesses of the good news of resurrection (24:1–9). God finds us, is there with us, even when we ourselves may not be looking for some experience of the Holy, in the everyday tasks of family life.

In Genesis 29 the story of Leah is a story of God being present in the midst of family life, even the lives of very troubled families. Leah was Jacob's unloved wife, Rachel's older sister. Jacob's father-in-law tricked Jacob into marrying Leah when Jacob really wanted Rachel. Many of us know well the romantic story of Jacob's love for Rachel and his faithful fourteen years of labor in order to purchase her. We don't think much about Leah, other than perhaps to ponder how Jacob could have slept with her on their wedding night without realizing that his father-in-law had switched sisters on him! Leah is a tragic figure, dumped by her father into a marriage to a man who had to be tricked into taking her. She is unloved.

In desperation Leah hoped providing Jacob with children would make him love her. And so she bore him son after son, four in all. Instead, her motherhood simply caused her younger sister and Jacob's favored wife, Rachel, to be more competitive with her, to hate her more, because Rachel could not get pregnant.

Where was the God of justice for Leah? The scriptures do not indicate that Jacob ever loved Leah, no matter what she did. Although it seems as though the miserable relationships continued with her sister and husband unabated, something happened inside of Leah. When Leah's fourth son was born, Leah changed her attitude. She realized nothing she could do could make Jacob love her. We can't change other people, only ourselves. And so she said to herself, "This time I will praise the Lord" (Genesis 29:35 NRSV). As theologian Renita Weems has pointed out, mothering four little boys in a household full of tension and hatred somehow opened Leah's eyes to God. In the end, perhaps even in some way as a consequence of this change in Leah's attitude, it seems that something also changed in her relationship with Jacob. Jacob's last request from his deathbed to his sons was to take him home and bury him next to Leah (49:32). His last thoughts before death were of Leah. What happened? We don't know, but perhaps Jacob learned to respect and love this woman who praised God in the midst of all the struggle and misery of her life.

When I asked them, the families I met in this project told me their own stories of praising God. "When have you experienced the presence of God?" I asked. Some talked about feeling the presence of God at church as they sang or participated in communion. Others described moments when they were in natural places of great beauty that filled them with awe at God's creation. They told these stories about their experiences as individuals more than as families recounting a shared experience. But there were also the stories of experiencing God in family life. A mother in the midst of a divorce described how living with her children has "enabled her to see miracles." Jesus made it clear that welcoming children to participate with us is, in essence, welcoming God's presence with us (Mark 9:36–37). As it did for Leah, the birth and presence of children brings an awareness of God's presence and our need to express praise.

In Family Crises

Sometimes in crisis, families glimpse full face the ever present (yet easily overlooked) holy ground of their lives.

Standing in the Kitchen Crying

Sitting in their sunny family room on a winter afternoon with Lisa, the retired store clerk, and Brad, the retired truck driver, I had listened to them tell me about their struggles with their children, the way that they have supported their little congregation financially, their pride in their son for finding and caring for a homeless teenager (see Chapter Five).

When I asked them to tell me about a time they experienced God in their lives, Lisa told me,

> About five years ago, Brad was in the doctor's office being diagnosed with diabetes. The doctor sent him from his office over to the nutritionist to give him some instructions on his medications and his diet, and I had an appointment at the same time with a neurologist. I had to have some tests run, so we were waiting. I had called the neurologist's office, and I said, "I am just down the hall. When you are ready for me, will you give me a call?" because I wanted to sit in on what the nutritionist was explaining to Brad. So they called me, and I went to his office and found out that I had multiple sclerosis. We came home and just stood in the kitchen, put our arms around each other and half-laughed and half-cried, and said, "Boy, when it rains, it pours." We both were so thankful that we were both under this umbrella together, and we knew God was going to take care of us. And He has. It's a horrible feeling to not have control over your body physically, but it has strengthened my faith. It has helped me to grow.

Kitchen Linoleum as Holy Ground

Although the illness each of them was facing was very individual, it played out on the canvas of family relationships, in a terrible mirroring of bad news. Trying to absorb the implications of these life-threatening diagnoses, they went home and found themselves holding one another in the kitchen and crying together. In that moment they also were able to laugh because they experienced assurance of God's care, the "umbrella" protecting them both, wrapped close together in one another's arms, an umbrella protecting them from being drenched by the crises facing them. They knew God had been their umbrella all along, taking care of them, but the downpour of bad news made God's presence keenly felt as they stood there on the kitchen linoleum crying and laughing together.

Growing Up with Mental Illness

Ginger and Allen, the couple in their twenties who have teenagers in and out of their home and who are making plans to go to seminary, told me about Ginger's experiences with her father's mental illness. "My father suffers from manic depression, and he has relapses every so often," Ginger began. "I remember praying and praying for my father to be delivered from being a manic depressive. I think about Christ saying, 'My grace is sufficient.' As I prayed for my father, I felt the peace of actually being closer to God. He didn't remove the illness, but He gave us strength to deal with it."

Allen added, "And that's a victory right there."

Ginger went on:

Accepting His will and realizing that things are actually going to be OK like He promised. Not OK like we would make them OK. But I've learned from growing up with a manic-depressive father. It's just been a part of our life. I watched a girl at work crying and real upset. I said, "What's wrong?" and she said, "My mom's sick." Usually people say "sick," and they'll usually say what from. But when people talk about mental illness, they're not going to say what they're sick from; they just say, "She's sick." And I said, "What kind of medicine does your mama take?" and she said, "Haldol." That's the medication they give for manic depression. So I said, "You know what? My father suffers from the same thing. Let's talk about it." And my family's experience became a witness, when I think about it.

Earlier, Allen had told me about praying for his dying father to live, and his father died anyway. He believes that instead of healing his father, God gave him the strength to cope and learn from this experience how he could care for others in grief. Ginger's story is somewhat different, but the theme is very much the same. God doesn't deliver us from suffering but is present with us through the suffering, giving us strength. She sees that now, although she did not in the years she prayed for her father's recovery and was disappointed. Both of them have found these experiences of illness and death of their fathers to be experiences for connection with others, for more effective service—like James and Marianne in James's dive into and recovery from drug and alcohol abuse, like Doreen and Clarence's terrible experiences of caregiving and loss of their first spouses to Alzheimer's disease, like Dorothy's grief and rage over losing her husband and being left alone in a city far from the place she knows as home.

In the Last Moments of Life

Many families described the sense that God was in the room with them at the time of death of a beloved. Lynette, the divorced mother you met in Chapter Five, shared with me the experience of her mother's death:

> She had been very sick with congestive heart failure. She had been in the hospital for two straight months before she got to come home. She and my dad had never talked about what they wanted for each other or for themselves until then. She was sixty-eight. Those thoughts were far off. But to watch them through all of those kinds of things and do it peacefully and without being afraid, it was just wonderful to watch it. I felt a part of it. The

169

peace seemed to transfer. Dying in her sleep was a shock to my father and to me, but it was blessing and a relief. To think, "Oh, she's with my grandmother—her own mother—she hasn't seen since she was fourteen." I was reassured by what I had been taught and what I believed. Occasionally it felt just like a really strong arm around my shoulder, and at times it just felt like a light, calming touch. It was very soothing at times.

Many experienced the presence of God as almost an audible or visible presence. A young mother described the death of her grandfather this way: "It was really strange, I hadn't had any feelings like that in the past. The room was dim, and there was light all of a sudden, and it wasn't for long. And it wasn't real light. It was just a different feeling. It wasn't so heavy." Every family experiences death, and perhaps no life experience so causes us to ponder the mysteries of our faith. We think of these times as heavy, turbulent, and exhausting—and they are. At the same time, these families spoke of a sense of lightness, peace, and even of calling to learn from the experience of losing a beloved.

Several couples spoke of their wedding days as times when they felt God's presence. Often they were stories of a sense of presence and awe in the moment. Others told funny stories. Many told stories that reflected the jumble of tension and joy that characterize weddings. Eleanor and Ed's wedding story was a little different from that.

Alone at Her Own Wedding

Eleanor and Ed invited me to visit with them late on a Friday evening. They both work long hours in their real estate business. Now that they are in their early forties, Eleanor said that somehow they decided without really deciding at all—it just happened—to have a business instead of children. Now she wonders if that was a good decision. Despite the long work hours, they both are very actively involved in leading and working in their congregation. "I don't know if I've ever experienced God's presence when we've been together like I did at our wedding," said Eleanor.

I don't know how to explain our wedding. There were all the people in the pews wishing us well. But for me, there was just this presence, this rightness, this other kind of hug that wasn't really from anyone. I felt a presence of calmness even though it was all crazy around me. Five minutes before the wedding, my mother was trying to make me change my mind because she didn't want me to leave home. She had always planned that when I left home, we would get an apartment, she and I. She would come and live with me so that she didn't have to live with my father. So she had been planning this all my life. So for five minutes she followed me around saying, "It's not too late." My dad and I were really never that close, and when I walked down the aisle, I felt like there was somebody else or something walking with me.

I felt something was holding me. I used to feel that same way as a kid. I always felt like I was being held. When I was really little, my parents would get into some tremendous fights, and my mother usually won. They were verbal and physical. And my brothers and sisters would always get in on it, and everyone had their weapon. My sister had a baseball bat that was hers, and my brother had a toy gun. I'd always sit on the steps, scared to death, and all this stuff would be going on, and I would always feel just this feeling of being held. If you can imagine, it was like arms. I felt like that on my wedding day. It was a kind of send-off thing.

Her mother was chasing after her, practically begging Eleanor not to get married in order to give her mother some kind of escape from her own marital miseries. The distance between Eleanor and her father—even as they walked down the wedding aisle together— made Eleanor feel alone, even while surrounded by all the well-wishers packing the pews. And in that moment, she physically felt the familiar arms of a Heavenly Parent. She had felt that feeling as a little girl and now as she started into a new family, protecting and guiding and blessing her in the ways her parents had failed to do.

Families talked about many other kinds of crises as being times that they felt God in their lives, giving them strength: custody battles between ex-spouses over children; a spouse's affair, the marital separation and then reunion that followed; divorce; the involvement of beloved children with drug abuse or cults; a husband being sent overseas by the military just after their first baby was born; a daughter's marital difficulties and parental attempts to help; and the attack and rape of a daughter walking home from school. Although the experiences differed markedly, the sense of God's presence was the same. These families were not delivered from the crisis so much as they found strength beyond what they knew they had on their own to cope, to carry on, and, for some, to use their experience to care for others.

IN DREAMS AND VISIONS

Some families told me of believing that God had been present to them through dreams and visions that they shared with one another.

A Dream Before Dying

Irene, whom you met in Chapter Two, shared this story with me. She is the widow working as a volunteer staff member and leader in her church, taking daily walks with her neighbor, Doris, who is like family.

> My husband [George] always got up for work at about 6:00 in the morning, and I always got up with him and made his coffee. He never ate anything; he just drank coffee and smoked cigarettes. I blame cigarettes for his death. He had been sick for two days. That Wednesday morning, he got up, and I asked him how he felt, and he said, "I don't feel very good. I had a dream last night." And he told me his dream. He said he was walking

down this lane, and he saw this man standing with this robe on and holding this stick in his hand, and the closer he got to him, he could hear someone in the background saying, "Go back, George. Go back." He said he saw this brilliant light in the back of him. He told me that story twice that morning, and he said, "I don't think I'm able to go to work today. I'm going to go back to bed."

I said, "You go on back to bed, and I'll go downstairs and ride my exercise bike." I was riding my bicycle when I heard this thump, and it was George. He had fallen out of bed. I ran upstairs and saw that he had had a stroke. I called my son-in-law, who is the county dispatcher. He dispatches fire and Life Squad and all that. He got the Life Squad here right away. I really feel to this day that my husband was telling me where he was going. He had seen the Lord, and he was going there. And I feel that was my saving grace when my husband died.

"Did you realize that when he told you the dream?" I asked.

No, but later I was able to relate that to my children, and that was so good. It carried us through. It was so different from when my mother died from a stroke. She was only forty-six. I blamed God; I wondered where God was, to take my mother. Looking back on it, I know differently. I know that she was in terrible turmoil at the time. My brother was in Korea, and his wife was living with us. She had a two-year-old child, and the day my mother had the stroke, my sister-in-law told my mother she was pregnant by someone else, and she was giving the baby up for adoption. I blamed her for a long time for my mother's death, and that wasn't right. And I think the Lord taught us the lesson that life goes on. My mother was where she belonged, and we had to

Kitchen Linoleum as Holy Ground

learn from that to live the kind of life that she wanted us to live. But I think that was the lowest point in my life.

Irene chose stories about the death of two beloveds, two times that have opened her eyes to the seemingly contradictory experiences of God's care as well as God's abandonment, or at least it seemed so at the time. Death does not automatically evoke a sense of God's presence for families. Rather, it is the family experiences around the beloved's death, and the stories they tell one another and others of that experience, that evoke the melodies of faith, of God's care and presence. I had asked Irene to tell me about her experience of God, and that question triggered a story that included much more than what I had asked, a substory about the exercise bike in the basement, a substory about how she had given up smoking herself and blames cigarettes for her husband's death and how she fussed at him, and yet another substory about her son-in-law, the county dispatcher. In the midst of all those details of family life—coffee pots and exercise bikes and cigarettes—God sends a dream. Not only did her husband have the dream, but he told it to her twice, and that was a significant message for her.

After his death Irene remembered the dream and found comfort in it and shared it with their children. Their family was one that could share and accept dreams. In telling me this story, the melody of faith of her life with George continues, even after his death. It even doubles back, pulling from the earlier experience of her mother's death a new sense that God was there all along, even in that terrible loss when she felt so abandoned.

A Reassuring Good-bye

Nell is the woman whose husband died, after which she married John; now John and Nell are heavily involved in helping Nell's daughter, Amy, and her husband raise their granddaughters. It was John who urged Nell to tell me the story of her father's death. "I was alone," Nell began. "My father was dying of cancer in Atlanta."

"My own dad was in the hospital in Lafayette, so I had to be there," John explained.

Nell continued,

It was pitch dark, and I was staying in a motel right next to the hospital. I had been at the hospital all day, so I went to catch a few hours of sleep, and all of a sudden I was sitting up in bed, and I saw my father just like an oval-shaped portrait. He said, "I'm going now, Pumpkin, don't worry about me. Everything is all right. I'm not going to be lonesome anymore." He had always called me Pumpkin as a pet name. My mother had died before. As he talked to me, he began to look healthy again. Then it wasn't scary. He was in the hospital, and I was at the motel. I was not dreaming; I was awake and saw him. Then I didn't see him anymore. I got up and smoked part of a cigarette. The telephone rang, and the hospital told me he had died. And I knew he had. I was waiting for the telephone to ring.

"You will never make me believe that was not real," John said.

Nell added, "I didn't tell anyone for a long time because I thought everyone would think I was crazy. But it wasn't scary. It was peaceful."

Clearly this was an experience that Nell had alone—staying somewhere in a motel where her father was hospitalized, with her husband and the rest of her family many miles away. And yet it is a family story. The occasion was death in the family. And the visitation, like Irene's telling of George's dream, has been told and believed and embraced and adopted as a family story. In a highly rational culture where a story of visitation like this might well raise eyebrows, John confirms his belief emphatically: "You'll never make me believe that was not real."

IN PRAYERS ANSWERED

Families also told me stories of God answering their prayers. Sometimes the situations sound like a coincidence to an outsider, but for the family it was God at work.

Kitchen Linoleum as Holy Ground

Angels in a Pickup Truck

Dorothy is the widow in her seventies who wonders if God remembers that she needs a man in her life. Now she is providing care for her ninety-year-old mother with the help of her own thirty-year-old daughter. She began by saying, "I know that there are people that don't believe that God speaks to people, ordinary people like me. But this particular time . . ." She went on:

> My husband died in January, and in March we had a violent storm. At the time, at the back of the house, there was a huge oak tree. The whole tree wasn't uprooted, but branches broke, and there was debris and stuff all across the patio, and when I got up and went out the back door that morning, I stood there, and I looked at all this stuff, and I thought, *Lord, what am I going to do? I don't have anybody to help me do anything.* I didn't actually say this, but I was thinking it, and just as I'm finished thinking these thoughts, he revealed himself to me through the heart, and he said, "I will be your strength." I knew the thought wasn't mine.
>
> I knew the thought wasn't mine. So I thought, *Yes, Lord, you will be my strength,* and I started picking up the little stuff that I could pick up.
>
> A pickup truck came down the street. Two fellows got out, along with a little child about four years old, walked in my yard, said, "Ma'am, we're in this neighborhood looking for houses to paint."
>
> I was standing there with the sticks in my arms, and I said, "I don't have anything for you to paint. I just don't have that kind of work."
>
> He said, "Well, looks like you need a little help picking up your patio."

I have always thought they were angels unaware. Those
two guys got out there, and they had it all cleared up,
and they threw it in their truck, and they took it off. I've
never seen them before or since. I've really learned,
because before his death, my life was my husband. But I
have learned to lean and depend on Jesus since he died.
It has strengthened my faith. I have more resolve. I've
become the kind of woman that believes she can do anything. I pick up a hammer and a saw, and I say, "Lord,
you know what to do with this." I do these things
because I live on a fixed income. I can't pay somebody to
do every little thing that needs to be done for me. So I've
learned to do things. And every time I get the hammer,
my daughter says, "Oh, God, not the hammer!" but you
know, I manage."

Angels driving a pickup truck with a preschooler in tow?
Dorothy qualified her story with the disclaimer that some will undoubtedly question whether or not these were angels or even simply
kind mortals provided as an answer to prayer. She has no husband to
say, like John did about his Nell's story, "You will never make me believe that that was not real," and so she emphasizes her points herself.
Finally she makes it clear that she trusts Jesus to help her, but she
doesn't depend on angels always being there; she can also wield a
hammer.

A House to Call Home

Christy is the mother of preschoolers; her husband is Aaron, the
lawyer. They are the family that likes to go out for breakfast on Saturdays. Christy told the following story of feeling God's presence
through answered prayer:

This happened right after we moved here, before our
second baby was born. Martha, our associate minister,
had just come to serve our church. She's just a little
bit older than we are. We were living with Aaron's

grandmother and had been for almost a year, since we moved to town. I was pregnant and already had a preschooler. We were living in this teeny tiny house, and we were desperately trying to find a house to move into. I was eight months pregnant and pretty much temporarily insane. I was obsessing about finding a house and couldn't, and I was badgering Aaron to death and couldn't pray about it. I couldn't get past, 'Dear Lord . . .' You know how it is. Sometimes you just can't.

One day I was going somewhere and passed the church, and I just pulled in the parking lot. I was going to go talk to my minister. *This kind of stuff is* their *job,* I thought. The pastor wasn't there, but Martha was, and she said, "What's up with you?" and I told her, and she said, "I know exactly what you mean. I've been pregnant. I've been desperate for a house. I was in real estate, and I know they're hard to find. You're looking for the perfect house, and you can't find it. Just don't try to pray. I'll pray for you." I was so relieved, and we talked a little bit more, and she said, "Do you want to pray right now?" and I said, 'Yeah, I want you to pray.' And she did, and the next day our real estate agent called me and said, "This house went on the market. I just want you to drive by and look at it, and if you like it, I'll see if we can go see it." It was this house. I drove by, and I loved it, and it was like God said, "OK, I've been jerking your chain long enough. Here."

It's a funny story, one with which I could identify and so could the minister and many other women who have felt "temporarily in-sane" in the last weeks of pregnancy, trying to get their nests ready for a new baby. Did God hear Martha's prayer because Christy couldn't pray for herself? Did God somehow arrange for that house to go on the market just at the right time? No doubt there are many different ways to explain what happened. But the point is that this is a family story, a time that this family felt God's care, and they now tell this shared funny and poignant family story about the mundane but perhaps also sacred business of finding a house to be a home for a family.

THROUGH THE MINISTRATIONS OF OTHERS

Like Christy, some families with whom I talked did not attribute the intervention of others as angelic, but they did experience God's presence through the ministrations of others.

An Angelic Nurse

Lynette is the divorced schoolteacher raising her two daughters and also visiting a young woman sentenced to a detention facility on drug charges. Lynette told me that after divorcing her, her husband married the woman with whom he had been having an affair. And when that marriage failed, Lynette's ex-husband committed suicide. Their daughters were devastated, and Lynette was both grieving and furious that her ex-husband would be so selfish as to take his own life without thinking about the impact on their children. Her congregation responded to her ex-husband's death by being present with food, with visits, with concern for the girls and for Lynette. They recognized that despite the divorce, he was still family not only for the girls but also for Lynette.

Moreover, Lynette talked about the care a nurse gave her daughter when her ex-husband was near death after attempting suicide. Lynette had rushed her daughter to see her father before he died:

> I talked to the nurse who was on duty, and I told her
> what my situation was and that my daughter wanted to
> see her dad, and I didn't know how she would react.
> She went out and talked to Patsy first and told her what
> to expect. He was unconscious. The three of us went
> back into the ICU unit, and Patsy asked every question
> imaginable about all the attachments that were in him.
> The nurse answered every question that Patsy had, and

it was like an angel being there for my child because she needed it so desperately. It was just an incredible thing. Hours before, I felt like God was absent, but as the nurse talked with Patsy, I knew God was with us. He was there, without a doubt.

Supported, Protected, and Kidnapped by Friends

Another woman who had experienced an abusive marriage and finally had strength enough to seek a divorce told how her Sunday school teacher had gone to her divorce hearings with her. She had dropped into a deep depression,

> and I guess the people at church saw the classic signs or something because they came to me. They were dropping by and calling in the middle of the week. I had a couple of people that came over and stayed with me until Mom could get there. When she left, I had people coming over to stay with me, making me eat. I couldn't eat or sleep. That went on for about a month. The guys at church came and changed my locks because I was afraid. A group of friends would come over on Friday night and kidnap me and take me out for movies and supper and would call me on Saturday and ask if I needed things. They just dragged me back to life.

As several people said, "God puts people there for us when we need them."

Many times, answered prayers came in the form of financial provision: staff at a doctor's office calling a family who needed medicine to say that they had just received free medications that the family couldn't afford for a child, a check in the mailbox of a divorced mother who had just run out of food and money, a car provided free by a church's "car ministry" to a single mother who needed transportation to work. There were also stories of healing because a congregation or a Sunday school class or Bible study group prayed for them: a child sick with *E. coli* bacteria recovering; a child regaining the use of his legs following a car accident, after doctors said he would never walk again; babies born with defects, who survived impossible odds and are living normal lives; spouses and children recovering from alcohol and drug addiction.

IN STRENGTH TO HANDLE LIFE'S DIFFICULTIES AND CRISES

After I asked the question "When have you felt God especially close to your family?" came the question, "When have you experienced God's absence?"

On Icy Roads on a Dark Night of the Soul

Brad and Lisa had just told me about their diagnoses of multiple sclerosis and diabetes. Brad, the retired truck driver, then told me this story.

> The trucking company called me to go to work one night, and the weather was bad—snow and sleet. I was supposed to be running to Atlanta. But they called and said, "You're going to have to go to Chattanooga tonight because we don't have a load to go to Atlanta," so that kind of upset me. Then they put me in a tractor I didn't want. It was just one little thing after another. In the meantime my mom and dad called me to come over to their house, and they broke the news that Dad had cancer. Oh, gee, everything was heartbreaking, and nothing was going right. So I started out, but I was so overwhelmed with the bad news. I even doubted myself. Of course, I was praying to the Lord, and I thought, *I must be lost. Nobody should feel like this just because they receive bad news,* and I questioned my salvation. I really did. That was a terrible feeling. Anyway, I was driving, and

Kitchen Linoleum as Holy Ground

all of a sudden I realized that I didn't see any traffic, and I hadn't met any. Still, I was just driving as hard as I could go, and I was going through the hills in Kentucky. There was a group of cars and trucks sitting on the side of the road, and at the top of the hill, I came to myself. I thought, *Gee, this road must be slick,* so I stopped on the side of the road, and I got out. I couldn't stand up, it was so slick.

This truck pulled in behind me, and the guy got out and said, "Driver, are you all right?" and I said, "Yeah." He said, "Don't you realize how slick this road is? I've got special tires." He was hauling fuel, and he had spikes in his tires. He said, "I have never seen anybody drive on a road like this."

And when I got back in the truck, I prayed to God for forgiveness because nothing but God could have kept me on the road that night. The load that I didn't want, it was heavy, and it stuck. The tractor I didn't want is the best one we have for ice. I got to the next motel, and as soon as I got in my room, I dropped to my knees and prayed to God for forgiveness. From then on I prayed, "Lord, if you'll just let me take it one day at a time, that's all I'm asking, for the faith that I need." So I guess that was the crowning point of my faith, how He watched over me because it was impossible. If you couldn't walk on a road, how could you drive it?

Lisa added, "I've been not just down in my faith but I've been really angry with God, and I let Him know I'm angry with Him. He knows it anyway. I've even thought God wasn't there too, especially when we were going through the problems with our son. I was having dizzy spells and falling around, and it was the multiple sclerosis, but we didn't even know what it was. I was sick and having problems with that child, and Brad was gone all the time, and I would think, *What is the use? Why is this happening? Are you there? Is there really a*

God? And like Brad said, there would be something all at once that would just totally turn you around."

Like so many others, Brad describes a personal crisis and a dark night when he wondered where God was and yet discovered at some turning point that God had been with him all along; Lisa affirms his story with one of her own. In one sense, these are not family stories but individual stories: they are stories Brad and Lisa told about individual experiences. And yet they took place with a backdrop of family crises. And the stories, though of different experiences, have the same theme and thus are linked and part of their common melody: when we are at our lowest, when we doubt that God even exists, something comes along to just turn us around or, rather, keep us stuck well to the road we don't even know is slick.

Questioning God

Dorothy, who told the story of the angels in the pickup truck, is still struggling as she tries to adjust to being a widow:

> I wasn't ready to turn him loose. There are days when I do really well, and then there are times when I just get so lonesome for him that I can hardly bear it. And I'm not alone in this. I understand that millions of women have gone through this, not only women but men too who have lost mates. But this is my experience, and there are times when I keep asking the Lord, "Why? Why didn't you take my husband when we lived where I had all his sisters for support and knew more people and everything?" You know, it's like Shakespeare: we are just players on this big stage, and when the puzzle gets all together, it's going to be fine, but while it's being put together, it just keeps poor little human beings confused. I keep screaming at the Lord, "Why? He was a good person."

She believes and hopes that the meaning of it all will be clear later, because she certainly is questioning God now.

Others echoed Dorothy's struggle. Anne, the young single woman who put so many miles on her car driving home during a year of family crisis (see Chapter Two), told about the experience of hitting a pedestrian who stepped into the street in front of her. She prayed fervently for him, and then a stranger who had witnessed the accident began to pray with her. The man died despite their prayers. When the police told her that the man had died, she said, "I talked to God for a while. 'Why? You said pray for what we want, and you'll give us what we ask for. And I prayed for him. I prayed *hard* for him. Why aren't you listening to me?' I found myself questioning God." This happened five years ago, and although she still doesn't understand where God was in that experience, she lives with knowing that we don't know from one minute to the next "where our souls will be."

Dorothy and Anne find themselves questioning God, raging at God for not intervening to change what have felt like unbearable burdens. They have not stopped asking those questions, and in the very asking, the praying for understanding, somehow they find the strength to go on with their lives. Someday the pieces will fall in place, Dorothy believes, and Anne has learned that someday can be any day.

FAMILY LIFE PROVIDES A WINDOW INTO THE NATURE OF GOD

The only time in my life that I have diligently kept any floor clean was when my daughter, Sarah, was a creeper, the stage before crawling, when babies scoot along on their stomachs on the floor. She and I spent most of our waking hours in the kitchen and family room. I was doing my work as a writer at the kitchen table, with her scooting around under my feet. Each day I would wash that kitchen linoleum floor on my hands and knees so that she would not be so dirty from wriggling all over the floor. I remember almost a quarter of a century later the sunny afternoon when an awareness dawned in that experience: the smell of the lemon soap and the feel of the hot sudsy water, the warm sun coming through a window open to the springtime, the quiet while Sarah napped, seeing the shiny floor and feeling *right* about caring for another in this very mundane way. Jesus washed the feet of the disciples he loved and taught to become the first church leaders (John 13); I washed a floor where my beloved baby crawled, a little one I too was responsible for discipling. Somehow there was a connection in my mind.

It was like any other afternoon, and yet the moment was out of time, connected with the ebb and flow of life and shot through with meaning. I later told a friend about this moment. Putting words to it, creating a very small story gave it an enduring significance that might otherwise have been fleeting and forgotten. And I still remember. The richness comes not from the experience of scrubbing the floor but from the thinking about and telling about what the experience meant to me. I had never thought about scrubbing a floor as being something spiritual, except somehow I experienced it that way in that moment. Did I *make* meaning for that moment? Or did I find the meaning that was already there in an act of caring for another, a meaning simply waiting to be discovered? Is meaning something we invent, that is not inherent in the experience? Or does that meaning exist, and we miss it if we do not open ourselves to seeing and feeling it?

The relationship between experience and meaning goes both ways. Not only does the spiritual emerge from the experience, but finding the meaning consequently influences future experiences. If scrubbing the floor becomes an experience with some connection to faith and spirit, I am more likely to keep up that practice in my life. It is keeping a floor clean, and it is so much more. That moment literally on my knees in the kitchen was a moment of joy.

When I asked families I interviewed to share moments they experienced God's presence, they shared both joyous occasions (births and weddings) and times of crisis: the diagnoses of multiple sclerosis and diabetes in the same day, the suicide of the ex-husband, the critical illness of a child. Whether little moments or big, moments of joy or of deep disappointment or despair, however, family life provides a window from our own experience into heaven, a glimpse of what God is like. And different persons, including different family members, experience the meaning in their shared experiences differently.

Beverly and Art are the parents of Catherine, the divorced young mother whose husband is in prison and whose grandmother blessed

185

her. More than two decades ago, it was Beverly who fled her marriage with infant Catherine, going home to her own parents, only to realize that she had made a commitment and had to go back to her marriage (see Chapters Three and Four). Beverly and Art described the tremendous stress they had experienced when their daughter, already pregnant, got married, and the young couple came to live with them. Their son-in-law was in and out of trouble, involved with drugs and stealing. Several times he left and returned, and finally when he was sent to prison, their daughter divorced him. Beverly said, "I felt the last time that he left, I said I just feel like a little bit of what Jesus felt when he was on that cross and we sin. He doesn't understand why we do it. And I didn't understand why Doug had done what he did."

Art added, "Her favorite scripture is, 'And we know that all things work together for good to them that love God, to them who are called according to his purpose.' And we love God, and we are called according to his purpose, so everything that has happened to us in our twenty-nine years of marriage, we've always come out higher and stronger, and we've seen a lesson."

Beverly and Art share in telling this story, and yet its meaning, their melodies, differ. Beverly believes that through the suffering they have endured with Doug, she understands God better. She glimpses what the experience of the crucifixion must have been like in some small way and how God may not even understand why people do what they do. Art seems to agree by quoting "her favorite scripture" and yet adds a melody of his own, even while he calls it Beverly's: goodness will come to those who love God, in the form of strength and understanding. Beverly's story tells of compassion with the suffering of Christ; Art's shifts to a theme of suffering creating strength.

Rough family experiences provide the ground for rethinking our understanding of God. In Chapter Four you read the story of Corrine, the mother whose son became critically ill after very minor surgery. This was a crisis of faith for Corrine and a turning point in her marriage. Her husband had dismissed the child's deepening illness as "just a virus." Their marriage is one in which he clearly dominates, and it took considerable courage for her to override his lack of concern and take the son to the emergency room despite her husband's objections. It became a turning point in their marriage, as well as in her faith, "I was so hurt with God and so disappointed. I thought I had the right faith formula worked out to have a happy life, and I didn't. I remember I was so touched that my husband was so remorseful that he hadn't been more concerned and hadn't paid attention to my worries, and it was really a turning point for him. Something good did come of it, but I will never believe that God made my son suffer. What could be the best thing to come out of this? Everything really has gone so much better for our family; my husband realizes how precious the children are."

WHEN GOD FEELS ABSENT

When I asked the question "When have you felt God's absence?" many said that they have never felt God was absent. Some said that they had distanced themselves from God, but God was always there. Some were afraid to accuse God of being absent. One young single adult said, "I've never said, 'God, where are you?' I feel like every time I've called Him, he's been there. Every time. I can't even imagine God not being there. I'm even scared to let that roll off my lips or accuse God. I know some did in the Bible in their desperation. But still, I just can't identify with that. It's always, 'I know you're coming by, but when?'"

On the other hand, some shared that they had experienced a sense of God's absence. Patrick is the stepfather whose stepdaughter gave him the paper titled "My Dad" for Christmas (see Chapter Two). He experienced his divorce as a time of God's absence in his life. "One day I would feel God's presence, but the next I'd be saying, 'Where have you been, God? Why did you let this happen to me? Didn't I do everything right?' Whether I did or not! The family was just a disaster. My ex was involved sexually with my best friends. It was a way of hurting me. I finally said, 'This is enough. This is crazy. Everyone is getting hurt here.' I guess that was one of those times that I felt God and I didn't feel God."

As Patrick explained, families can feel both God's presence and absence, all at the same time. Some of those who experienced the absence of God were also those who had experienced God's presence in tangible, miraculous, or almost miraculous ways. Lynette is the mother who described the nurse as being like an angel for her daughter. She said that she felt God's absence when she received the phone call that her ex-husband had shot himself and was in critical condition in the hospital. She was angry with God because she felt God's absence in her ex-husband's life more so than in her own:

> I know he had to be searching because we had had too many conversations. He had had a childhood friend that committed suicide, and I had had a childhood friend that committed suicide while we were married. We had many conversations about how there's always someone else to talk to, always somewhere else to go. You always pray and get that reassurance. I know he had to be looking. And in the very next minute, as certain as I knew that he had shot himself, I thought, *I have to get up and tell these children.* I had to wake them up in the middle of the night, and I had to have the strength to be there. I felt like I was in a constant state of prayer.

At the very time she was questioning the very presence of God, the family demands of the moment drove her to pray continuously.

Virtually all of those who talked about experiencing God's absence wondered where God was in the lives of others more than in their own lives. A middle-aged woman questioned God over the struggles her sister has had in her marriage and with her children. A retired father wondered why God hadn't intervened in the life of his son, who is involved in a cult. He and his wife have done everything they know to do to try to help their son. "We wonder why God hasn't done anything yet," he said.

Experiencing God's absence is not something reserved for the big crises of life; it comes with the trying crises of daily family life as well. Corrine explained her experience with her first baby. "I thought he cried a whole lot. He preferred me to anyone else, so it was hard for people who really wanted to help to help me. I had worked right up until the time he was born, so I really didn't have a lot of community connections. I remember looking at the ceiling and wondering where God was. I just didn't understand why relief didn't come in the form I was looking for. I wanted that baby to stop crying!"

An eleven-year-old who lives with her divorced mother and only occasionally sees her father said, "When my father was leaving, I really wanted him to stay. I was asking God to keep him here, but he still left. I kept thinking to myself, *How come God didn't come in right then when I asked Him to keep my father here and get him back on the right track?*"

BARRIERS IN THEIR FAITH LIVES

In Chapter Five, we explored the ways in which faith practices can be a part of family life and in fact can be the means of opening a family to experiencing God. One of the questions I explored with families was "What gets in the way of your family living its faith?" Families talked about their failure to make faith practices such as Bible study and prayer together a part of their family life, about competing values and stressors that crowd out the faith practices they do share, and, for some, the challenge of belonging to different faith traditions.

Faith Practices Are Not a Part of Family Life

Many of the adults in these families have times of private Bible study and prayer, but leading the family in such a practice is an entirely different matter, calling for interpersonal skills and a willingness to open their spiritual lives to the people closest to them. One Southern Baptist father was candid about his own sense of failure:

> I have not worked to establish a family home-prayer time or Bible study time of any sort. I feel like that's my place, and I haven't done that. I don't know how to go about it, to get everybody together. I talked to the pastor about it, and he's given me some good advice and some books and things, but I guess I got scared. I didn't know

how everyone would react to it or if they would cooperate at all. I just let it slide. I do worry a lot, and I get frustrated because I can't make it happen.

Many are afraid that they do not have the knowledge they need to provide such family leadership or even, for that matter, to study the Bible and pray privately. Karen is the divorced mother who also has an exchange student and a houseful of pets living with her (see Chapter Two). She told me that she knows she needs to make Bible study and prayer a part of her life, but studying the Bible on her own just creates frustration. She answered this way when I asked her to share a favorite Bible passage or story: "I don't guess I know the Bible well enough to say. I am learning the Bible with the kids in my Sunday school class because I was never a devout Bible reader, and I've learned the stories by reading a children's Bible. And I try and try and try, and I pick up my Bible and read through this stuff, and I don't understand it. I like the adult Sunday school class that I go to occasionally, but now I'm teaching the children's class every Sunday."

In these two families and others like them, the lack of knowledge of biblical narratives and teachings may not be only the result of a lack of Bible study but also a cause of it. The Bible is not easy reading, and those who don't have the tools and skills for reading it in ways that bring insight and meaning for their daily lives often shy away from trying. However these factors interplay with one another, the result is that many of these families do not have much knowledge of the scriptures to inform their faith. When I asked families if they have a favorite story or verse from scripture, many persons gave quotations or stories from current popular religious literature. More people named the poem "Footprints in the Sand" than any single Bible story. It is a poem about feeling all alone, seeing only one set of footprints in the sand, and then realizing that God was carrying the person all along. A widow said, "Let's see; I've got something over the refrigerator that I love. It says something like, 'I asked Jesus how much he loved me. He opened his arms and died for me.' Is that a quote out of the Bible, or is it just something I have on the refrigerator?"

I was particularly struck by the contrasting experience I had with many of the National Baptist families with whom I talked.

Their stories were filled with biblical metaphors and peppered with scripture quotations. Many of these families attend a weekly Bible study together as a family, led by their pastor. Together they walk through passages of scripture verse by verse, word by word, hearing and repeating back in the conversational style of the group session the stories and phrases and meanings that then become a part of their family's language.

Some families experience chronic conflict in the various sectors of their life together, and their faith life is not immune. Beverly and Art described their marriage as full of conflict since the very beginning, when Beverly had taken the baby, Catherine, home to her parents, only to decide to return to her marriage with Art.

He explained, "I'm a Jesus freak. She and our daughter would tell me, 'You talk too much about God.' And I said, 'What are you talking about? It's my house, I'll talk about God if I want to.'" I thought, *Oh, Lord, have mercy, have mercy on them. What the problem with this world is we don't talk about God enough.* When I get into a spiritual battle with my wife or with my daughter, I get mad, because I know that I'm right."

Earlier in this chapter, I shared Beverly's story of their struggle with their son-in-law, who is in prison. Even in their sharing of that story, they found different meanings. Beverly has found in that experience an understanding of God's compassion; Art focuses, quite differently, on God's victory over suffering and bringing good out of everything. In many ways the melodies they sing even in telling this story are not in harmony, like so much of their lives.

Competing Values and Stresses

Many families rarely eat together, and in the families I talked with, the families that did not eat together did not have a time for prayer together. Nor did they name other patterns in their lives that I could identify as faith practices. Some of these families expressed that they typically had a daily meal together when children were younger, but the demands of parents' careers and children's activities had crowded out the evening meal when their children became teenagers. A blending family described how everyone eats separately, whenever each person chooses to, between 3:00 in the afternoon and 9:00 in the evening. The father in this family is the one who expressed his sense of failure that he had not established a ritual of family prayer and Bible study. I asked if there are particular television shows they watch together, but everyone in the family has his or her own television and stereo system, and so they prefer watching on their own. As the mother said, "We don't have the same likes of anything."

Many described how they have struggled unsuccessfully to establish a family mealtime. One woman said, "I cook, not every day but about three times a week. I've been trying my best to work on one family night. When we first got married, I told everybody, 'We're going to have one night.' But we are all just on our own. It was nice, the few times we did eat together. We had the chance to relax a little bit and feel free to say whatever. I heard that on a talk show somewhere where it's good for families to sit down together and eat dinner together."

A common theme is that children's extracurricular activities—music lessons and organized sports and church groups—have crowded out the family dinner, much less time for prayer or other faith practices, although most of these families do attend church worship most weeks. During the week, one parent eats and runs with the children, and the one who works later eats later, alone. As one father said, "Sometimes they leave my food on the stove. When she's home, we usually gather unless we have a church meeting or a school banquet."

"Which is about every night," added his wife.

Single parents face the enormous challenges of balancing full responsibility for both financial support, maintaining the home, and providing emotional and physical nurture. A single mother of teenagers is trying to work and go to school:

We don't eat together on a regular basis. I work late a lot, and I can't tell you when the last time was that I actually cooked and we all sat down together. Probably the holidays. Not even Easter. I think probably Christmas. I buy things, and they cook. Everybody cooks for themselves. I don't like that. I really would like to be able to come home every night and prepare a meal and sit down and see how everybody's day went. On a regular night, I usually get home at 7:30 or 8:00, and I go in at 7:30 or 8:00 in the morning. It is hard, and I would like for it to be normal. I'm tired.

An unrelenting schedule like hers beats on parents, crowding out all but what they must do to keep money coming in to pay for food in the refrigerator for teenagers to grab when they are hungry. She needs a church community to come alongside her, understand the weight of her load, and help her figure out how faith can be woven into the survival march of her life path.

Different Levels of Involvement, Different Faiths

Several adults had spouses who were not involved in the faith community. One mother of young children longs for her husband to go to church with her and the children.

He's been to church one time, and that was for the Christmas cantata that I sang in with the choir. I want him to go, and I ask him, but I know that if I push, he's going to go the other way. It's not that he doesn't believe in God. He does. He believes in almost everything that I believe in; he just doesn't think that you have to go to church every Sunday to do this. He's right in a lot of ways, but I always thought that church was where you went to fellowship with other Christians. He sees it as a bunch of hypocrites sitting in the church, and in a lot of ways he's right there too. But it's like I've tried to explain to him that church is not for perfect angels; it's for sinners. They go in there, and that's a part of life. He wants the kids to be there, but he wants me to take them. I think eventually he'll go.

Darlene and David are the parents and stepparents of Paul and Pete. He is Catholic, and she is Presbyterian and an elder in her church. They have felt pressure from the community to unite in one church but decided not to do so. Darlene said, "I seriously considered becoming Catholic a couple of times, but I never got to the point where I thought I could. David never put any pressure on me."

David added, "She wanted us to all go to church together, and I said, 'We're only going to be together [before the boys are grown and gone] four or five more years.' Why do it for that reason?'"

Darlene went on,

> But most people that know me well will make the comment eventually, "It must be difficult to support two churches; wouldn't it be better if you could all go to church together?" I start to think, *Well, would it be better?* I've come to the point that I don't think it's better for anybody to settle. I married David knowing he was Catholic. It hasn't been a struggle between the two of us. It's more an outside pressure. I have really become comfortable in our decision. I like the way we do it. It's good for our family. It may not be good for every family. We often go to both churches. He sings in the choir, so we always make a point to go when he sings, but we don't sit together anyway, because he's up there. There are times we avoid—I don't go to his church on Right to Life Sunday, and he doesn't come to mine on Reformation Sunday! What we tend to do is come to some consensus on most issues in general, and when we don't, we just agree to disagree.

They have used their own experience as the foundation for teaching tolerance to their children. "One thing we try to tell them is that everybody believes something different," said Darlene. "You could be Muslim or Hindu. You've got the right to think and believe what you think. You should never look down on somebody for what they believe. They may have an avenue to the truth that you don't have, and you should always try to listen to them."

David expands this tolerance to include not only religious but also political tolerance: "I get a lot of newspapers and magazines with

SACRED STORIES OF ORDINARY FAMILIES

different viewpoints. I want to read everything. That's one thing I learned from my father. Read everything, and then decide what you think. That's what I try to tell them. You're not always right, and everybody else is not always right. Try to find out what you think, and don't think something just because that's what your parents think. You need to find out for yourself what you think."

Most extended families welcomed new family members from different Christian traditions with considerable tolerance and even relief that they have remained within the broader Christian tent. For example, Irene said about her sons marrying Catholics,

> It was fine with me. They met good girls, and I had no qualms about it at all. My friend has ten children, and she's Catholic. She said, "I couldn't have accepted that the way you did." I said, "Well, at least they were going to church. They aren't staying in bed every Sunday morning." Our oldest son said to me, "Mom, would this hurt you if I did this?" and I said, "No, James. You're an adult now. You're going to have your own family. I think it's better if you're all the same than one going this way or maybe one not going at all."

Doreen is the wife of Clarence; they both lost their first spouses to Alzheimer's disease. Doreen told me,

> My daughter is a Taoist, so we don't have religion in common. She married two Jewish men—not at the same time! They've both been very nice people. It's helped me not to be so judgmental and to feel that our religion is the only religion. I went to school with a bunch of Jewish people, though, so it's made me more broad-minded. I was concerned at first, though, when my daughter wanted to marry a Jewish person. In fact, I was concerned when she wanted to marry a Catholic! But I've reached this stage where I think, *Why was I concerned?* "In my Father's house are many mansions," and that means to me that there's going to be more people

Kitchen Linoleum as Holy Ground

than just us there. I would rather they believe as I believe, of course.

Many other parents of adult children expressed their concern and disappointment that their grown children have left the church. Unlike Irene and Doreen, some mothers grieve that their children have married outside their religion and even their denomination.

Kathryn and Darren, the biracial couple that are so involved in their son's life, told me how they worry about Kathryn's son from her previous marriage, whom they raised together. They take comfort in their observation that he is a good person, that he is making a positive contribution to the world, even though he is not a churchgoer. They see evidence that many young people drift away and then come back. Still they worry and wonder if they should do something to encourage him. They clearly regard it as deeply personal and sensitive, and therefore almost inappropriate for them to broach with him. Yet they clearly have talked about it with one another. They have mulled it over together. Darren said, "If you hassle somebody too much about doing those things, they get resentful."

"I feel inadequate," said Kathryn. "I know that he knows that I have a deep faith. I know that I believe that if I was supposed to do something, something would tell me how. But then I just can't sit back and wait."

Her husband comforted her, "I think there's a time in most everybody's life when they . . ."

She interrupted, "Slow down?"

"Well," he said, "start drifting. Nine times out of ten, they will come back if they've been reared that way."

"I don't know. I just don't know," she said.

She went on to tell me that she often prays for her son because she doesn't know what else to do.

"Tell me about those prayers," I asked.

"Oh," she said, "It's often when I'm doing chores and have time to think and to pray. Standing at the sink at the kitchen or wiping up the floor because I'm such a messy cook."

Moses was busy with his daily chores, tending his father-in-law's flock of sheep in the desert, when he saw the burning bush and heard

God say, "Remove the sandals from your feet, for the place on which you are standing is holy ground" (Exodus 3:5 NRSV). Kitchen linoleum too seems to be holy ground, one of the many places of daily life where families meet God, scrubbing the floor in care for a wriggly baby who plays there, holding one another and crying together while troubles rain down, praying for a wayward son.

Chapter 7

THE CONGREGATION AS A COMMUNITY OF FAMILIES

🌿

By this point you have not only read many stories of the families I met in this project, but you have also reflected on some of your own family's stories and perhaps shared them with others. As you have read the experiences of the families I met, you may have recognized stories in your own family's life with the same kinds of melodies of meaning just waiting to be told.

Families need to tell their stories to one another. Stories are how we say who we are; they are a part of our celebrations; they give us something to cling to in hard times. They are carried by the melodies of our faith, melodies we can sing together and pass on. As important as it is to tell our stories to one another in families, we also need to share our stories with others, to pass them on and share them and compare them with those of a larger community of people who confirm, challenge, and sing those melodies with us in our faith journeys. If a congregation is truly a community of faith, then it is a place where people and families know one another not just by name but also by their stories. Just as my sharing with you the stories of these families and of my own family has reminded you of your family's stories, so your stories encourage others to share their stories. We give one another melodies to sing, melodies to which we can apply our own words. Those stories become prayers, praise, and encouragement to keep on in the faith. Sometimes we sing our stories of lament, perhaps in a minor key, as we deal with family crises and catastrophes. How do congregations become communities where people know one another not only by name and occupation, but by family and by story? How can congregations encourage families to practice their faith with one another?

FAMILIES NEED COMMUNITIES

Just as individuals need to have families, families need to have communities. The people in our community know us. They are people from whom we can borrow yard tools or camping equipment, or who will take care of a child in an emergency. Community includes the physical environment that also, by being familiar, communicates a sense of belonging. The smells of the sanctuary upholstery or the boxwood shrubs around the door of the church are much like the smells we remember from childhood homes, part of the canvas of daily experience so familiar that we hardly notice it except when we miss it in a strange place or until we return after absence. We do not need a map or an usher to find our way around in our own community. We sit in the same pew on Sunday and look at the same stained glass windows from the same angle, and we can predict who else will sit where. Anyone who has tried to change the color of the sanctuary carpet or add or remove banners from worship has run into the emotions that bubble up in church folks when someone tries to change the physical environment they have come to know as their spiritual home.

Congregants are like freshman college students. Parents who have sent a child off to college know that child wants "home" to be just the same when she comes back—the same furniture arrangement, the same food on the table, everything just the same. The first year of college is not the best time for the family back home to redecorate the house! In the same way, congregational members, particularly if their lives are turbulent in other ways, may have an emotional attachment to the physical space and ritualized experiences that represent their spiritual home.

That spiritual home is a place where people know our stories too. As Lynette, the divorced woman whose ex-husband committed suicide, said about the outpouring of care from her congregation, "I have a history with those people." They knew what a crisis this death would create in her life and the lives of her daughters, and they knew how to care for her in ways that mattered. Connections with others strengthen a family's ability to cope with life stressors. There are people who care, who listen to our struggles, and who offer assistance. The security that community connections give families not only helps them to manage life stresses but also to muster the courage to make changes when they are needed. A community provides models of others who have dealt with similar circumstances. It helps a family to have community connections with others who have cared for an older family member with Alzheimer's disease or an adult child with AIDS.

The community that a congregation can become is particularly important in an age when geographic neighborhoods are not really communities for many families. Some children still walk to a neighborhood school and so have friends within the neighborhood, but most ride school buses or are driven by parents out of their neighborhood to regional schools. Although some adults are once again working at home, most are still driving to work somewhere beyond their local neighborhood. One can imagine a time-exposed aerial photograph of a family's daily movements that would provide a map of the family's community: various places of employment and schooling, shopping centers and grocery stores, other neighborhoods for visits with friends and family, a fast-food restaurant for a family meal, soccer practice or ballet lessons or the pediatrician. A family's automobile is the family encapsulated, moving from one node of community to another, often through "foreign" territory (those places that aren't part of the family's community). The streets of the neighborhood used to be the place where neighbors met neighbors and community developed and functioned. Now, in most communities, streets are passageways that connect geographically separated nodes of community life, but they themselves are not locations of community.

For many families congregations are the only community that knows them as a family. Adults have workmates, but those workmates may have little relationship with one another outside of the workplace and may not know one another's families beyond a picture on a desk or polite conversation at the annual office family picnic. In such a fragmented social world, congregations can have a significant role to play in the lives of families as contexts for informal sharing of work, recreation, resources, and help in times of need. They provide families with the opportunity to belong to something larger than their own small, separate family unit.

Nevertheless, community does not come without a price. It means having others to share our burdens with but also being expected to help carry the burdens of others, more freedom from having to do it all ourselves but also less control over our own lives. The swapping of services and tangible resources carries obligations. If you help me with something I'm struggling with, then you will probably expect that you can call on me sometime, in one way or another. Community does not mean simply being supported in times of stress and crisis; it also means supporting others. It means not only receiving welcome information and advice; it also means being the recipient of unwelcome meddling on the part of well-meaning or perhaps not so well-meaning community members. When neighbors share, items shared are sometimes damaged or not returned at all. That is the cost of community. In some ways communities are like children: they disrupt, stress, and bring high price tags that are often not considered beforehand. On the other hand, they can bring a deep sense of fulfillment, rootedness, and even joy that makes the price seem insignificant.

What These Families Said About Their Congregations

All of the families with whom I visited were engaged in congregational life. That is how I found them, so that is hardly surprising. Some were peripheral members, but many were very active, and twenty-nine of the 110 families had a member in some leadership role: serving on a committee or board, teaching Sunday school, leading or singing in a choir. Most of them, though not all, believe that the congregation has been important in shaping their faith commitments. Darlene said,

Faith is just who we are. It's what we learned as children. It's what we want our children to learn. It's beyond being my anchor. David and I were both pretty much like all Americans, I guess. You go through that period when you sort of drift off, and then when you get married and have kids, then you come back to wanting your kids to be in church and realizing that they need that foundation because you have it, and you need all the help you can get giving it to your kids. So you come back to church. Sometimes I get disgusted with church and get bored with church and get put out with the politics of it all and put out with organized religion sometimes. But I don't think that I could be a religious person without church, and I used to think I could. But I don't now. I think you can revel in God's glorious creation without church. But I still need to go and be there at least that hour, and sometimes I've said, 'Gosh, I wish I could just stay here and never leave, because it's safe, and it really is sanctuary." Sanctuary—home base.

How Families Connect with Congregations

Some families "inherited" the congregation from the families in which they had grown up; a few had been connected to the same congregation for three or more generations. As one woman said, "I became a part of that church because it's part of my family. It's part of my family's history. My great-great-grandfather was one of the first members, and we've been in that church ever since." Such long histories were unusual among these families, however.

For most the all-American pastime of shopping describes how they ended up belonging to a particular congregation. As Shamika said,

Charlie and I wanted to get married when he got home from the service, so we actually just kind of shopped

around. We went to different churches. When we went
to Douglass Presbyterian, we liked it right away. It was
familiar. A lot of the things in the service were familiar
to me from my childhood, and a lot of it was familiar to
him too. So it was just like bits and pieces of both. And
it was very comforting. Everyone there was very nice.
The pastors are so nice! And it's not far away. My mom
had been going with us, and about six months after we
had joined the church, she decided to join the church.

The seeds were sown for both of them as children, although both had
distanced themselves as teenagers and young adults. They needed a
church for their wedding. That sent them into the shopping mode,
trying on different churches. They chose this Presbyterian church because there were elements of familiarity for both of them: it felt like
home. People were kind to them, and they felt included (they are a
biracial couple); the pastors (a husband-wife team) were "nice," and
it is not too far away. Her mother then followed them there.

Jan and Harold chose their church simply by looking in the yellow pages of the phone book. They needed a new start after the death
of their spouses with Alzheimer's disease and their remarriage. "Most
of the churches we visited, though, were by word of mouth," said Jan.
"Friends of his, friends of mine. But we picked Glen Haven out of
the yellow pages. Now we look back and think God was pointing us
there, because we were comfortable immediately."

Many parents found their way back to church—or went for the
first time—with the birth and growth of children. Corrine is the
mother of two boys, one of whom became so seriously ill after what
was supposed to be minor surgery. She first began looking for a
church when the boys were preschoolers.

We visited around as much as I could get my husband to
church because he works so hard during the week that
he would rather play on the weekends and sleep late. So
finally I just got the feeling *I've got to go home, to find a
church that can be that for me.* I would visit in some
churches, with these little wiggling toddlers, and nobody

would welcome me; nobody would help me with them. I felt really ill at ease leaving them in the nursery. But at the Presbyterian church, the little lady that's been there forever would turn around and say, "Your children are so precious," even when they hadn't been. People were just so warm and loving. It didn't matter that they were pillars of the community and we were nobodies. They were just so open and welcoming, so I decided to join the church and brought my husband along too.

Family after family talked about how they chose a congregation because people were friendly; they felt welcomed; it was familiar, and somehow they felt like they had come home. Pastors were very important in drawing families and keeping them. Jacob, whose infant son died in the fire at the babysitter's house, said, "The pastor was the first white person that ever just walked up and threw his arms around me and made me feel like he was genuinely glad to see me. He is not a small man. He can just smother you, and he does. I just felt at home with him."

The importance of the pastor was highlighted in interviews with families in one small congregation, which had recently lost a pastor and currently was searching for a new one. The sense of loss and uncertainty of the congregation had invaded their family faith life as well. This sense of identification and inclusion of the pastor as a significant figure in the family's life together was most pronounced in smaller congregations, congregations that varied in size from eighty to 350 people.

In larger congregations family members often identified with a community of other congregants and paid or volunteer church leaders that are one of several such communities in the congregation. But these groupings are often segregated by age: the youth group, the couples class, the singles group. Larger congregations have to be much more intentional about thinking in terms of families, thinking about consistently mingling generations, swimming against the current of age-graded, gender-specific, life-situation-oriented programs that are marketed as ministry but may actually undercut the ability of families to be families in the congregation.

The Congregation as a Community of Families

What the Congregation Means to Families

Over time the sense of comfort and familiarity of the congregation develops into a sense of belonging and attachment, the same kinds of belonging and attachment that bind us together as families. Peggy and Bill are the couple who had been in the real estate business all their lives with their neighbors until a fuss split them apart; they are also the couple whose son committed suicide. Married and involved in their congregation for more than fifty years, Peggy said, "That church has a special feeling for us. We're not just the ordinary person." They feel special in their congregation, even though they may seem rather ordinary as families go. They belong there, and they would be missed if they were gone.

Bill went on to talk about how the church has been the center of their lives, "Church is the focal point of our lives outside of family. It always has been. Now let me clarify that. If we had had money, I don't know if it would have been. The people that I know that have money, the church is second or third in their priorities. We have friends that love to travel, and they take off weeks at a time. If we had the money to go and spend as we pleased, church might not have been the important thing that it is to us now and has been all through the years." Bill went on to describe the many roles they have had in their congregations: teaching in a variety of programs, serving on committees, and his role working as a deacon.

Bill then talked about changes that have been taking place in the programming format in their church, as in many Baptist churches. They are cutting out the Sunday night and some of the weekday programs, programs that have been a part of Southern Baptist churches for many decades. Clearly Bill doesn't like it: "We're trying to make ourselves Methodist: go on Sunday mornings and live like the dickens the rest of the week. I'm not judging, and yet I am."

They might as well put purple and orange carpet in the sanctuary and encourage the pastor to wear a robe, I thought to myself, knowing that members of this rural Baptist church in the Deep South would identify a robed pastor with a non-Baptist tradition. When the world is changing all around, we want the center of our lives, the community where we feel we really belong, to hold steady, to be unchanging.

If we are Baptist, we don't want to feel like our church is "going Methodist." And I am certain that a Methodist would say much the same if it seemed the congregation's worship was beginning to look Baptist!

Sharing Life Struggles and Joys

Patrick described his experience in Kansas, when he and his first wife were going through a divorce, before he moved to Louisiana. "We loved our church there. I didn't want to move. But when I was going through the divorce, I could count on one hand the times that people came up to me and said, 'We know you're suffering, and we're not really sure what to do, but we're just going to pray that you'll have the strength.' They just didn't do it; people are afraid to get too personal."

In contrast, Heidi is a single Anglo-American mother with three young adult children. She is now cohabiting with Derrick. They have not married because of the financial repercussions: she would lose the child support she is currently receiving from her ex-husband. She shared an experience of several years before, when her teenage son had run away from home.

> I had been meeting with a class at church, and we shared our concerns, and we prayed for each other. We did all the things that a class like that does. And then my son Ben just went nuts at some point, I think when he became a sophomore in high school. He actually ran away. We found him after one day, but he wouldn't come home. So he stayed with this other family in the group. The minister started going every night to the home where Ben was and was trying to mediate everything. We got everything fixed, and I started taking Ben to therapy, and it all worked out great. When Ben was suffering all these traumas of trying to turn himself into a young man under the thumb of this controlling woman, me, I used to tell him that the class was praying for him. I didn't kill him with it, but I'd just

The Congregation as a Community of Families

say sometimes that we had prayed. And the people in the class always pay attention to my children. Some time later Ben actually said to me, "I know that if it hadn't been for your class and the pastor, I never would have made it. They really helped."

Later on, Ben got this car for his sixteenth birthday from his dad, and the minister was coming. I remembered hearing him talk about blessing somebody's house, so I just said to Ben, "The pastor will be here pretty soon. Would you like him to bless your car?" and he said, "Yeah!" When the pastor got here, I asked him if he would. He had never blessed a car before. So he said, "Go get me some olive oil." We called some friends over, some folks from the class that live in the neighborhood and some of Ben's friends, and we all went out to the street. We all held hands. The pastor made this wonderful prayer for this car. He had Ben stand with him. He asked Ben these questions, whether he'd use the car for good and all these things and even if he'd let his sister use it. Ben waited a long time before he said "Yes" to that one! And then we prayed, right out there on the street with all these teenagers and adults from my class. When Ben came home that night, I said, "Did your friends think we were all crazy?" He said, "They did at first, Mom, but everybody thought that was really good."

Many families talked about how much it meant to them for the pastor to visit during times of family crisis. Families mentioned the pastoral visit over and over during these interviews as being a powerful and meaningful expression of support. I understood; I remember vividly the overwhelming gratitude when I saw my minister sitting on my cold, dark front steps that night I lost John and it took a police bloodhound to find him.

Not only the pastor, however, but other congregational members provide the sense of being wrapped in community in times of crisis.

Lynette expressed her amazement at the support she received from her church when her ex-husband committed suicide. "Everybody has been there for me. They helped in every way imaginable, from just being there to notes of encouragement to food. Even now somebody will ask, 'How are you? Are you really doing OK?' And it's wonderful to know that they know me, that they are really concerned."

Suzanna and Darren moved almost three years ago to a community thirty miles from the city where they grew up. Anglo-Americans and both with deep roots in the Southern Baptist church where they both were raised, they quickly found and joined a Southern Baptist congregation in their new community. A few months later, Robert was born, and he was critically ill. Just two hours after his birth, a helicopter flew Robert to the children's hospital in the city a hundred miles away. Suzanna had to stay behind in their town's hospital, seriously ill herself. She and Darren spent the night crying and praying together for their baby, now so far from them. She believed that if the baby survived, it would be because God had intervened. And if the baby died, God would take care of them.

Suzanna told me about the support her new congregation gave her in the weeks and months after Robert was born,

> A lot of people at prayer meeting wrote what our baby meant to them and how they were praying. They brought us meals when we started staying at the hospital with Robert, all day every day. For five weeks, every night, seven nights a week for five weeks, somebody from that church brought us supper to the hospital. And it wasn't a casual thing to drop by the hospital. We lived thirty miles out of the city and they had to fix something, drive it in, find somewhere to park, pay parking. If you've ever had a long hospital stay, you know it will financially drain you, eating meals out. But they brought us supper, and I'm talking T-bone steaks, baked potatoes, salad, and dessert. For five weeks. Not only was it a godsend to us, but the people in the waiting room of the intensive care unit were saying, "Where do these people come from?" "Would you get your church people to

come to our church and do a seminar on how to be good Samaritans?"

Later she described the long months during which they could not take the baby outside their own home because he could not be exposed to the risks of disease. During this time friends from the church frequently came and stayed with the baby so the parents could get out or alternatively would call when they were going to the store and offer to pick up things the family needed. For the baby's first Christmas, a church member rented a Santa suit and came to visit in the home so they could take pictures, since they could not take Robert out to the mall for this American family ritual.

It is easy to discount the home-cooked and carried-in supper response of congregations to family crisis; after all, fast foods and carry-out restaurants are available, at least to middle-class families who can afford them. Yet families mention the ministry of meals over and over as a significant support, and even a sign of God's love, during family crises. Families also told of other forms of tangible, basic help they received. Patricia's teenage son (see Chapter Two) was involved in gangs and drugs, and she found herself evicted from public housing because of her son's behavior. Her pastor collected money so that she could stay in a hotel for several days. Friends then invited her to live with them and connected her with a program for low-income families to purchase homes.

Being part of a community does cost, though. Perhaps the financial giving to help others in the congregation is the easiest part; having others to share life's struggles with also means sharing theirs. Aaron and Christy told me about a couple in their church having marital problems; the wife left and the husband was "devastated," said Christy. "When one hurts at church, everybody hurts," she said. "They were both involved in everything at church. It's a scary thing; they're supposed to have it together. We didn't expect anybody to be perfect. It was just a terrible thing."

Aaron explained further, "When you see something like this happen, you're reminded of how vulnerable your marriage is too. All families go through stuff. The difference is that in our church we don't have to go through it alone." They have found support for their family life in the faith community. But the community also suffers when one of its families suffers. Communities are costly; we must bear one another's hurts and difficulties, and they sometimes challenge and even frighten us. Nevertheless, as Aaron said, "The difference is that we don't have to go through it alone."

Cross-Generational Friendships

Amy is the adult daughter of Nell and stepdaughter of John; Nell and John provide care for Amy's children before and after school, and they often all eat dinner together. Amy and Don are in the middle of a disagreement about where to go to church. He wants to take their children to a congregation with lots of children and children's programs, to give their daughters more opportunity to participate in strong children's programs. Amy is content to go to the same small congregation where her parents are members.

Amy and Don's daughter, Agatha, age twelve, describes the church she visited with her father, "There were tons of kids. They had four classrooms, and there were tables where you would be elbow to elbow with kids. I didn't like that. Everyone knows me at our old church. I'm the oldest."

"She gets a lot of attention at our church," Nell added.

For Agatha, being known by people of all ages and having a special role in the community—the oldest kid—was more important than being a part of a congregation with lots of programs and activities for children her age.

Brad and Lisa raised their sons in their little Southern Baptist congregation. Lisa explained, "We just took them to whatever we were doing. They toddled and played all over the church, and older people spoiled them. My one big thing was, What's going to happen in this world when these boys find out that the whole world doesn't love them?" With pride, she went on, "It didn't seem to hurt them." Indeed, Brad and Lisa are proud of their sons, and one is now the volunteer youth minister in their congregation.

They had some doubts and wanderings, though. Brad and Lisa left their little congregation and joined another for three years so their sons could be in a church with lots of young people. Lisa said, "Our boys were in junior high and beginning high school, and we knew we had to do something because at Forest Glen, there were only two or three kids in the youth group. They had no incentive to go. So we left Forest Glen, which broke our hearts because we love the people up there. And that was our home."

"And it probably wasn't a good move really," Brad added. "We thought that might solve a problem."

Lisa countered, "He thinks it wasn't a good move, but I think it was very good. At Forest Glen, as they got older, the boys didn't want to go. But after two weeks in the new church, they were doing everything with the youth group, and they became very involved. So we moved our membership. For a year I sat and didn't do a thing because I didn't feel like I fit in. But the move kept the boys involved in church, which was very important to me." Later, the oldest son met and married a young woman from Forest Glen. The middle son also moved back to Forest Glen, and the parents and youngest son then followed. They are home again, led back by their children.

Children certainly need strong, supportive peer groups, but they also need cross-generational friendships, and so do their parents. Parents need the support of people who will hold their children, bless their children, and see their gifts and promise. Parents today already have to rely on lots of paid substitutes—babysitters and day care teachers. These people are important in children's lives, but children need "aunting and uncling and grandparenting" as well as parenting. They need to be spoiled by adults who think they are special, not just another member of the day care group or the soccer team they coach.

The stories of Jesus' own childhood tell of the importance of adults other than his parents in his life. Luke 2 tells the story of Mary and Joseph taking the infant Jesus to the temple for the purification rites after his birth. When they walked into the temple, two prophets greeted them, each in turn taking the child out of the arms of his parents and praising God. Each of them blessed Mary and Joseph, telling how wonderful their child was, how important he would be, but how hard it would be for them to love and care for him. It is a story of a community blessing and strengthening the family. God breaks in, filling these two old prophets with the Holy Spirit, who then turn and bless the child and the parents.

Years later the story of the child Jesus in the temple (Luke 2) underscores the significance of the community in the life of this family. Jesus' family walked up to Jerusalem for the holidays with a bunch of friends and relatives. Jesus was twelve years old. On the way home, already a full day's journey down the road, they realized they had left him behind. They lived in a world in which the community of friends, neighbors, and relatives shared in the care of children. They had just assumed Jesus was traveling with someone else in the clan. Today we would charge them with child neglect. Jesus' community, however, made no such accusation. He was not in a children's shelter alone and frightened and wondering when they would come for him. A community of faith instead surrounded him.

These are not stories primarily about parenting at all. Mary and Joseph certainly were committed and willing to follow where parenting this child led them, but they did so with the support and involvement of the community. Jesus learned and began to teach himself in the nurturing community he found in the temple. He studied and talked and tried out ideas with the adults in the temple. Jesus is still with us, in each child toddling and playing in and around our congregations. Jesus said that as we care for each little one, we care for Jesus. "Whoever welcomes one such child in my name welcomes me" (NRSV). A congregation is the company of travelers, the fellow learners in the temple, for Jesus—and for Agatha; for Brad and Lisa's sons; for Ben with his new car; for James and Marianne's four children, including their toddler, Ariah, who sings around home the praise songs she learned at church.

HOW CONGREGATIONS CAN NURTURE THE FAITH LIFE OF FAMILIES

Clearly, even if they are not very aware of it, congregations are already addressing the needs of many families who express the belief that they are stronger, more resilient in the face of crisis, and more faithful in their life together because they are a part of a congregation. Many congregations can be even more nurturing of the faith life of all congregational families with some not-so-major programming adjustments. Most of that nurture does not mean adding new programs; it means considering what a congregation is already doing from the perspective of the impact it has, not only on individuals but also on the families of the congregation.

Look for Family Relationships Beyond the Of-Course Family

In many congregations, the term *family ministry* often really means "ministry with married couples and their children." As important as those families are in a congregation, if we stop with the of-course definition of families, we miss the rich diversity of families that extend across households and include not only biological and legal kin but also others who function as kinfolk for one another. This may be most obvious for single adults, but as many of the seemingly traditional families described to me, their family relationships are also more varied than they might seem. These relationships are rich resources for family life and sometimes sources of stress.

These relationships serve as a crucible for learning the principles of Christian faith: love, grace, confession, forgiveness, and managing anger in ways that are truthful and that are "helpful for building others up according to their needs" (Ephesians 4:25–30 NIV). Family relationships are a rich focus for educational programs in congregations, particularly giving recognition to those who are examples of the adoptive model of family that Jesus taught. These programs need to include *all kinds* of families, because all kinds of families have these opportunities for living the principles of faith: blending families, childless couples, grown children and their older parents and relatives, friends who have become like family.

Families may need recognition and encouragement in defining themselves, even when that definition bucks cultural norms, as in the example of Shamika and Charlie, the young couple who wants to maintain a close relationship with Shamika's mother despite the disapproval of those in their community who label this as interference by the mother-in-law. Families themselves need to tell us who they are, and when their relationships fall outside what our culture normally

214

recognizes as family, it helps to have a congregation that tells them that not only are they OK, but that there is strength in their connections.

I learned too that there are cohabiting couples in our congregations, even in more conservative congregations. They are unmarried for a variety of reasons that also range widely: from the young couple not in any hurry to make a commitment to the senior adult couple protecting financial assets. Recognizing these couples' presence as congregational members creates some difficult dilemmas for many congregations. Ignoring their presence, however, means ignoring the most significant relationships in the lives of these members. As we provide leadership in these congregations, we may not be able to resolve these dilemmas, but we can at least present them as yet another very practical life issue with which congregations must struggle if they are really to know and care for families.

Look for the Strengths of All Families

Because our culture defines family as marriage and children, some family structures—divorced families, never-married parents, and stepfamilies—bias us to look for their problems and brokenness rather than their resiliency and strength. This bias is reinforced when the family is in crisis and looking for help. In fact, all of the families I talked with who told powerful stories of resilience and coping had also experienced troubles, all kinds of troubles in all kinds of families. There had been drug and alcohol abuse, infidelity, juvenile delinquency, mental illness, dysfunctional conflict, criminal conduct, financial irresponsibility, poverty, and abandonment. If I had been interviewing them to learn more about the crisis and difficulties rather than their identity and their faith, they might have appeared to be dysfunctional. Because I came looking for strength and faith, however, I found it in even the most unlikely families. Moreover, as they told me stories of faith and resilience, they defined themselves differently, accentuating their strengths, underscoring for themselves their own resources for tackling the challenges that confront them. The task for the congregation, then, is to find ways to identify the strength of *all* families—even when they are in the midst of crisis, even when they have had troubles or been troubling to others.

Catherine, the young divorced mother of a preschooler, whose ex-husband is in prison, said of her congregation,

> They teach a lot about family values and marriage, and they don't realize that there's a lot of people who don't have that, and not by their own choice. I feel out of place. There are times like Father's Day, and as the preacher is preaching, I'm thinking that my son doesn't have that, and I just don't want to hear it. I just can't hear it. I want to hear something that relates to my experience and to others like me. My son and I are a "broken family." But I don't feel broken; I feel whole. A lot of people at church don't know what to say, so they avoid me. Their fears cause people like us to move away and not feel a part of anything. They are quick to judge. I was like that for a long time, but when I went through my experience, I began to think, *You sweep under your own back porch before you start sweeping under mine.*

Catherine's frustration at her family's being seen as a broken family comes because she feels like she is making so much progress in her life, developing a career and making a secure home for her son. But no matter how much progress she makes, this world will call her family broken. It struck me what a vivid description "broken" is and how ironic its use is in the church, where we are promised wholeness, regardless of what situations have shaped our lives. Can Catherine's congregation find a way to define her and her son as a redeemed family? Can they teach her that she can share the deep laugh of recognition Marianne shared with me at having a niece call her family "perfect"—a second marriage with a history of drug and alcohol abuse, living just beyond the edge of poverty?

Karen, another divorced mother who has taken in a South American exchange student, told me,

> In our church there's a Pairs and Spares group. That's what they call it. I never did much with them because it's mostly pairs, couples. Who wants to be called a

spare? I said something about it to the director of Christian education, and she said, "But we don't act like we're pairs. We don't even think that way." But I told her that's my hang-up, but it's how I feel. It's not how they make me feel. Pairs and Spares. It's cute. It rhymes. But there are a lot of things you don't want to feel like. Who wants to be a spare tire?

Blending families also often feel either ignored by the church or perhaps even labeled as examples of failure. As one father in a blending family said, "The church doesn't see us; it isn't very open to blended families." When congregations do "see" blending families, it is often as targets of ministry: seminars and counseling services for those experiencing grief after the death of a spouse or the rupture of divorce and then the challenges of remarriage. Clearly such seminars and services are valuable. In addition, however, many of these blending families taught me the significant ways they can be channels of service to others and to the community: Jake and Jana's family and their involvement in the life of the congregation and community, and Patrick and Tess's family with a ready supply of warm blankets for homeless people on cold nights. These families need to be recognized not only for the struggles they have experienced but more importantly for the witness they provide to God's grace and redemption—and examples of faithful service.

Encourage Families to Develop Their Own Faith Practices

Christy talked about her Bible study group of mothers of young children at church.

> One of the other mothers was upset because she can't seem to find time for herself for anything, much less to pray or read her Bible. We basically talked about the seasons of our life and how this was just a season and that it would pass. And rather than getting angry about not getting time for our little personal studies, why not

do a study with the kids where the family has a scripture
verse that it memorizes? I have learned more scripture
memorizing it with my kids than I've ever learned on
my own. My son was always bringing scriptures home
to learn. He writes it out, and we put it up on our board.
We have a scripture verse of the week up there. What's
really bad is if Mom doesn't know the scripture and the
kids do. It keeps me on my toes.

Christy wisely recognized the seasons of her own spiritual life
and the spiritual life of her family and refused to feel less spiritual because her responsibility for young children made private devotions so
difficult. Notice, however, that coming to this understanding and feeling good about it happened in the congregational context. She needed
other mothers to acknowledge and bless her approach to the faith
practice of studying scripture. The twelve family faith practices in
Chapter Five could be a framework for families to explore together—
at church—the ways they can be more intentional in practicing their
faith together.

Provide Ways for Families to Serve and Learn Together at Church

One of the most significant ways to help faith families to form and to
undergird existing family relationships in a community of faith is to
encourage persons in the same family and persons of different generations and life situations to participate in community life with one another, benefit from one another's gifts, and care for one another's
needs. Family and cross-generational groupings are ideal for what we
are trying to accomplish in community life: caring for one another,
ministering to others, worshiping God. Both children and adults learn
best about God's love by being loved by God's people, about being a
child of God by belonging in a faith family embedded in a community of faith, about worship by worshiping in a gathered community,
about ministry by serving in partnership with others. There are times,
of course, that age-graded, specialized groups work best for accom-
plishing particular objectives. But these peer-group experiences need

to be balanced by groups that bring together persons of different ages and life situations, and above all, that allow families to participate in congregational life together. Unlike the early Christian families, for whom church was for the most part an extension of family life, too many families today experience church as something they do that pulls the family in different directions. They may drive to church together but then not see one another again until the drive home. Yet worship, Christian education, Christian care, administration, and ministry all lend themselves to being inclusive of family groups.

Faith and faithful living is not cognitive knowledge; it is lived. We learn the knowledge and values and skills of Christian living, including family life, by a combination of hearing, conversing, and experiencing. People need to experience the principles of Christian living as a part of our Christian discipleship training. That means we need to be educating whole families together. Intergenerational Christian education is vital to the ministry of the church because younger persons need to hear and learn from older persons (Deuteronomy 6:6–7), and older persons need to hear and learn from younger persons (Isaiah 11:6). And it is even more effective when those older and younger persons are family to one another day in and day out.

Age-graded programming is limited in what it can do to help disciple Christians for faithful living in families. It is important. Adult children of frail elderly parents need to be with peers to talk about the stresses and joys of their lives. But they also can learn and grow as Christians by being in experiences with elderly adults, even those who are not their parents. Teens need a place to talk about their parents, but they need also to be with their parents at church, where in the safety of the church community they can learn to live patiently and lovingly with one another.

Although intergenerational family learning is essential, not all programming should take place this way. There are also values to traditional age groupings for some religious education. People of all ages learn certain things best from and with their peers, not from another generation. In addition, personal and social issues and readiness for learning are different at different ages.

Intergenerational educational experiences may seem to present a number of challenges to Christian educators. It is difficult to meet the wide range of knowledge, interests, and motivations for learning. Family-oriented Christian education is intergenerational, but it is also perhaps less of a challenge, because it involves natural groups. It implies that at least some of the time, we encourage families to participate in education together, as families and faith families. Thus, it is not simply throwing the adults and the youth classes together, but instead the youth class inviting their parents and faith parents (or vice versa) to join them for educational experiences. It means providing a rocking-chair Sunday school class so that parents of babies who have been in child care all week can sit together with their babies for the Sunday school hour, sharing the Bible lesson of the week while they rock and feed and play with their infants.

In essence, family-oriented Christian education means studying the Bible together in family groups and applying it to family life. It is a much less structured approach to education that communicates sensitivity for family life experiences. In other words, the educational experience is built around and for family and faith-family relationships. In many respects it takes what has been learned in congregations that use cell groups and home fellowships and applies it to the Christian education that takes place in the larger congregation.

One of the values of family-based Christian education is that family members can relate Bible study directly to their lives together. They have opportunity and language and encouragement to discuss their faith and their ministry in the sacred space of the congregation; such conversation might never take place at home because they don't know how to get it started. The structured, sanctioned opportunity provided by a church program can be a powerful catalyst for family conversation. Over and over families I interviewed told me they had never talked about their faith together before, but they immensely enjoyed the interview. My questions and presence (and I was just a stranger, a researcher they had allowed into their homes) opened the door for new discussion.

Nevertheless, too many church activities are for adults only. Even if the church provides child care, the congregational activity separates parents and children; families are pulled apart. One Presbyterian, who is currently an elder serving on the session, the church's governing body, said, "All of those things begin to add up where serving on the session is almost an antifamily commitment." Sometimes church programs seem to simply ignore the conflict they may create with family responsibilities. For example, Patrick said, "One of the older gentlemen in the choir said, 'I never missed a choir practice in the twenty years I've been doing it,' and I said to him, 'Parent-teacher conference at my children's school is on choir night, and I'm not missing it.'"

Many families have responded creatively to the demands of congregational service by making one family member's responsibility a family responsibility: teaching Sunday school as a couple, parents being the directors of their children's choir, parents involving their children in service activities. Of the 110 families with whom I talked, twenty-nine had a leadership role in the congregation, working as Sunday school teachers or choir leaders, or serving on a governing committee or board. Among these twenty-nine, nineteen were actually serving in partnership with a spouse or were leading a group in which a family member (usually a child) was a participant. These family members have turned individual appointments into family ministries!

Rather than leaving a family-leadership approach up to families to invent, however, congregations can consider how they might involve family units in the various roles and responsibilities of congregational life, at least for those who want such involvement. Families should not have to make a choice between being family and being involved in their congregation. Family units can be involved in the committees and other business of the church and in the Christian care of visiting other members who are sick or homebound.

A number of families mentioned that they wish they had Bible study together in their church or other activities that included them as family units. Several also mentioned how valuable church programs had been that helped them to wrestle with family life issues. A young couple with preschool children said they wished there were more Bible teaching with practical application to family. She has organized a parent education course because she wanted something like that for herself. She said, "I led the Parenting in the Pews series; we weren't happy with the children's worship. The children are just given crayons to color. It just wasn't meaningful. So I read this book, and then we did a class on it at the church. And it was just so exciting, because now we have all these parents who are 'parenting in the pew,' and it's really changed our whole direction of how to worship. It was a new idea for the pastor, and he kind of had a hard time with our kids being in there, but now he's kind of more into it, and he's even said out loud, 'How can I help the parents?' It was exciting to see things change."

A father of young children echoed what others said: "We get a study of theology every week, and I just want to say, 'How can I apply that to my life and kids?' Just get down to the application level. Don't teach me about what the car engine can do. Teach me how to drive safely. That's what I need to know every day."

Provide Ways for Families to Minister Together

A family's ministry may be simply centered in the activities of members as they live their Christian faith in work and play, at home and in the community. The congregation can combine those opportunities for families to be involved in community ministries with Christian education that ties faith and service together. Aaron said,

> When it comes to missions, we have your "lifers" over here who do missions all over the world, some of my dearest friends. Then you've got your people that go off for a month at a time and some for a week down in Mexico. But our family can't get away. There are a lot of things that we can do locally in our community. Maybe we can work as a family doing family missions. Even if it's just getting two families together to go over to Mrs. Wilson's house and rake her yard on a Saturday, that's a mission right there. I think getting those two families together does as much as all of the money that you could give to somebody that's going to be going down to Mexico. You're bringing the two families together, plus you're helping a third in the community.

In addition to the church asking families to send their members on the congregation's mission, they are suggesting that the congregation support the ministry of families in their own community in ways that not only reach out in ministry but also reach inward in family faith development.

Use Church Conflicts as Opportunities

Most congregations face conflict at one time or another, and the majority of the congregations with which I worked in this project were actually dealing with some conflict during the time I was with them. Church leaders are often in the thick of it, usually feeling besieged themselves, and may not be aware that families in the congregation are also carrying the conflict home with them. For example, Eleanor and Ed are the childless couple who have poured themselves into their business. Ed said, "I think the ministers are trying to ram new ideas down our throats, especially the inclusive language. I have a problem with that. At Christmas time, we had to change the three wise men to the three wise ones. I don't understand. They were still men; that will never change. Why not just call them the three wise men?"

Eleanor explained, "I was serving on the governing board, and I was one of the ones that said, 'OK, we've got to change things slowly.' But then we couldn't sing 'God Rest Ye Merry, Gentlemen'; some of us wanted it changed to 'Gentlefolk.' And the little hairs on the back of everybody's necks started standing up. It hit my husband and a few other people hard. There has been conflict between the two of us—because I want the gender-inclusive language!"

"Before, we both enjoyed Sundays, but not now," said Ed. "The pastors didn't know they were such a support to us, but to us it was a big loss."

Eleanor went on, "I think the church gave us a sense of belonging, feeling like we could share, and all these people would care. He feels like they've taken away that sense of belonging, and we needed to belong." Ed has stopped going to church, and Eleanor slogs on alone.

Kathryn and Darren told me how they have struggled with a conflict in their church that erupted when people learned that the pastor had been sexually involved with a young single woman in the congregation. Darren was on the governing board and therefore very much involved in dealing with the conflict in the congregation over what action to take. Kathryn said,

> I don't think we've ever tried to shield the children. We just said to them, "We've got a problem here. We're going to have to pray it through, and God's in this church, and we have to see it through." We have been so stressed, and it's not our home life; it's not financial; it's church. At times it did get between the two of us. We yelled at each other over it, but then we had to step back.
>
> It's very difficult. There were a lot of people who stayed and toughed it out because they love the church, and they love the people in the church, and they were willing to stay through it. But it's such a hurt. There's no place else in the world that you can go besides your own home that you are that vulnerable. When you go to church, you're laying everything on the line because these are good people and this is your community. So it's hard to heal after that, very hard. Some people left and never came back.

Because conflict is inevitable in every congregation and in every family, congregational leaders can use church conflicts as opportunities to help families to explore and apply Christian principles of anger management and conflict resolution. Otherwise, conflict not only tears apart congregations but also stresses and sometimes tears into the core of the lives of congregational families.

Provide Ways that Families Can Eat Together or Simply Be Together

Families value eating together not only at home but also as a part of congregational life; the church fellowship meal is a powerful symbol and important event in their life together. In congregation after congregation, families named the fellowship meal as one of the most important experiences of congregational life, whether it was the

Wednesday night church supper, a quarterly potluck dinner after church, or in some congregations, the gathering at a local cafeteria each Sunday for dinner. Perhaps one of the reasons is that it is often a time for faith families to gather around tables. It ties to the core of our faith and to the stories of Jesus' miraculous feeding of the multitude, his last supper with his disciple, and the breakfast fish fry with the disciples after the resurrection (John 21).

Many congregations today appear to be looking for some powerful family ministry program that will strengthen and heal families. Perhaps there is something to be learned from these families, who were almost apologetic in describing how "boring" their favorite activities are: eating together, playing board games, going to the zoo, watching television together. In the same way, perhaps the most significant family ministries of a congregation are those regular programs—church suppers, Bible study, worship, ministry—reconceptualized for family rather than individual participation.

Be a Place that Evokes and Listens to Family Stories of Faith

Jesus chose stories to communicate the great truths of the Christian faith. When family life is difficult, theological principles are probably not all that helpful. What we lean on are the stories we have learned: stories of a discouraged Peter who thought he was so strong and then found himself lying through his teeth because he was afraid (Luke 22:31–34, 34–42), a woman with a broom (in my mind, poking under the refrigerator) looking for a lost coin (15:8), a loving father welcoming a wayward son (15:11–31), two sisters fussing at Jesus for not coming before their brother died (John 11:17–32). Author Ina Hughes says that the only way we can find our way, to remember who we are and whose we are is to share our stories with one another. My family has risked sharing some of our stories with our congregation and now with you in hopes that together we can understand our story and how it connects with The Biblical Story.

When Moses asked to see God, God placed him in the cleft of a rock and covered him until God had passed by. Moses saw the back of God, not the face of God (Exodus 33:18–23). Rabbis commenting

The Congregation as a Community of Families

on this text say that it means we can see God at work in our lives only by looking back, not by looking to where God will be in the future or even where God is at work right now. Our stories allow us to glimpse the back of God passing through our own lives. We hear the melodic themes that connect with stories of our childhoods, with stories of our biblical ancestors. When we have opportunity to reflect on what has happened to us from the perspective of time, we can see more clearly and we can see God's presence in our lives.

I hope this book has given you opportunity to reflect on and remember out loud the stories of your own family and to see God at work there. I hope you have also had the opportunity to share your family's stories with others in your congregation. This is not a high-tech activity; the questions that evoke family stories can be quite simple:

- What does faith mean in your family?
- How does your family try to live its faith?
- When have you felt God close to your family?
- When have you wondered where God is?
- What Bible story or teaching do you think of when you think of your family?

These are simple questions. Any one of them could keep families and congregational groups talking for hours. Nevertheless, answering them is very risky business. It means we allow the community of faith to know us as families. To tell our stories to one another also commits us to living those stories as the truth in our lives. In other words, stories have the power to shape our lives.

Earlier in this chapter, I shared the families' stories about the ways their congregations have been places they experience belonging, where they can share life struggles and joys, where they can develop relationships that span the generations. Telling those stories means that these families are now living into these stories, shaping the future of these congregations to fit their stories. The same could be said for any of the stories they shared with me. Peggy and Bill, the couple wrestling with who their neighbor Mary is to them, friend or family member, are now living with the story of how their relationship is family-like. By telling the story, they will experience Mary even more as family now than they

SACRED STORIES OF ORDINARY FAMILIES

have before. Renee, the mother in the story about the sick dog, has told a story of faithfulness that will continue to shape her relationship with her ex-husband as the coparent for her children.

AN ENDING STORY

I began in the first chapter of this book with a story about my son and the night I lost him, at least for a few hours. He is grown now, and with his permission, I share another story about him from his sophomore year in college.

The Garland family needed a new washing machine. Several weeks before, I had forgotten the last load of towels, leaving them damp in the washer for several days. When I finally found them, they were covered with rust spots: the tub had rusted through. It was time. Twenty-five years ago that old washer washed creepers' and crawlers' snap-bottom coveralls, the baby clothes I tried to keep from getting so dirty by scrubbing the kitchen floor. On occasion I would throw in a load of overly loved stuffed animals, frayed and dirty from being carried and loved and played with as imaginary characters in make-believe play. I always imagined I could hear muffled cries of "Help! Help! She's trying to drown us!" as they were tossed about in the undulating water of the washing machine. For years after that, that washer cleaned muddy jeans and field hockey and soccer uniforms, and then it was backpacking gear. It washed Grandpa's clothes each week, when I brought them home from the retirement community and returned them fresh to him. Of course, there were also the hundreds of loads of regular family clothes, linens and towels and underwear and shirts. It was finally time for a new one. I was delighted; I'd been harboring a secret desire for one of those front loaders.

But I had to think twice. John had come home from college on a Tuesday night to wash his clothes, not a frequent visit but always one that brought me joy. I had not shared with him my plans for a new washing machine. We were both quietly reading in the living room, he studying for a quiz, talking occasionally, and the spin cycle came on in the laundry room. He looked up from his book and said,

"What a wonderful sound! That's the sound of being home on a Saturday. That *is* home." As was true in so many families, both of his parents worked outside the home during his growing-up years. Saturday was the day for all the chores, including the laundry. We moved away from his "home" when he was sixteen, and the washer came with us from Kentucky to Texas. But the spin cycle sounds the same in Texas as it did in Kentucky.

What makes a place or a time home? Obviously, it isn't really the sounds of appliances or even the wind in the pine trees outside or whatever the sounds and smells and sights are that trigger the experience of home in our imaginations. Rather, it is all the mundane caregiving and sharing and squabbling and loving that takes place that tell us who we are and who we belong to, surrounded by those sounds and smells and sights that are often just on the edge of our consciousness, yet reminding us when we encounter them again of home.

I always felt guilty when my children were little. Like many other middle-class moms, I was the first mother of young children in the generational march of my family to be employed outside the home. I went to work full-time when John was not yet two years old. The concept of quality time was floating around then, but I was not sure I really spent any time that could be called quality with my children on a regular basis either. I was not very good at playing with my children; I hate board games and all of that. Instead, I just gathered them into my activities; we folded laundry together and shopped for groceries, and they "helped" me cook meals. We were together, just busy about the ordinary business of living, talking about the important and not so important as we went. Somehow, in the conversations and noisiness and quiet moments of our days, however, I think there was a sacred melody, and my son felt its beat, heard it in the spin cycle of a washing machine. Saturday after Saturday, week after week, year after year, we washed clothes. We cared for one another, and we still do. And we tell stories to one another about very important matters, like the sound of a washing machine chugging away on a Saturday morning, and hearing that sound again on a late evening when all else is still except the turning of pages in a college textbook.

YOUR FAMILY STORIES

QUESTIONS FOR REFLECTION

CHAPTER ONE
MELODIES FOR DAILY LIFE

If possible, ask other family members to read this chapter and those that follow with you. You may even be able to read it aloud to one another, pausing to talk as you read. Our family has found car trips, whether across town or across country, to be good times for reading and talking. Lying in sleeping bags at night on a family camping trip is also a good time for reading and talking together.

What family stories have come to your mind as you read the stories in this chapter? Are they stories your family has told, or are they potential stories? If your family is not interested and roll their eyes at the suggestion of reading together, perhaps you can just read one of the stories from this chapter: the story of the sick dog and sad boy, the night I lost John, or Paulette Berry's story of her great-grandfather. What do these stories remind your family of in your own experience?

What are the times you find your family telling stories? At the supper table? On errands in the car or trips together? Working in the kitchen or doing laundry together? How can you make those times you are together times for sharing stories? Some of the easiest stories to start with are stories of beginnings. Even resistant family members like to hear about the special day when they entered the family.

Ask family members to share one of their favorite memories about the family. Listen for the melodies in these stories, the meaning that "This is who we are." It doesn't have to be said; let it rest in the story.

Does your family have heroes? Ask who, and talk about when family members have been heroes.

If you are an adult, who were the family storytellers when you were a child? How did the family participate—or not—in story-telling? What stories from your childhood have you shared with your family?

CHAPTER TWO
THE CHALLENGE OF BEING FAMILY

Bill pondered and struggled with whether or not Mary, a next-door neighbor, business partner, and friend for more than thirty years, had become family. Are there people beyond parents and children and spouse who are like family to you? Are these people you count on to care for you in times of crisis or illness? Are there people you have cared for—or would be willing to—if they needed you to be like family?

What are the experiences, the stories, that mark in your mind how a friend or neighbor or work colleague began to cross over into being family? What difference does it make to think of that person as family? Consider sharing this story with your family.

Who do others in your family think of as family?

In the family in which you grew up, who was your of-course family? Were there also people who were like family to you as a child? Did you have special names for them?

How does your congregation fold people into adoptive families, pointing to the good news that in Jesus no one should be without family? If they don't do this currently, what are some ways they might?

CHAPTER THREE
BINDING FAMILIES TOGETHER

If you were asked to paint a picture of your family doing something together that shows who you are as a family, what scene would you paint?

Does your family have rituals like Christine's, which plays an endless game of cards, or Aaron and Christy's Saturday morning ritual of breakfast out, or watching certain television shows together?

Does your family have meals together? Is it a time for conversation? What are the kinds of things you talk about? Have these conversations changed over time? What effect does having mealtimes together—or separately—have on the rest of your lives as a family?

What are your favorite memories around the dinner table?

When you were a child, did your family pray together? What are your first memories of praying alone? With your family? Did anything funny ever happen?

Does your family pray together now? What is that like? What makes it hard?

Does your family involve itself together in activities in church or community, serving others, or do you do those things alone? Are there ways that you could make individual activities something you do together?

Has there been a time that you felt loved by your family no matter what? If you have the opportunity, share that memory with your family.

CHAPTER FOUR
FAITH THAT SUSTAINS US

Catherine believes that God has a reason for her ex-husband ending up in prison. What do you think?

Marianne said that she identifies with Moses' wife, and her daughter Sandi named David as her Bible hero. What Bible stories come to your mind when you think of your family? Or if not a story, what verse or passage seems to speak to you about your family?

What happened that made Peggy and Bill believe that God was at work in the tragic loss of their son? If you had been in their place, would this have felt like God at work? Have there been times when you have felt God's presence in the midst of terrible circumstances?

Paul tells the story of the family argument over the soaked papers as a time when he felt like God was absent. How would you feel if a child in your family told such a story? How did his telling of this story communicate the security he now feels? The story has now become one of redemption and grace, a testimony that this family has weathered and redeemed difficult stories. What stories in your family might be stories of redemption?

Chapter Five
The Challenging Practices of Living Faith

Which of the twelve practices has been a part of your life as an individual? As a family? How did you learn the practices that are a part of your life? What practices have been most fulfilling for you? What practice have you tried and struggled with?

Jake told stories of how he has woven family involvement into community and church activities. He sees these as ways they are living their commitment, practicing their faith. What are some of the activities of your life that *could* draw on the themes of faith to give them more meaning? Could you find ways to involve others in your family in these practices?

What are one or two faith practices you would like to make a part of your family life? How could your congregation help you with these practices? What church leader can you go to for help in developing faith practices at home?

CHAPTER SIX
KITCHEN LINOLEUM AS HOLY GROUND

Have there been times in your own family's life when you have felt the presence of God? You may want to look at the categories from the chapter to help you think: in family crises, in dreams and visions, in prayers answered, through the ministrations of others, in strength to handle life's difficulties.

The chapter concludes by looking at some of the barriers families in the study have faced in their faith lives. What barriers have confronted you and your family in your own life of faith together? How have you worked to overcome such barriers in the past? Are there any recurring barriers that surface in your family's life together?

CHAPTER SEVEN
THE CONGREGATION AS A COMMUNITY OF FAMILIES

The families in this chapter were all active in their congregation, at least to some extent, and they described what their congregation meant to them: belonging, a community in which to share life's struggles and joys, cross-generational friendships. To what extent do you think these qualities describe the experience of families in your congregation?

The book ends with eight suggestions for how congregations can nurture the faith life of families. In what ways is your congregation already doing some of these? Are there ways that your congregation could be more effective in its nurture of family faith?

THINKING ABOUT
FAMILIES AND FAITH

A DISCUSSION GUIDE FOR GROUPS

My hope is that this book will encourage congregations to become communities for the telling of family stories—stories of family struggles and resilience and redemption, stories of family faith. This sharing may take place among individuals who represent families but are not with their families in the congregation, such as in age-graded Sunday school or other study groups. Ideally, however, you will be able to gather persons in cross-generational family units to discuss the book, to share how it resonates with their own experiences, and to share their own stories with one another and with small groups or even the congregation as a whole.

Of course, congregational groups are frequently places where we tell our stories. As we read a Bible lesson together, we talk about our own experiences and challenges; we tell stories. The best sermons tell stories of faith: stories from the Bible, from the preacher's own experiences, from the life of the community. Often, however, because so much of our time at church is spent in age-divided and even gender-divided groups, we are telling stories of our individual and family lives to others, but not with our families themselves.

Seek to make places and times for families to be with one another in the context of the congregation. The possibilities are endless: the weeknight church family meal when family groups can be encouraged to sit together, recreational evenings, and even Bible study or seminar groups that welcome families to participate together. The greatest challenge is to be sure that everyone is folded in, that those who seem alone are encouraged to bring with them those that are their families, and if that is not possible, that they will be folded into groups that can, at least for a while, be home base for them in the congregation. After all, Jesus promised that those who follow him would find ample mothers and brothers and sisters in the community of followers, and it is our challenge to make it so (Matthew 12:48–50).

This book is designed to be read chapter by chapter or section by section and discussed as a group. The ideal group for discussion is a group of families: the families that come together, that family home base that God folds us into in the community of faith, whether in a seminar group, support group, Sunday school class, or just a group that gathers for a time. A section of the chapter can be read ahead by everyone or even presented by a church leader to family groups gathered around a weeknight church supper table, by a Sunday school class to a group of adults who have become faith brothers and faith sisters to one another, by a youth minister to parents and children and grandparents gathered for an evening of conversation and fun. The settings are as open as your imagination. Chapter by chapter, suggestions follow that will help launch the conversation. But the launch is an easy one: trust families to have stories to share that will encourage others to share and to find the common melodies to all the unique stories of their lives. I will present suggestions for a small group of families that are reading and talking through the book together, but feel free to adapt these suggestions to fit your setting and the way families engage the process of sharing the stories of their lives with one another in the community of faith.

CHAPTER ONE
MELODIES FOR DAILY LIFE

If this is the first time the group has gathered, there may be some initial reluctance to share personal stories. Therefore, you may want to focus most on the stories in this chapter. You can also focus on other stories that have been important in the lives of readers: stories they were told or read as children, stories they have read or told to children, stories they have read or heard as adults, and then perhaps stories that were or are a part of their own families. The following questions may help launch discussion, but feel free to abandon these if the discussion takes off in a direction you want to encourage.

Ask someone to tell the story of the sick dog and the sad boy. Encourage others to help out in the telling (like families do). You may want to assign roles; ask the person telling the story to take on the voice of Renee, the mother, and two others to take the voices of the children. Once the story has been told, ask the tellers to step out of their roles and share what it was like to hear this story as one of the family members. What do you wish you knew about this family and their life that the book hasn't told you? Why is this information important? How did you choose what to tell and what to leave out? What feelings did you have as you read this story? How is it different to hear the story told than to read it?

Storytellers have a great deal of power in that they choose what is important to tell and not to tell in shaping family stories. Who were the family storytellers when you were a child? How did the family participate—or not—in storytelling?

Ask someone to tell the story of the night I lost John, again taking the mother's role, with others taking Sarah's role and John's role, encouraging others to help out. What did the tellers leave out? What do you wish you knew to include?

What feelings did you have as you read this story and now as you heard it told?

This story has changed in its meaning for me over time. What kinds of other meanings do you think it might have or would have if it were your story?

Did you think of your own family stories as you read this chapter? Ask for a volunteer to tell a family story that he or she would like to share with the group, something that came to mind during the reading. Don't try to say what the story means; just tell the story!

After a group member has shared a story, discuss what the story says about this family's sense of identity. In addition to describing who

Thinking About Families and Faith

the family is, what else does the story do? Does it fit one of the story types defined by the author: beginnings and new beginnings, endings and loss, heroes and ancestors, survival, cautionary, funny, or sacred? In what ways?

Ask the teller: Has the story changed over time? In what ways?

CHAPTER TWO
THE CHALLENGE OF BEING FAMILY

This chapter begins with family stories and then moves to a brief look at Jesus' life and teaching about what families are. Therefore, your discussion may begin with reviewing some of the stories in the chapter, reading and talking through some of the scripture passages referenced, and then discussing participants' own experiences of faith families. The session can end with discussing the implications for your congregational life of the need for faith families.

Ask someone to tell the story of Peggy and Bill and their relationship with the couple next door.

Discuss whether Mary is friend or family to Peggy and Bill. Why is the distinction important?

The chapter tells the story of two blended families, one formed by remarriage after divorce (Patrick and Tess) and the other formed by remarriage after the death of a spouse (John and Nell). In what ways are these processes of becoming family similar to and different from other ways we add family members: marriage, adoption, friends becoming like family?

What experiences has the group had with the processes of becoming family?

Several families were described that live in more than one household, and there are also people who live in the same household who do not consider one another family. For example, sometimes children, stepchildren, or roommates consider one another family, and sometimes they don't. In what ways does living in the same household define your family—or not?

Do any members of the group have special relationships in their families, where siblings are more like parent-child, or grandparents are more like parents, or friends are like family?

The teachings and life experiences of Jesus radically redefine family. *Radical* means cutting to the root. Ask the group to talk about how Jesus defined family, recalling the events from his adoption by Joseph to his death. Discuss how your congregation defines family. What are the ways your church nurtures the development of faith-family relationships? How could your church encourage and strengthen these relationships?

CHAPTER THREE
BINDING FAMILIES TOGETHER

This chapter explores the ways families solidify and deepen their relationships with one another: developing daily and special rituals, eating together, taking trips together, praying together, communicating unconditional love and acceptance, and participating in programs together. Their stories refute the myth of quality time as meaning condensed into some planned experience in the press of the weekly calendar. Instead, these are people who are family to one another on the way to other places, doing together the mundane chores, taking care of one another, even watching television together.

Have someone recall the game ritual that Christine's family has developed for holidays together. Discuss the purpose of this continuing game in defining her family. Ask the group to share their own holiday or other special rituals that came to mind as they read about Christine's family. Have the rituals changed over time? If so, how? What brought about the change?

Review some of the other family rituals and activities in the early section of the chapter: watching television together, attending children's sporting events, sitting with a child practicing the piano, taking a drive on Saturday and going out for lunch together. What does faith have to do with these everyday activities? Ask members briefly to share some of their ordinary family rituals with one another.

The most common picture families gave to describe themselves was having a meal together, whether a special celebration or an everyday supper. How were these families' meals similar to and different from the family meals of group members?

Ask the group to recall Margaret's daily prayer for her daughters. Are there times that group members pray with their families? What challenges make it hard to pray as a family?

Several of the families have transformed children's programs, which have the potential of pulling the family away from one another, into family programs. Have any members of the group done that? What has that experience been like? What if the church were more intentional in planning for families to participate together rather than in age- and gender-segregated groups? What are the drawbacks?

How would your family answer the question, What are your dreams for the future? Break into family groups and discuss this. Provide poster board or paper and markers, and have families write out their goals and post them for sharing with the group.

CHAPTER FOUR
FAITH THAT SUSTAINS US

This chapter tells the stories of how family life provides a context for the development and maturing of members' faith. It also tells family stories of faith, in which the story—and the faith—was a dimension of family life, not just of individual members.

Ask the group to define *faith*. Watch for the three aspects of faith mentioned in the chapter: belief, trust, and action.

Family experiences challenge and reshape our faith. Ask someone to review the tragic death of Kate and Jacob's son and the effect it had on their faith. Where did they look for answers? What kinds of answers did they finally settle on? How did the church help? How did they help one another?

Invite group members to share stories of how their own families have been crucibles that have shaped and reshaped their own faith. If there are families in the group, have them talk among themselves first to see what stories come to their minds. Together, families can choose one story to share with the larger group.

Ask the group how they have experienced God when they acted in faith. Have things worked out because they pray or because they act in faith? Have any experienced being disappointed in their prayers or belief that God would change things?

Catherine believes that God has a reason behind her ex-husband ending up in prison. What do you think?

Marianne said that she identifies with Moses' wife, and her daughter Sandi named David as her Bible hero. Ask families in the group to gather together and talk about Bible stories with which they resonate.

Ask the group to recall the highlights of the story about Peggy and Bill's loss of their son. What happened that made this couple believe that God was at work in their tragedy? If members of this group had been in Peggy and Bill's place, would this have felt like God at work?

Paul, Darlene's son in the stepfamily, tells the story of the family argument over the soaked papers as a time when he felt like God was absent. Ask the group how they would feel if a child in their family told such a story. What might they do now in response to this story?

CHAPTER FIVE
THE CHALLENGING PRACTICES OF LIVING FAITH

The chapter tells stories of families working on the twelve faith practices listed in Chapter Five. Write up each of the practices, and have the group recall some family story from the reading of how families engage in that faith practice.

Ask the adults in the group to volunteer to share one of the faith practices that was a part of their family life growing up. Ask them to tell a story or give an example that will help the rest of the group picture what that was like.

If teenagers and children are in the group, ask them to share a story of one of these faith practices in their family life today. After they have shared, ask the adults to share their experiences. In what ways have they carried on what they learned as children? How are the faith practices of their families today different? Why do you suppose that is?

Why does the group think that none of the families in the book talked as much about confession, forgiveness, and restoration as a faith practice in their family?

As each practice is shared, invite families to talk about how they engage in that practice, if they do.

Ask the group which of the practices they find most difficult or perhaps even not appropriate in their family's life. What is it about these practices that make them difficult?

Divide into family groups to discuss: What are one or two faith practices that each family in the group would like to make a part of their family life? What kinds of help do they need?

Share family discussion with the larger group.

CHAPTER SIX
KITCHEN LINOLEUM AS HOLY GROUND

This chapter begins with references to Bible stories in which people who were going about their ordinary lives encountered God. Select one or more of these stories to read aloud or to tell. Ask the group to reflect on what it is that prepares us to encounter God in our daily family lives.

Do these stories from the Bible connect in any way with the stories families told of their experiences of God's presence? They are ordinary stories in many respects: the death of a parent, driving on icy roads, parents snarling up a daughter's wedding, men stopping to help a widow clean storm debris from her patio. Yet these families felt the presence of God in these moments.

Ask the group to share times they have felt God's presence in family life. You may want to put the categories from the chapter in front of the group as prompts: in family crises, in dreams and visions, in prayers answered, through the ministrations of others, in strength to handle life's difficulties. If the group consists of families, begin in family groups, asking family members to share their memories with one another first, then with the group.

The chapter concludes by looking at some of the barriers families in the study have faced in their faith lives. Ask the group to recall some of these barriers. In what ways have they found barriers in their own faith lives? How can the church help?

CHAPTER SEVEN
THE CONGREGATION AS A COMMUNITY
OF FAMILIES

This chapter begins by looking at how families in this study came to be a part of their congregation. Some seem to inherit church membership from their families of origin; they grew up in the church. Many others found the church after shopping around during key points in their lives when they felt drawn back or drawn for the first time to be in church. How did the families in your group end up in this congregation? How about others in your congregation? Encourage group members to tell the stories of their own involvement in the congregation.

These families were all active in their congregation, at least to some extent, and they described what their congregation meant to them: belonging, a community in which to share life's struggles and joys, cross-generational friendships. To what extent does your group think these qualities describe the experience of families in your congregation? This question may elicit more family stories!

The book ends with eight suggestions for how congregations can nurture the faith life of families. Take each in turn and talk about ways your congregation is already implementing that suggestion and perhaps other ways the group thinks the congregation could nurture the faith life of families.

REFERENCES

PREFACE

For research studies on finding a relationship between family resiliency and family spirituality and involvement in a community of faith, see Gene H. Brody, Douglas Flor Stoneman, and Chris McCrary, "Religion's Role in Organizing Family Relationships: Family Process in Rural, Two-Parent African American Families" (*Journal of Marriage and the Family,* 1994, 56[4], 878–888); Vaughn R. A. Call and Tim B. Heaton, "Religious Influence on Marital Stability" (*Journal for the Scientific Study of Religion,* 1997, 36[3], 382–392); William P. Deveaux, "African Methodist Episcopal: Nurturing a Sense of 'Somebodyness'" in *Faith Traditions and the Family,* P. D. Airhart and Margaret Lamberts Bendroth, editors (Louisville: Westminster/John Knox, 1996), pp. 73–84; Marilyn A. McCubbin, "Family Stress, Resources, and Family Types: Chronic Illness in Children" (*Family Relations,* 1988, 37[3], 203–210); Hamilton I. McCubbin and Marilyn A. McCubbin, "Typologies of Resilient Families: Emerging Roles of Social Class and Ethnicity" (*Family Relations,* 1988, 37[3], 247–254); and Froma Walsh, editor, *Spiritual Resources in Family Therapy* (New York: Guilford Press, 1999).

James Fowler's work on the stages of faith development can be found in *Stages of Faith: The Psychology of Human Development and the Quest for Meaning* (San Francisco: HarperCollins, 1981); "Faith Development Through the Family Life Cycle," in *Catholic Families: Growing and Sharing Faith* (New Rochelle, N.Y.: Don Bosco Multimedia, 1990); "Perspectives on the Family from the Standpoint of Faith Development Theory," in *Christian Perspectives on Faith Development,* J. Astley and L. Francis, editors (Grand Rapids: Eerdmans, 1992), pp. 326–346; and *Weaving the New Creation: Stages of Faith and the Public Church* (San Francisco: Harper, 1991). The phrase "ecologies of faith consciousness" that Fowler uses to describe families can be found on p. 337 of "Perspectives on the Family." Those critiquing Fowler's work who are cited include Craig Dykstra, "What Is Faith?: An Experiment in the Hypothetical Mode," and Randolph A. Nelson, "Facilitating Growth in Faith Through Social Ministry," in *Handbook of Faith,* James M. Lee, editor (Birmingham, Ala.: Religious Education PressReligi, 1990). Peter Benson and his colleagues have focused on the behavioral consequences of faith in the development of the Faith Maturity Scale, which is described in "The Faith Maturity Scale: Conceptualization, Measurement, and Empirical Validation" (*Research in the Social Scientific Study of Religion,* 1993, *5,* 1–26).

The definition of "family schema" can be found in Hamilton I. McCubbin, Marilyn A. McCubbin, and A. I. Thompson, "Resiliency in Families: The Role of Family Schema and Appraisal in Family Adaptation to Crises," in *Family Relations: Challenges for the Future,* T. H. Brubaker, editor (Thousand Oaks, Calif.: Sage, 1993), p. 154. See also Hamilton I. McCubbin and Marilyn A. McCubbin, "Resilient Families, Competencies, Supports, and Coping over the Life Cycle," in *Faith and Families,* L. Sawyers, editor (Philadelphia: Geneva Press, 1986), pp. 65–88.

Reports from the Faith Development of Families in Congregations project can be found in the following publications by coauthors Diana R. Garland and Pamela Yankeelov, "Families in Congregations: A Survey of Demographics, Strengths, Stressors, and Faith Behaviors" (*Review of Religious Research,* forthcoming); "The Strengths, Stresses, and Faith Practices of Congregational Families" (*Family Ministry: Empowering Through Faith,* 2001, *15*[3], 28–47); "The Church Census" (*Family Ministry,* 1998, *12*[3], 11–22); "The Families in Our Congregations: Initial Research Findings" (*Family Ministry,*

1998, *12*[3], 23–45). See also Diana R. Garland, "Faith Narratives of Congregants and Their Families" (*Review of Religious Research,* 2002, *44*[1], 68–91; "The Faith Dimension of Family Life" (*Social Work and Christianity,* 2001, *28*[1], 6–26); and "'Who Is Your Family?' Membership Composition of American Protestant Families" (*Social Work and Christianity,* forthcoming).

The following resources were foundational to the development of my interview method: Norman K. Denzin and Yvonna S. Lincoln, editors, *Handbook of Qualitative Research* (Thousand Oaks, Calif.: Sage, 1994); Jerome Kirk, *Reliability and Validity in Qualitative Research,* Qualitative Research Methods Series 1 (Thousand Oaks, Calif.: Sage, 1986); Herbert J. Rubin and Irene S. Rubin, *Qualitative Interviewing: The Art of Hearing Data* (Thousand Oaks, Calif.: Sage, 1995); and Robert S. Weiss, *Learning from Strangers: The Art and Method of Qualitative Interview Studies* (New York: Free Press, 1994).

The resources I found most helpful for developing grounded theory were Barney G. Glaser and Anselm L. Strauss, *The Discovery of Grounded Theory* (Chicago: Aldine, 1967); M.L.B. Miles and A. M. Huberman, *Qualitative Data Analysis,* 2nd ed. (Thousand Oaks, Calif.: Sage, 1994); Janice M. Morse and Peggy Anne Field, *Qualitative Research Methods for Health Professionals* (Thousand Oaks, Calif.: Sage, 1995); and Anselm Strauss and Juliet Corbin, *Basics of Qualitative Research: Techniques and Procedures for Developing Grounded Theory,* 2nd ed. (Thousand Oaks, Calif.: Sage, 1998).

CHAPTER ONE
MELODIES FOR DAILY LIFE

I gleaned the insight about the melodic nature of the stories we read to small children and how children's stories develop as children age to more focus on drama and the reader's expression from Brian Sutton-Smith's essay "Children's Fiction Making," in *Narrative Psychology: The Storied Nature of Human Contact,* T. R. Sarbin, editor (Westport, Conn.: Greenwood, 1986), pp. 67–90. Other essays from the same work that I found particularly helpful for understanding family storytelling included T. R. Sarbin, "The Narrative as Root Metaphor for Psychology" (pp. 3–21); and E. G. Mishler, "The Analysis of Interview Narratives" (pp. 233–255). Other publications that informed my understanding of how stories are constructed, how they are chosen from the larger stream of human experience, and the role of storytelling in families include Thomas Leitch's book *What Stories Are: Narrative Theory and Interpretation* (University Park: Pennsylvania State University Press, 1986); Megan McKenna, *Keepers of the Story* (Maryknoll, N.Y.: Orbis, 1997); Alan Parry and Robert E. Doan, *Story Re-visions: Narrative Therapy in the Postmodern World* (New York: Guilford Press, 1994); John A. Robinson and Linda Hawpe, "The Analysis of Interview Narratives," in *Narrative Thinking as a Heuristic Process,* T. R. Sarbin, editor (New York: Praeger Scientific, 1986), pp. 111–125; and David Yamane, "Narrative and Religious Experience" (*Sociology of Religion,* 2000, *61*[2], 171–189).

Louis Smedes's concept of a family as a "community of memory" can be found on p. 249 of his essay "The Family Commitment," in *Incarnational Ministry: The Presence of Christ in Church, Society, and Family. Essays in Honor of Ray S. Anderson,* C. D. Kettler and T. H. Speidel, editors (Colorado Springs: Helmers & Howard, 1990), pp. 241–253. Insights about the difference between truth and fact in stories and the different functions storytelling has from history and science came from George S. Howard, *A Tale of Two Stories: Excursions into a Narrative Approach to Psychology* (Notre Dame, Ind.: Academic Publications, 1989).

The story of the night I lost John has also been published in my book *Family Ministry: A Comprehensive Guide* (Downer's Grove, Ill.: InterVarsity Press, 1999) and in an article entitled "Family Stress: Reflections on Personal Experience and Implications for Congregational Ministry" (*Journal of Family Ministry,* 1994, *8,* 4–19). I have written and published this story, and in many ways it may seem to be *my* story about my family more than it is a family story. Yet I knew before I wrote it that I would be asking all of my family members to read it; they would be the first audience. Therefore, it is our story. The other stories I tell about my family have been shared with them; they approve my sharing them with you.

Frederick Buechner's insight that stories make the distinction between past, present, and future ultimately meaningless and allow us to taste eternity can be found on p. 55 of "The Dwarves in the Stable," in *Listening for God,* P. J. Carlson and P. S. Hawkins, editors (Minneapolis: Augsburg Fortress, 1994), pp. 40–56. The story of Paulette Berry is told by Elizabeth Stone in her book *Black Sheep and Kissing Cousins: How Our Family Stories Shape Us* (New York: Times Books, 1988), pp. 144–145. This book is an instructive report of Berry's research on family stories.

The concept that just as we read the Bible to learn about God, we should read our own experiences to find our role in the vast purposes of God, comes from Peter S. Hawkins's introduction to the work of Frederick Buechner in *Listening for God* (cited in the previous paragraph), pp. 37–39.

I learned from Eileen Silva Kindig that stories told well live on in the listener, as she explains in her book *Remember the Time? The Power and Promise of Family Storytelling* (Downers Grove, Ill.: InterVarsity Press, 1997). The thought that pictures and symbols help us convey more meaning than our words can hold comes from Joyce Huggett's book *Praying the Parables: A Spiritual Journey Through the Stories of Jesus* (Downers Grove, Ill.: InterVarsity Press, 1996). Michael White and David Epston explore the significance of an audience for family stories in their book *Narrative Means to Therapeutic Ends* (New York: Norton, 1990).

The story of a sick dog and a sad boy, as well as the other stories in this book, other than those of my own family, came from a research project funded by Lilly Endowment, Inc. That project is explained in more detail in the Preface and its notes. I have changed identifying information such as names, occupations, and locations that do not seem to have a direct impact on the significance of the story itself to protect the privacy of the families who shared their lives with me.

Chapter Two
The Challenge of Being Family

An earlier version of this chapter was published in the journal *Social Work and Christianity* as an article entitled "'Who Is Your Family?'" (cited in the Preface). The discussion of biblical material was originally presented more comprehensively in my book *Family Ministry* (cited in Chapter One).

Of the twenty families I interviewed in which at least one spouse had been previously married, sixteen of these families had children in the home; fourteen included the biological children of one or both parents, and the two other families were raising grandchildren and nieces.

Our research with congregational families found that parenting creates the most significant source of stress in the lives of families. This holds across the diversity of family types, whether the adults in the family are in a first marriage or later marriage or single. Further discussion of this and other findings from our congregational research can be found in Diana R. Garland and Pamela Yankeelov, "The Strengths, Stresses, and Faith Practices of Congregational Families" (cited in the Preface).

Maurina's description of the Delany sisters comes from the book by Sarah Delany and A. Elizabeth Delany (with Amy Hill Hearth), *Having Our Say: The Delany Sisters' First One Hundred Years* (New York: Kodansha, 1993). I developed the discussion about godparents based on Maurice Aymard's essay "Friends and Neighbors" in the book *A History of Private Life,* vol. 3: *Passions of the Renaissance,* Roger Chartier, editor (Cambridge, Mass.: Harvard University Press, 1989), pp. 447–491.

For other references to the "beloved disciple," see also Matthew 26:37; Luke 9:28; John 13:23.

CHAPTER THREE
BINDING FAMILIES TOGETHER

The research on television watching as a shared activity was conducted by Kerry J. Daly and reported in the book *Families and Time: Keeping Pace in a Hurried Culture* (Thousand Oaks, Calif.: Sage, 1996). Samuel Vuchinich reported his research on the length of family dinners and amount of conflict in the article "Starting and Stopping Spontaneous Family Conflicts" (*Journal of Marriage and the Family,* 1987, *49,* 591–601). Further discussion of the concept that self-sacrifice has as its aim mutuality can be found in Christine Gudorf's essay "Parenting, Mutual Love, and Sacrifice," in *Women's Conscience: A Reader in Feminist Ethics,* B. H. Andolsen, C. E. Gudorf, and M. D. Pellauer, editors (San Francisco: Harper San Francisco, 1965) pp. 175–191; and Bonnie F. Miller-McLemore's book *Also a Mother: Work and Family as Theological Dilemma* (Nashville: Abingdon, 1994). The idea that we are sometimes surprised that we can be better than we thought we were comes from Elizabeth Achtemeier's book *Preaching About Family Relationships* (Philadelphia: Westminster Press, 1987).

CHAPTER FOUR
FAITH THAT SUSTAINS US

For discussion of the baptism of whole households and the household worship of the early church, see Peter Lampe's article "'Family' in Church and Society of New Testament Times" (*Affirmation: Union Theological Seminary in Virginia,* 1992, 5[1], 1–19); and Carolyn Osiek's article "The Family in Early Christianity: 'Family Values' Revisited (*Catholic Biblical Quarterly,* 1996, 58, 1–24).

Craig Dykstra suggests that to study faith, one needs to look for the patterns of intentionality that constitute a person's fundamental orientation in life. One would try to discern in a person's life narratives the themes, events, and experiences that hold together. "The result, rather than stage assignment, would be a 'faith biography' that revealed and represented that person's faith life in its wholeness and complexity," from "What Is Faith?: An Experiment in the Hypothetical Mode," *Faith Development and Fowler,* Craig Dykstra and Sharon Parks, editors (Birmingham: Religious Education Press, 1986), pp. 45–64. Other resources that I have found helpful in shaping my understanding of faith and its manifestations in family life include Monika K. Hellwig's essay "A History of the Concept of Faith," in *Handbook of Faith,* J. M. Lee, editor (Birmingham, Ala.: Religious Education Press, 1990), pp. 3–23; C. Ellis Nelson, "Does Faith Develop? An Evaluation of Fowler's Position," in *Christian Perspectives on Faith Development,* J. Astley and L. Francis, editors (Grand Rapids: Eerdmans, 1992), pp. 62–76; and, in the same volume, Sharon Daloz Parks, "Faith Development in a Changing World," pp. 92–106.

Erik Erikson's work on developmental stages can be found in his book *Identity: Youth and Crisis* (New York: Norton, 1968). The reference to Sharon Parks is to her article "Faith Development in a Changing World" (cited in the previous paragraph). The research on family resilience in the face of crises and catastrophes can be found in Hamilton I. McCubbin and Charles R. Figley, editors, *Stress and the Family,* vol. 1: *Coping with Transitions* (New York: Brunner/Mazel, 1983); and Hamilton I. McCubbin and Marilyn A. McCubbin, "Resilient Families" (cited in the Preface).

Parents directly and indirectly affect God-images in children. When children perceive parents as nurturing and powerful, especially when they perceive the mother as powerful and the father as nurturing, children perceive God as both nurturing and powerful, according to research by Jane R. Dickie and colleagues, as reported in their article "Parent-Child Relationships and Children's Images of God" (*Journal for the Scientific Study of Religion,* 1997, *36*[1], 25–43).

CHAPTER FIVE
THE CHALLENGING PRACTICES
OF LIVING FAITH

Useful sources on faith practices include Craig Dykstra, *Growing in the Life of Faith: Education and Christian Practices* (Louisville: Geneva Press, 1999); Craig Dykstra "No Longer Strangers" (*Princeton Seminary Bulletin,* 1985, 6[3], 197); Dorothy C. Bass, editor, *Practicing Our Faith: A Way of Life for a Searching People* (San Francisco: Jossey-Bass, 1997); Craig Dykstra, "Reconceiving Practice," in *Shifting Boundaries: Contextual Approaches to the Structure of Theological Education,* B. Wheeler and E. Farley, editors (Louisville: Westminster/John Knox, 1991); and Richard Foster, *The Celebration of Discipline* (New York: HarperCollins, 1978). I adapted the list of faith practices from Craig Dykstra's *Growing in the Life of Faith*. See also John Westerhoff, *Bringing up Children in the Christian Faith* (Minneapolis: Winston Press, 1980), pp. 36–52; and Dorothy C. Bass, *Practicing Our Faith* (cited earlier in Chapter Five).

Aria's story was previously published in Diana R. Garland, "What's the Perfect Family?" (*FaithWorks,* 2000, *3*[6], 20–21).

The insight that no one in the New Testament stories grasped the meaning of the resurrection better than Stephen, the man whose daily job was running the first church's feeding program for widows, came from Marianne Sawicki, "Recognizing the Risen Lord" (*Theology Today,* 1988, *44*[4], 441–449).

The research on the role of service in the development of faith and compassion in children and youths can be found in Eugene Roehlkepartain, *The Teaching Church: Moving Christian Education to Center Stage* (Nashville: Abingdon, 1993); and Peter L. Benson, *All Kids Are Our Kids: What Communities Must Do to Raise Caring and Responsible Children and Adolescents* (San Francisco: Jossey-Bass, 1997). See also Robert Wuthnow, *Learning to Care: Elementary Kindness in an Age of Indifference* (New York: Oxford University Press, 1995).

The discussion of hospitality can be found in Christine Pohl, *Making Room: Recovering Hospitality as a Christian Tradition* (Grand Rapids: Eerdmans, 1999); and her earlier work, "Welcoming Strangers: A Socioethical Study of Hospitality in Selected Expressions of the Christian Tradition" (unpublished doctoral dissertation, Emory University, 1993). The work of Robert C. Roberts can be found in his book *Taking the Word to Heart: Self and Other in an Age of Therapies* (Grand Rapids: Eerdmans, 1993).

Lewis B. Smedes's work on forgiveness and "redemptive remembering" can be found in "The Family Commitment" (cited in Chapter One); and in *Caring and Commitment: Learning to Live the Love We Promise* (New York: HarperCollins, 2001).

Chapter Six
Kitchen Linoleum
as Holy Ground

Renita Weems opened the story of Leah to me in her article "Leah's Epiphany" (*Other Side,* 1996, *32*[3], 8–11, 44–46). The poem "Footprints in the Sand" was written by Mary Stevenson in 1936. The poem and its author's story can be found in Gail Giorgio, *Footprints in the Sand: The Inspiring Life Behind the Immortal Poem* (n.p.: Gold Leaf Press, 1997).

CHAPTER SEVEN
THE CONGREGATION AS A COMMUNITY OF FAMILIES

For a fuller discussion of my reflections on the role of community in the lives of families and on the role of family and community in the life of Jesus as an infant and child, see my book *Family Ministry* (cited in Chapter One).

One of the most well-known models of family-oriented Christian education is the family cluster, consisting of four or five families who meet weekly. Margaret Sawin developed clusters among Protestant congregations in the 1970s and is considered the founder of the family cluster movement. Participants are involved in a learning event designed for a cross-generational group, often through art materials or games, and then discuss their experience of that event. Often the session together is accompanied by a meal. For more information about family clusters, see Margaret M. Sawin, *Family Enrichment with Family Clusters* (Valley Forge: Judson Press, 1979); and Barbara Vance, *Planning and Conducting Family Clusters* (Thousand Oaks, Calif.: Sage, 1989). For more ideas about how to involve family units in the various roles and responsibilities of family life, see my book *Family Ministry* (cited in Chapter One). Robbie Castleman is the author of *Parenting in the Pew: Guiding Your Child into the Joy of Worship* (Downers Grove, Ill.: InterVarsity Press, 1993). The research of the Search Institute is reported in Eugene Roehlkepartain, *The Teaching Church* (cited in Chapter Five). The reference to Ina Hughes's work is to "Doing Theology Through Personal Narrative" (*Witness,* 2000, *83*[12], 8–11). For a discussion of Exodus 33:18–23 and its relationship to our stories, see Carol Ochs, *Our Lives as Torah: Finding God in Our Own Stories* (San Francisco: Jossey-Bass, 2001).

THE AUTHOR

Diana R. Garland, Ph.D., is chair of the School of Social Work at Baylor University in Waco, Texas, and director of the Baylor Center for Family and Community Ministries. She is the editor of the journal *Family Ministry: Empowering Through Faith*; senior editor of *AM/FM: Audio-Magazine for Family Ministry*, a quarterly audiotape publication that reviews current developments in family ministry; and coeditor, along with J. Bradley Wigger, of the Families and Faith book series published by Jossey-Bass. She is also the author, coauthor, or editor of sixteen books, including *Family Ministry: A Comprehensive Guide*, which won the 2000 Book of the Year Award from the Academy of Parish Clergy. Diana and her husband, David, have two adult children, Sarah and John.

INDEX

Binding families together: by communicating love and safety, 82–86; by developing rituals, 58–75; overview of, 57–58; reflection on, questions for, 231; by serving together, 75–79; thinking about, discussion guide for, 239–240; by working toward dreams and goals, 79–82

Blended families: bias against, 215, 217; redefining relationships in, 35–39

Blending, implication of, 37

Boundaries around experiences, 23

Brody, G. H., 245

Broken families, being labeled as, 215, 216

Brown, M. W., 3

Buechner, F., 20–21, 248

C

Call, V.R.A., 245

Caregiving: absence of mutual, 47–49; in faith families, 51–54; importance of, 44–46; Jesus on, 46–47

Caring and kindness, roots of, 147–148

Castleman, R., 254

Cautionary tales: example of, 14–19; types of, 22–23

Celebrations, 59–60

Child-parent faithfulness, 25

Children: birth and presence of, effect of, xiv, 166, 203, 204; dreams for, 80–81; guiding, toward faith, responsibility for, 101–102; and perception of parents, 252; at play, watching, together, 62–65; reading to, 3, 12; stories for, melodic nature of, 3, 247; welcoming, 213

Choosing family, 33

Christian hospitality, 150–154, 253

Christian story, telling and reading the, 133–136

Chronic stress, 17

Church attendance, encouraging, 118–119

Church congregations. *See* Congregations

Church family, being, 78–79

Church programming format, changing, feelings about, 206–207

Commitment, 50, 109–110, 128, 202–203

Communities: creating, in accord with God's will, 159; need for, and role of, 200–202, 254. *See also* Congregations

Community: importance of, in defining family, 18, 20; of memory, 12, 248

Competing values and stresses, 191–193

Confession, 17–18, 160, 161, 162

Confidence, 89

Conflict, 71, 79, 90, 191, 223–224, 250

Congregational conflict, 79, 90, 224

Congregational groups, discussion guide for, 235–244

Congregational service, 218, 221

Congregations: feelings about, 202–203; finding family in, 47–49; how families became connected with, 203–205; involvement in, different levels of, 193, 196; meaning of, 206–213; and need for community, 200–202; and nurturing family faith life, 213–227; overview of, 199–200; reflection on, questions for, 233; sharing stories with, 19, 27, 199–200; thinking about, discussion guide for, 243–244

Connection: with The Biblical Story, 225; with congregations, how families established, 203–205; to family members, 11; with other families, 25–26; in rituals, 59, 60; strength from, 201; through praying together, 74

Context, 13

1 Corinthians 1:16, 88

1 Corinthians 13:8, 85

2 Corinthians 12:9, 111

Counseling, 19

Crises: faith, 103–108; family, xiii, 108, 167–172, 207–211, 245, 252; life, 181–184

Cross-generational friendships, 211–213

Stepfamilies. *See* Blended families
Stephanas, 88
Stephen, 142, 253
Stevenson, M., 253
Stone, E., 21, 22, 249
Stoneman, D. F., 245
Stories, melodic nature of, 3. *See also* Family stories
Storytelling: process of, 3–4, 248; time together for, 26
Strength: from community connections, 201; from experiencing God's presence, 169, 172, 176, 177; in faith, xiii, 89, 101, 108–111, 252; to handle life's crises, 181–184; looking for, in all families, 215–218
Stress: coping with, 201; significant source of, 17, 36, 250
Stresses and values, competing, 191–193
Surprising oneself, 85, 251
Survival stories, types of, 22
Sutton-Smith, B., 247
Symbols and pictures, 26, 249

T

Talking and listening, attentive and empathic, 155–157
Teaching together, 76–77
Television: as barrier to praying, 140, 192; turning off, 67; watching, together, 61–62, 250
Thompson, A. I., 246
Thoughts about faith, sharing, 136–138
Tolerance, religious and political, 194–195
Traditional family: decline of, 55–56; defined, 31; looking beyond, 214–215
Tragedy, faith-shaking, facing, 96–100
Trust: belief and, family, 111–118; and cycle of developing faith, 93, 104; faith as, xiv, 89, 90, 91; and mistrust, families teaching, 95–100
Truth, 10, 248

U

Unconditional love, 83–86
Unforgiving servant parable, 161

Untold stories, 13

V

Values and stresses, competing, 191–193
Vance, B., 254
Visions and dreams, experiencing God's presence in, 172–175
Volunteering together, 77, 90
Vuchinich, S., 71, 250

W

Walsh, F., 245
Weakness, 111
Weddings, experiencing God's presence during, 170–171
Weems, R., 166, 253
Welcoming others, 150–154, 205, 213
Westerhoff, J., 252
White, M., 249
Windows: into nature of God, 184–187; into within, 13
Witnessing stories, 19, 27
Worshiping God together, 131–133, 218
Wuthnow, R., 147–148, 253

Y

Yamane, D., 248
Yankeelov, P., 246, 250